THE DISCIPLE-
MAKING PASTOR

Also by Bill Hull

Anxious for Nothing

Building High Commitment in a Low-Commitment World

Choose the Life: Exploring the Life That Embraced Discipleship

The Complete Book of Discipleship: On Being and Making Followers of Christ

The Disciple-Making Church

Jesus Christ, Disciplemaker

Revival That Reforms: Making It Last

Right Thinking: Insights for Spiritual Growth

7 Steps to Transform Your Church

Straight Talk on Spiritual Power: Experiencing the Fullness of God in the Church

Experience the Life: Making the Jesus Way a Habit curriculum
1. Believe what Jesus believed—through transformed minds
2. Live as Jesus lived—through transformed character
3. Love as Jesus loved—through transformed relationships
4. Minister as Jesus ministered—through transformed service
5. Lead as Jesus led—through transformed influence

THE DISCIPLE-MAKING PASTOR

LEADING OTHERS ON THE JOURNEY OF FAITH

BILL HULL
REVISED AND
EXPANDED EDITION

BakerBooks
Grand Rapids, Michigan

Published by Baker Books
a division of Baker Publishing Group
P.O. Box 6287, Grand Rapids, MI 49516-6287
www.bakerbooks.com

Printed in the United States of America

Library of Congress Cataloging-in-Publication Data
Hull, Bill, 1946–
    The disciple-making pastor : leading others on the journey of faith / Bill Hull. — Rev. and expanded ed.
      p.   cm.
    Includes bibliographical references.
    ISBN 10: 0-8010-6622-0 (pbk.)
    ISBN 978-0-8010-6622-1 (pbk.)
    1. Church growth. 2. Pastoral theology. 3. Clergy—Office. I. Title.
BV652.25.H83 2007
253—dc22
                                                    2007015770

To the chorus of thousands
who have read this book
and are now singing the same song

Contents

The church today is in crisis. What does it need, and how do pastors perceive that need?

Further Reflections

Before a pastor can make disciples, he needs to count the cost. Nine forces militate against discipleship, and he needs to be prepared for them.

Further Reflections

What are the biblical foundations of disciple making, and what does a disciple look like?

Further Reflections

How does Scripture define the role of pastor? What does he do?

Further Reflections

Foreword

It is no secret that the organized church today is in trouble. Not only has the institution lost momentum, but by and large, it has lost direction. Unless persons come forth who can lead the church to renewal—which puts the heavy end of the load on pastors—there is little hope that the situation will change for the better.

Unfortunately, pastoral leaders with apostolic hearts are in short supply. Indeed, in far too many instances, clerics in privileged positions to shepherd the sheep themselves flounder in aimlessness and frustration.

This is not to say that the church lacks conscientious workers or that nothing worthwhile is happening. For as we can see, all kinds of things are going on. But somehow, it seems to me, ecclesiastical programs and membership promotions have been mistaken for fulfilling the Great Commission. Where are the laborers in the harvest, constrained by the love of God, moving out to make disciples of all nations? I am afraid that in all too many instances this measure of a New Testament church has been obscured, if not forgotten. In fact, we have drifted so far from the mandate of Christ that persons who take it as the pattern of their lives are looked upon as fanatics.

Bill Hull may be such a man. Convinced that the command to make disciples has lost none of its authority or relevancy, he has tried to set the course of his ministry by it.

This book describes the rationale for his choice and what it means for the local church. It is scriptural. It is realistic. And though the author does not mince words, he writes with understanding and compassion.

Giving the story a ring of authenticity is Mr. Hull's personal experience. He does not speak as a theoretician, but as a practitioner—an active pastor who has sought to build a church around disciple making. The validity of his ministry is attested in the way the congregation has grown in numbers and vision and has now reproduced itself in several daughter fellowships.

Here is a message men and women aspiring to church leadership need to hear and ponder. Not all will agree with his conclusions, but no one can read the account without getting a new appreciation for the discipling pastor. For some, it may be the birthday of a new conception of ministry.

Robert E. Coleman

2007 Introduction

Even though this work was published in 1988, I wrote it in 1987, so twenty years have now passed. A lot has happened in those two decades. My children have become adults, my hair has turned white, and I have succeeded and failed. I have seen trends rise and fall, movements come and go, and so many efforts to reach the world for Christ—as ambitious and grandiose as they seemed—disappear. I have changed my mind about some things, as evidenced by the reflections at the end of each chapter. Overall, I believe we have made some gains, but they are balanced by the losses. We have gained in better training and in wonderful materials such as books and DVDs. There seems to be a greater unity among evangelicals; the leaders are more focused on what matters. The playing field has been leveled in business competition: India, China, and others can now compete for business with the West. The church in the developing world is greatly enhanced as cell phones and the Internet make information available to them. There are technologies that now can provide needed training to millions of Christians around the globe.

However, the losses are connected to the same technologies. The spread of the consumerism mentality has poisoned much of the good training. The reliance on technology for worship and teaching competes with the need for the personal touch and the development of sacrificial community. As I will mention several times in this book, people cannot be formed in Christ in a climate that is dominated by a consumer mentality. Jesus calls us to come and die, whereas consumer Christianity calls us to come and improve our lives and enhance our personalities. In light of this, I have reserved two overarching observations for the introduction. They are not long, but I pray they will interest you in reading on.

The church continues to try to reach the world without making disciples. I know that all who believe in and follow Jesus are disciples, technically or theologically. I think this kind of belief is far different, however, than what many Americans call belief. The American gospel understands faith as agreement, so saying the prayer or walking down the aisle is the finish line rather than the starting line. I am convinced that everyone who believes in Christ follows Christ. When Jesus commanded us to "make disciples," He meant more than converts or church members; He meant those who take up their cross daily and follow Him. It has taken hundreds of years and thousands of theologians to diminish this simple fact. We have too many people arguing about what doctrinal statement you can sign rather than what you can do. I find George MacDonald's words useful at this point:

> I will tell you; so make yourself his disciple at once. Instead of asking yourself whether you believe or not, ask yourself whether you have this day done one thing because he said, Do it, or once abstained because he said, Do not do it. It is simply absurd to say you believe, or even want to believe in him, if you do not do anything he tells you.[1]

The church concentrates on getting people to say a prayer or adhere to a theological formula. It is a focus on convincing people to sign up for the ride to heaven without the road of discipleship. I must again point out that this is inadvertent, a product of the consumer culture in which we live. The gospel has been stripped of repentance and the basic call of Christ to deny oneself and follow Him.

Yet there are some encouraging signs that pastors are more interested in making disciples. By *interested* I mean they want to spend time on it, to focus more on the care of souls than the more conventional measures of success. Discipleship is now being conducted under a different name, such as *spiritual formation, mentoring, coaching, spiritual direction,* and so on.

Making a disciple has three dimensions. The first is *deliverance,* which is accomplished via evangelism when a person is reborn and baptized. The second is *development*—what most people call *discipleship* or *personal development*—in which a person is established in the faith. This is ongoing and lifelong, necessary for the care of the soul. The third dimension is *deployment,* in which the developing disciple is commissioned to a mission in the harvest field. A church or pastor committed to making disciples would be focused on this process as the first priority.

Second, it is more important to be a disciple than to have a plan to make disciples. There must be a landfill where all unused or failed plans to make disciples now rest in peace. Those plans had been started with different motives—some to grow the church, others to reach communities, still more to bring depth to the church members—so that anyone coming in contact with them would be changed. But for one reason or another, the plans went sideways, spun off into a ditch, or were shredded by the resistance of a threatened congregant at a late-night meeting. But most of them failed because the pastor was not developing as a disciple. How can one make disciples without practicing the very things he or she advocates?

Before you try to answer that question, let me do so. Hardworking pastors really care about their work and people, but they are too busy organizing, motivating, preaching, and putting out fires to attend to their own souls. So the fire gets low, and sometimes it might be but an ember. This has happened to me at times. It has made me feel like a creaking, old, broken-down car that is sputtering on the side of the road with smoke billowing from beneath the hood and the water gauge on red. Usually I need to be towed back to safety. The challenge for pastors is to be a disciple first, seeking God daily and practicing the spiritual disciplines he or she advocates. Yet that is getting harder to do.

Thomas Friedman, the brilliant columnist for the *New York Times*, talked about this problem. His column's title was "The Age of Interruption." He reflected on spending four days in a Peruvian rain forest:

> I have to say, as a wired junkie myself, there was something cleansing about spending four days totally disconnected. It was the best antidote to the disease of our age, what the former Microsoft executive Linda Stone aptly labeled "continuous partial attention." That is, you are multitasking your way through the day, continuously devoting only partial attention to each act or person you encounter. It is the malady of modernity. We have gone from the Iron Age to the Industrial Age to the Information Age to the Age of Interruption.[2]

The key to our souls is contemplation, the acquired habit of being alone with God to hear His voice. I find it hard to start my day with God if the first thing I do is check my email or phone messages. I hear all the other voices more readily than God's. Friedman points out that a wired society means that everyone is always "in" and never "out." That calls for artificially creating "out." He quips that very soon we might see five-star hotels advertising that every room is guaranteed to come *without* Internet service.

My advice to all pastors is to simply rearrange your life around the practices of Jesus. Look at His life filled with the press of the crowd, the hatred of religious leaders, and the dullness of His disciples. How did He handle it? He prayed, He prayed alone, and He prayed at special times of pressure and decision. He lived a life focused on others, a life that was based on humility and sacrifice powered by love. When we live with a simple commitment to know God's will and do it, then many of those unused and malfunctioning plans begin to work. When pastors are active disciples, they make disciples. This book can be that plan, but it is just ink on paper without the heart and fire to do it.

Introduction

THE CRISIS AT THE HEART

That the church is in crisis is not news. It was born in crisis and has remained in that state until the present day. By definition, *crisis* means "to separate," "to be at a turning point." Crisis demands we make a decision, and what makes the decision critical is that the wrong one could lead to disaster.

Hundreds of leaders can name thousands of crises in the American church. Books have been written and messages delivered on the crisis in preaching, evangelism, the Christian family, integrity of both the clergy and Christian businessmen. Others point to crisis in world missions, theological education, Christian colleges, and some throw in the slow death of the Sunday school.

The word *crisis* has become so hackneyed that many have stopped listening to the warnings of modern prophets and feel great skepticism concerning the validity of many so-called crises. The Christian public has become jaded to the fervent cry of their leaders when they speak of life at the edge of the abyss. The nearing apocalypse somehow never seems to materialize; therefore, each subsequent warning of impending doom seems more and more like "crying wolf."

In spite of such cynicism, I must insist that the crisis at the heart of the church is deeper, more threatening, and more important than any other. The fact that the church can get by without being confronted with its ramifications makes it so dangerous. Ignoring the crisis is like a man who will not deal with a heart problem. He refuses to recognize the warning signs: his inability to climb stairs with ease, to exercise without pain, or to breathe normally. Life can go on in a limited way under such circumstances. But one day, his heart will suddenly quit, and then it will be too late to restore normal health to the diseased cardiovascular system.

To follow Paul's analogy of the church being the body of Christ, the crisis is not one of the extremities—the hands, the legs, the feet. In other words, it's not directly a crisis of function and task. It is a crisis of what governs the body's ability to do the function and task. *The crisis is at the heart of the church.* The church's cardiovascular system, its most crucial part, determines the health of the entire body. The condition of the heart, the free and regular flow of blood through veins and arteries, determines the body's ability to function normally.

The evangelical church has become weak, flabby, and too dependent on artificial means that can only simulate real spiritual power. Churches are too little like training centers to shape up the saints and too much like cardio-pulmonary wards at the local hospital. We have proliferated self-indulgent consumer religion, the what-can-the-church-do-for-me syndrome. We are too easily satisfied with conventional success: bodies, bucks, and buildings. The average Christian resides in the comfort zone of "I pay the pastor to preach, administrate, and counsel. I pay him, he ministers to me. . . . I am the consumer, he is the retailer. . . . I have the needs, he meets them. . . . That's what I pay for."

We can most clearly see this in our idolatrous worship of the American superchurch. The bigger it is, and the more its methods mimic the American entrepreneurial spirit, the better. The seduction is complete when the bigger, the more creative, and the more "successful" churches serve as the ultimate by which we measure all other churches.

The all-too-common measure of greatness is the number of people gathered for worship. If 3,000 people gather, some may make the snap judgment "this is a great church." Measuring greatness this way has two important flaws. First, numbers themselves do not indicate greatness. Large groups can gather for any number of events, such as lynchings, mob riots, or Tupperware parties. The more accurate observation concerning a large church gathering might be "the number of people gathered here indicates that those leading the church—the pastor and the music leader—must be highly talented." That would be a good and generally true judgment.

The second flaw of such a superficial measure is that you have asked the wrong question: "How many people are present?" The right question is, "What are these people like?" What kind of families do they have, are they honest in business, are they trained to witness, do they know the Bible, are they penetrating their workplaces, their neighborhoods, reaching friends and associates for Christ? Are they making the difference in the world for Christ that He expects? These are the right questions, the issues of the heart, and the criteria for greatness.

The evangelical church has lost the will to ask the right questions and the courage to face the answers. The critical decision facing the church is will we commit ourselves to the issues of the heart? Will we repent of our foolish ways and turn to the work Christ commanded? But what are the issues of the heart? What is the cardiovascular system of the church?

George Orwell wrote, "We have now sunk to a depth at which the restatement of the obvious is the first duty of intelligent men." In today's church, the obvious is revolutionary. Nothing is as treacherous as the obvious. Like walking a tightrope in a high wind, understanding and executing the obvious is tricky. The obvious restated and applied shakes the church at its foundation. When you state it, inoculated leaders nod their sleepy heads. When you apply it, they scoff and label you as radical, inexperienced, and parachurch.

What obvious truth causes the saints to squirm? Simply this: *The church exists for mission.* The church lives by mission as fire exists by oxygen. *The church does not exist for itself.* This collides head-on with the self-indulgent ego-driven psychobabble mentality that dominates evangelicalism. Look at the bestselling Christian books, listen to the television evangelist, talk to the average parishioner; the common thread is a preoccupation with felt needs. If the church is going to obey Christ, this must stop. Christians won't stop having needs, real or felt. However, the preoccupation and prioritizing of felt needs over Christ-commanded activity must stop.

The focus of a church's staff, leadership, and core congregation is not to be inward, but outward. The church's mission is penetration into the world, as its metaphors instruct us. Salt, light, leaven, army, ambassadors, pilgrims, all denote movement and penetration. The church grows when members become more effective in penetration.

Like any crisis of the cardiovascular system, this has left the church weak and dependent. It has placed pastors in the difficult role of coaches trying to field a basketball team from a hospital ward. The players may try hard and do their best, but they won't make the National Basketball Association. As a sad result, the church functions at a great disadvantage. Therefore, the church is much less than God intended. Tragically, it doesn't need to be this way, and we must gather the courage to fight it and change it.

The Cure Introduced

Only one kind of person will penetrate the world, and the failure of the church to produce this kind of person is the error that has thrown it into crisis. *The crisis at the heart of the church is a crisis of product.* What kind of person does the church produce? The Christ-commanded product is a person called a disciple. Christ commanded His church to *"make disciples"* (Matt. 28:19). Jesus described a disciple as one who abides in Him, is obedient, bears fruit, glorifies God, has joy, and loves (see John 15:7–17).

It makes so much sense. The kind of person who glorifies God best is called a disciple. The command of Christ to His disciples was "make disciples," because disciples penetrate their world. Disciples reproduce themselves, which leads to multiplication. Multiplication is the key to reaching the world and fulfilling the Great Commission.

How the church has missed this obvious mandate can only be attributed to a diabolical scheme. The crisis at the heart of the church is that we give disciple making lip service, but do not practice it. We have lost the integrity of our mission. The cardiovascular system of the body will not get better until we change our ways and prioritize the production of healthy, reproducing men and women who will penetrate their world. *The cardiovascular system of the church is the principles that produce the right product.* When it produces and reproduces the right product, like any healthy body, it will be able to carry out its function. When we obey Christ's commission, two good things happen: We create healthy Christians; healthy Christians reproduce, and the body grows, then multiplies, and the world becomes evangelized.

Not much will change until we raise the issue and create controversy, until the American church is challenged to take the Great Commission seriously, until pastors are willing to start reproducing themselves through others, to prepare people to be self-feeding Christians, until congregations allow pastors to spend most of their time on teaching and training the spiritually well minority, rather than servicing the whims and desires of the unmotivated and disobedient majority, until pastors can be unleashed from evangelical "busy work." It must be done; we can't allow this to continue; there must be change.

The Need

The Condition of the Church

I have thrown down the gauntlet. I maintain that the evangelical church is weak, self-indulgent, and superficial, that it has been thoroughly discipled by its culture. As Jesus said, "Every one when he is fully taught will be like his teacher" (Luke 6:40 RSV). Furthermore, I believe the crisis of the church is one of product, the kind of people being produced. I propose the solution to be obedience to Christ's commission to "make disciples," to teach Christians to obey everything Christ commanded.

Do I stand alone in my critical analysis of the church? Others more wise and experienced than I maintain the same thesis. The late Elton Trueblood has said:

> Perhaps the greatest single weakness of the contemporary Christian Church is that millions of supposed members are not really involved at all and, what is worse, do not think it strange that they are not. As soon as we recognize Christ's intention to make His Church a militant company we understand at once that the conventional arrangement cannot suffice. There is no real chance of victory in a campaign if ninety per cent of the soldiers are untrained and

23

uninvolved, but that is exactly where we stand now. Most alleged Christians do not now understand that loyalty to Christ means sharing personally in His ministry, going or staying as the situation requires.[1]

A 1980 Gallup poll indicated that of the 22 million churchgoing evangelicals, only 7 percent had taken any evangelistic training and only 2 percent had introduced another person to Jesus Christ. How would you like to march into battle with only 7 percent of your troops trained and only 2 percent with combat experience? While I pray these figures have changed over the years, I would guess that today's figures are much the same.[2]

This illustrates the need for asking the right question. How could the 3,000 gathered for worship compose a great church, if only 7 percent were trained to witness and only 2 percent had introduced another to Christ? The test of a congregation, apart from personal holiness, is how effectively members penetrate the world. American churches are filled with pew-filling, sermon-tasting, spiritual schizophrenics, whose belief and behavior are not congruent.

Christians are not well trained, largely because pastors have not worked out a means of helping people do what Jesus has told them they should. As a result they feel a great deal of frustration and guilt.

Most churches grow by transfer. The rule of the day is the rotation of the saints. The number of real conversions to Christ by some "great churches" is meager. Instead churches with strong preaching and great music programs attract large numbers. Therefore, people think that the church is great and the staff does its job. In reality the churches with the best programs are crowded, along with the best restaurants and theaters, because people like excellence.

In the relationship between clergy and laity, the clergy have become professional performers and the parishioners the audience. The better the show, the larger the crowd. All this proves is that outstanding performance attracts people. It means little more than that; in no way does it faithfully reflect the priorities of Christ for His Church. As Elton Trueblood has stated, "Cheap Christianity can usually pull a pretty good attendance on Sunday morning. It is cheap whenever the people think of themselves as spectators at a performance."[3] Trueblood goes on to point out that emphasis on how many gather for worship is pre-Christian and pagan. "We fall back into an Old Testament mind-set, in which we look mostly at how many people come into the temple for the ritual. That was what counted most under the Old Covenant. Meanwhile, we forget Jesus' words in Matthew 12:6, 'I tell you something greater than the temple is here.'"[4] You can always get a crowd, if you demand very little and put on a show.

Deceptively, such success blinds us to the real issues. Are the Christians healthy, is reproduction taking place, are people being trained to be disciple makers? What is being asked of the people, are they living and serving the way God planned? The purpose of gathering Christians is for training so that their penetration ability is improved.

Looking at the church twenty years ago, pollster George Barna commented:

> There is strong support among Christians for the notion that an individual is free to do whatever pleases him, as long as it does not hurt others. Two out of five Christians maintain that such thinking is proper, thus effectively rejecting the unconditional code of ethics and morality taught in the Bible. Three out of ten Christians agree that nothing in life is more important than having fun and being happy. Christians express such love for money, possessions and other material objects that their Christianity cannot be said to rule their hearts. For instance, more than half of the Christian public believes that they never have enough money to buy what they need, nor what they want. One out of four believers thinks that the more you have the more successful you are. *The fact that the proportion of*

*Christians who affirm these values is equivalent to the pro-
portion of non-Christians who hold similar views indicates
how meaningless Christianity has been in the lives of millions
of professed believers.*[5]

Even though Barna's findings are over twenty years old,
they still ring true. If anything, the problem is more acute
now than then. Not only are Christians untrained to penetrate their spheres of influence, their values have slipped
as well. Now the difference between Christians and non-
Christians has blurred and is fast disappearing. My own
experience as a pastor substantiates this belief. Christians'
use of money, priorities of time, attitudes about work and
leisure, divorce and remarriage, increasingly reflect culture
rather than Scripture. Therefore, the church is weak in
skills and weak in character.

When Os Guinness says, "We have left out substance,
it is no longer the holies of holies, but vanities of vanities
. . . we worship the god of the gut, no deeper than our last
experience,"[6] he speaks of a lack of strength in the church.
George Gallup's findings support this view. Only 42 percent
of Christians know that Jesus delivered the Sermon on the
Mount, and most of them know that because of television.
Those who could identify the writers of the Gospels or name
the Ten Commandments were fewer. Evangelicals show a
startling biblical illiteracy. Bible teaching and learning are
different. Among evangelical pastors a major myopia exists
on this very issue. Sermons do not prepare people to live
effective Christian lives. Christians evidence a serious lack
of depth of both knowledge and good experience.

Francis Schaeffer warned us: "Here is the great evangelical disaster—the failure of the evangelical world to stand
for truth as truth. There is only one word for this—namely
accommodation: the evangelical church has accommodated to the world spirit of the age."[7]

We see the bitter fruits of biblical illiteracy and subsequent accommodation in some sensitive ways. George

Barna recently did a study among 10,000 evangelical youth. The results show the alarming rate of decline of values among churchgoing evangelical teens. By eighteen years of age, 43 percent had experienced sexual intercourse. Twenty-four percent considered premarital sex as acceptable. Thirty-nine percent found other sexual activity as normal. Fifty-five percent could not state that premarital intercourse was wrong. A startling find was when those who had engaged in intercourse were asked if they were forced into sex against their will, 47 percent of the boys and 65 percent of the girls said they were pressured.

The transfer of values and priorities from parents to children is weak because the majority of parents in evangelical churches have an accommodated value system. They are not committed as a whole; therefore, the children reflect the same slippage of commitment.

George Gallup says that among evangelicals, there are a highly committed group of 10 percent. These people carry the load and will make the difference. These nonaccommodators are the "hell-bent for glory group." From them the 7 percent trained for evangelism come. Ten percent highly committed means that effective values transfer operates at ten percent efficiency.

I will develop this in full later, but for now I need only say that the truth we have sacrificed is the command for quality. The Great Commission has been worshiped, but not obeyed. *The church has tried to get world evangelization without disciple making.* The impetuousness of human nature and cultural pressure to get quick results have caused pastors to take every shortcut. Shortcuts don't work; most of the time we end up starting over again. Only one road leads to world evangelism: disciple making. The truth that disciple making is the key to world evangelization, because it is the key to reproduction and multiplication, refuses to go away. We have sacrificed disciple making on the altar of cultural success, ego gratification, and immediate need. This is my version of the great evangelical disaster.

I would cast my lot with the former editor of *Christianity Today*, the late Dr. Kenneth Kantzer:

> My opinion—unprovable, I admit—is that evangelicalism is weaker now than it was fifteen years ago, or fifty years ago. People often think it is stronger because they hear more about it in the public media. It certainly has a better press today than it had anytime since the First World War. Then, too, evangelicals now have a greater sense of their own identity than they did earlier in this century. But the influence of evangelical faith and evangelical ethics on our society is less. As a culture, our nation and, indeed Western Europe are moving away from Biblical Christianity.[8]

I can't prove that the evangelical church is in as much trouble as I say. But I am satisfied to cast my lot with these men: Elton Trueblood, Donald Bloesch, George Barna, Os Guinness, Francis Schaeffer, Kenneth Kantzer, and others. Years ago I heard Billy Graham say that 95 percent of all Christians live defeated lives. I was skeptical concerning such a high figure, but I am no longer. Something must be done about the sickness of Christianity, and I think the solution is obvious. We must upgrade our product; we must produce healthy, reproducing believers who impact their world for Christ. How to do that is the heart of this work.

The Expressed Desire of Pastors

Pastors want to do what is right. I don't know a single pastor who doesn't desire to produce healthy Christians. All agree with this book's thesis that the evangelical church needs revitalization. They want to make disciples and help fulfill the Great Commission, but many don't know how. That's right, it surprised me too. At first I was skeptical about the need for instruction in how to structure a church for disciple making.

Too often we pastors become jaded concerning semi-nars, books, and other professional helps, because we see the church through the narrow lens of the successful. We survey the major success stories of evangelicalism and conclude that the church is in pretty good shape. "Look at all those successful churches; they don't have that disciple-making philosophy. They have more people; they send more missionaries; they have tremendous programs for almost every need group in society." But this view has a huge blind spot, because when we look at the church through the eyes of the successful, we see only 5 percent.

Let me be clear: I don't expect to reach the upper 5 per-cent of evangelicalism. Highly talented and creative entre-preneurial pastoral models dominate the upper 5 percent. They are very effective, God greatly uses them to minister to the masses, and they can offer a few principles and hints that can assist others in their work. But as models, they do more harm than good. Most pastors would do better if they had never heard of or been exposed to the upper 5 percent.

The upper 5 percent present the average pastor with an unrealistic, unreachable, guilt-producing model that threat-ens his ministry. Pressure to be like them has destroyed many. Instead of blaming the upper 5 percent for their work, we should thank God for them, and leave it at that. While I hope the upper 5 percent will adopt the philosophy of this book, they are not my target. My message is to the 95 percent of pastors who want to build healthy, effective churches. I propose an obvious, simple thesis that a pastor with average skills can execute.

If we measured hunger for help among the upper 5 per-cent, we would get a low reading. But in the lower 95 percent, there exists a famished army of pastors, ready to consume helpful material. I base this on the contact I have with pastors. After the publication of my first book, *Jesus Christ, Disciplemaker*, I started getting phone calls, letters, and visits from interested pastors. The comments generally went something like, "I agree with what you are saying, but how do I implement this kind of philosophy in my church?" After speaking at conferences or talking with denominational leaders, again came the comments, "Yes, we agree; this is what we want, but how?" I found a great distinction between desire and know-how. This motivated me to do three things.

The first action was to plant a church. In June of 1984 I left an established church and started one in San Diego. My motivation was to see if installing disciple making at the heart of the church would work. Doing that requires three things:

1. The pastor must possess convictions concerning disciple making and declare it as top priority from the pulpit.
2. The philosophy and its goals should be published in church literature and should be reviewed by leadership and reported to the congregation annually. This provides for a form of accountability for all concerned, and it tells the church how it is doing.
3. The disciple-making philosophy must be modeled at the church-leadership level. The pastor and leaders should be effective disciple makers themselves.

I wanted to see these principles at work from the ground floor. God has richly blessed these priorities, because they are His. Today the church is healthy, growing, and many exciting ministries have emerged. From planting the church, the second important action was born.

The second action was to recruit other pastors and plant more churches. I did not want to plant them just to plant new churches. I wanted to plant churches that shared the same philosophy of disciple making, that would reproduce, that would produce a healthy product and multiply themselves throughout the world. Therefore, we actively recruited men who shared our thinking. They raised their

financial support and joined us in San Diego. I quickly
learned that while these men agreed with the philosophy,
like other pastors, they did not have a handle on how to
implement it. They asked the same questions I got in the
letters and phone calls.

As a result we developed a center that would give the
pastors on-the-job training. We started with ten people,
composed of existing local pastors and our recruits. The
training environment has been dynamic and challenging,
and teaching pastors on the job has demanded all my ability and more. I have had a great deal of help in developing this philosophy. In the future we would like to export
the training-center concept to facilitate planting disciple-
making churches in other regions.

The training remains so valuable to the pastors that the
third action was unavoidable. You are reading the third
step, the book *The Disciple-Making Pastor*. The book's objective is to give pastors the philosophical base and the
model by which they can implement disciple making in
their churches. It is not the only way; it is simply the way
we did it.

I have built the model around the training methods of
Jesus. Chapter 9, "Making It Work in the Local Church,"
will take the reader through a four-phase model that attempts to apply His training methods in the church. The
fuller explanation can be found in my first book, *Jesus
Christ, Disciplemaker*. The model shows how the principal
phases of Christ's training can work in concert with the
standard vehicles that already exist in most churches. My
experience in teaching others how to do discipleship in the
church has shown me it requires two things: The pastor
has to have a philosophical system and deep convictions
concerning the system; and he needs a model, a gridwork,
a means to apply his philosophy. That is the purpose of
the model.

I am thoroughly convinced God wants disciple making to
be the heart of local church ministry. My experience with

pastors confirms that most of them agree. I do not present a model or means for building a culturally successful church, nor can I guarantee that this teaching will give you a big church. In fact, I have good reason to believe that in the initial stages, the philosophy will retard your numerical growth. I am proposing the principles God esteems in His people and His church. I suggest that when the church prioritizes these principles and pastors resurrect their appointed roles as disciple makers, the church will be healthy and honor God. So I address myself to those hungry 95 percent of pastors who desire to build healthy Christians and dynamic, obedient churches that reproduce.

There are two compelling reasons to place disciple making at the heart of the church. First, the need is seen in the condition of the church; its weakness is a mandate for corrective action. Second, pastors have strongly expressed that they want to take corrective action and place disciple making at the heart of the local church. They are asking for a means and a model. This book attempts to give both. But before we plunge ahead, let us consider the obstacles.

Further Reflections

Twenty years ago I wrote that "the evangelical church is weak, self-indulgent, and superficial, that it has been thoroughly discipled by its culture" (see page 23). Is it still true? Was it true in the first place? It doesn't take a genius to criticize the church. You don't have to be smart to attack this imperfect group of people who seem slow to change and even slower to get into line with what God wants. What is so confusing about "make disciples"? What don't we understand about "teaching them to obey everything I commanded you"?

What a man sees at forty is different than what he sees at sixty. At forty a man is climbing the mountain, his family is young, his legs are strong, and he is full of dreams for his future and ambitious to do great things for God. Twenty years later his children have children, his knees ache, his feet hurt, he's on medication, and he's short on future. He has crested the hill and reached some goals, but he has also failed, and he knows his failings very well. Maybe he realizes that he has been weak, self-indulgent, and superficial. When he puts on his Faconnable shirt and Ralph Lauren slacks and races for his car, double-checking for his Treo 650 and iPod, he realizes that he has been thoroughly discipled by his culture. Therefore, now his judgments are less shrill and are tempered with humility, and they may be more accurate. His vision is still strong. It could be that what he now says is seasoned with wisdom. His heart still burns for God more than ever, but now perhaps he realizes it's not entirely up to him to fulfill the Great Commission. It might be that loving those near him is the highest priority.

Okay, I confess, I have changed. One thing that is consistent with my thinking, however, is that I am a fan of patience and perseverance—not for my benefit but for obedience to God. The past twenty years have proven that those who have both of those characteristics are the ones to admire. These qualities are essential if we are to teach people to obey everything that Christ commanded. Eugene Peterson puts it this way: "Forming people in Christ is a slow work, so it can't be hurried; it is an urgent work, so it can't be delayed."[9]

Is the church in as much trouble as I claimed twenty years ago? I must tell you, it is worse. There are many big churches—by most accounts around 1200—that host 2000 or more Sunday attendees.[10] Basic math tells us that this is about 0.35 percent of America's 350,000 churches. The megachurch is more characterized by talent than any other characteristic. God gives out the talent in different measures (see Rom. 12:6–8; 1 Cor. 12:11). Some people just have a greater measure of it, which creates its own dynamic. But talent doesn't make disciples. It gathers, motivates, and mobilizes, and what it creates is determined by conviction, environment, patience, and perseverance. Sometimes the corollary to talent is the anointing of the Spirit; other times it is creativity and clever packaging that create a buzz, which leads to a positive word-of-mouth movement. And when "spiritual lightning," or sudden growth, strikes, we get the "superchurch" that changes the religious landscape.

When leaders of a megachurch are committed to making disciples, the church becomes an encouragement to all within its influence. We can thank and praise God for that work. However, when they are committed to measuring their progress by bodies, bucks, and buildings, they demonstrate that they have been seduced by the culture.

An easy mistake to make is to think that the megachurch and its megastars can be reproduced and multiplied. The temptation for ordinary leaders to believe they are extraordinary is powerful. By *extraordinary* I mean equipped or destined to lead something large and well known. Many leaders with lesser amounts of gifting and buzz can be and are extraordinary in their realm. When leaders make it their goal to lead a large ministry, they commit themselves to something that works 0.35 percent of the time. This, I believe, is a fool's errand. The goal is not something that they can control. Also, it is devastating when leaders measure themselves by a megastandard. The measure of a person is faithfulness, not numerical success. The real issue continues to be the kind of people we are producing in our churches. What is the body of Christ like when the lights are out, the doors are locked, and the parking lot is empty?

The late Elton Trueblood's statement in 1979 still rings true today:

> Perhaps the greatest single weakness of the contemporary Christian Church is that millions of supposed members are not really involved at all and, what is worse, do not think it strange that they are not.[11]

George Barna confirms Trueblood's claim in his research. One of his best efforts was his 2001 book *Growing True Disciples*, in which he painfully extracted the real state of disciple making in the American church. His conclusion was a bit sobering:

> The chief barrier to effective discipleship is not that people do not have the ability to become spiritually mature, but they lack the passion, perspective, priorities, and perseverance to develop their spiritual lives. Most Christians know that spiritual growth is important, personally beneficial, and expected, *but few attend churches that push them to grow or provide the resources necessary to facilitate that growth.* Few believers have relationships that hold them accountable for spiritual development. In the end it boils down to personal priorities. For most of us, regardless of our intellectual assent to the importance of Christian growth, our passions lay elsewhere—and our schedule and energy follow those passions. *Most believers, it turns out, are satisfied to engage in a process without regard for the product.*[12]

Barna's research provides hard data to the claim that *the church is trying to reach the world without making disciples.* It didn't work twenty years ago; it doesn't work now.

Distracted Disciples

I don't want to make an argument that the church is in decline because attendance is in decline and then turn around and claim that what really matters in the church is not attendance. The decline is not as much about fewer people attending church as it is about them attending less. A number of years ago, faithful attendees were present eight out of every ten Sundays. More recently, that ratio has changed to six out of every ten Sundays.[13] Much of this decline is due to lifestyle options, the growth of alternative activities for families, and a diminished sense of commitment. It is indicative of church leaders' failure to challenge the congregation and, more importantly, lead them by example. This decline requires us to address the related pathology of consumer-based churches.

I continue to believe that pastors do not neglect making disciples on purpose. The daily grind of local church life drains the strength of leaders, and they can easily lose focus. Also, many of them have not received any training in how to lead others. And often pastors have a wrong notion of discipleship—that it is exclusively a one-on-one mentoring relationship.

Consumer-Based Churches

When I use the term *consumerism*, I am not thinking primarily about economics. I have warned Christians in India, Rwanda, Kenya, and Kazakhstan of its dangers. It is more the philosophy or worldview that shapes us into consumers.

To think of oneself as a consumer is natural. We all consume every day. It is obvious that to a degree, being a consumer and purchasing products is a necessity. Food, shelter, clothing, and related items are necessary to sustain life. The trouble begins when we take on this philosophy, namely, "It's primarily about me, I am in the center, and my needs are preeminent." The consumer mind-set is that whatever is manufactured is for me to consider buying. It puts the self in the center of life, and all the world's commodities are in orbit around the self. Advertising is designed to create needs in us that we didn't even know we had. The customer is always right; the customer is in the driver's seat.

Similarly, the consumer-based person believes that the ministry of the church is to meet his or her needs. "We are looking for a church that will meet our needs." Isn't that what most of us say? What is the music like? How can I worship? Do the sermons feed me? Will the youth program take care of my kids? And the questions and the lists go on. The church then gets caught up in meeting expectations, fearing that people will not visit or stay, or, even worse, will leave after a while because their expectations were not met.

The problem with all this is that we can't make disciples based on a consumer mentality. Sure, we can run programs, have a wonderful small group ministry, and have an exciting curriculum that people attend in droves. *But we cannot expect that people will truly be formed into the image of Christ.* Jesus lived for others, and as his disciples we are called to do the same. Our churches exist for others. We don't do missions for ourselves; we do them for others. And then our needs are met—our real needs for purpose, joy, and knowing that our lives are right before God. That is why we must drive a stake through the heart of consumer Christianity, and this act must begin with our leaders.

The Conflict

Suppose one of you wants to build a tower. Will he not first sit down and estimate the cost to see if he has enough money to complete it? For if he lays the foundation and is not able to finish it, everyone who sees it will ridicule him, saying, "This fellow began to build and was not able to finish."

Luke 14:28–30

Disciple making takes more faith than any other task of the church. Since it is top priority for God, it is top priority for Satan. No work of God's servant draws more resistance than disciple making.

That is why the above words of Jesus serve as an inaugural contract for the disciple-making pastor. More than most, he feels tempted to quit before he finishes. Jesus said to quit before you start, unless you plan to finish. The nature of His work requires long-term ministry; therefore, the enemy strikes at the disciple-making pastor's Achilles' heels of impatience and immediate results. The exhortation to count the cost is a tonic for discouragement, a reason to go on. But like a scorpion, it has a stinger in its tail. Before you start making disciples in the church, count the cost; don't start unless you plan to finish. For you will experience the sting of ridicule if you fade in the stretch. Most studies show that the average pastorate lasts between three and four years. With so much starting and very little finishing, it should be no surprise that our product is weak. The specter of starting and not finishing haunts the disciple maker most, because finishing can be measured.

The characteristics of disciple making are intentional, measurable, clearly communicated ministry. The benefits are realized only when the ministry has reached maturity, after a minimum of five years. Studies reveal the most productive pastoral time to be years four to seven. Disciple making takes longer; the results come slower; and its validity requires a long-term work.

Many forces militate against disciple making. In theory, disciple making is popular because it promises a quality product that honors God. In practice, however, it requires time, dedication, and patience that pastors living in American culture find difficult. In this section I will consider the conflicts that stand in the way of putting disciple making at the heart of the church. In addition, I will address why the disciple-making pastor must be totally committed to his work. Being the disciple-making pastor is the most difficult work in the church.

The Liberal Church

"Liberal theology started in the seminaries and then made its way to denominational leadership, next to pastors and finally into the pew."[1]

The liberal church is a product of liberal theology. First came the breakdown of absolute truth rooted in Scripture, leaving a rationalistic, humanistic base. The pluralistic nature of such a floating base redefined evangelism as a social agenda. It applied itself to solving the systemic causes of poverty, hunger, racism, and so on.

Flying in the face of the clear evidence, liberalism today continues to insist that man's nature is basically good and a better environment and the progress of evolution will lead to a better quality of life. Common sense clearly tells us this is false.

The liberal church wanted to change the world. Liberals fallaciously thought the key was to address themselves directly to social issues, so they plunged headlong into the arms race, civil rights, the war on poverty, and world hunger. While the needs were real and the issues valid, they approached it backward. They prioritized work outside the church over the basic scriptural agenda for inside the church.

In 1966 the World Council of Churches adopted as their motto, "Let the church be the church." What did this good motto mean? It meant what the council changed the motto to in 1986, "The world sets the agenda for the church." This terrible motto represents the deterioration and decline of the liberal church.

The truth that the more the church tries to change the world, the more the world changes the church has escaped the liberal church. The church is to be in the world, but not of it. The church is like a boat; the boat is to be in the water, not water in the boat. The liberal church took on too much water, and when they realized they were sinking, they didn't have enough hands and buckets to bail out.

Let us learn from the liberal church's mistakes. The church best influences the world by being the church. Richard Neuhaus adds the needed ingredient ignored by the liberals. "The key to the church's engagement with the world is the church's engagement with God."[2] Engagement with God is what the church is all about. The reason the church has not changed the world is not just because of warfare with the world, the flesh, and the devil. Blame goes to the good guys as well, for the evangelical church has failed to produce a healthy product. While the liberal church has edited out the biblical mandates to make disciples and to evangelize the world, evangelicals have disobeyed the mandates by neglect, church busy work, and the practice of "cheap Christianity"—promise a lot, require a little.

Making disciples in liberal churches presents special problems that do not exist in evangelical churches. In the evangelical church the issue isn't whether evangelism, Bible study, and world mission should be done, but what methods should be used to get it done. The liberal church battles over should these things be done at all. The disciple-making pastor who finds himself serving a liberal church fights both theological and methodological battles.

The cost in the liberal church is extremely high. A religious institution that has forsaken its reasons for existence is the most difficult of places to obey the Great Commission. Any person who ventures in should ponder the cost carefully and enter at his own risk.

Misconceptions about Discipleship

Discipleship has become a trendy evangelical term. Most people think of it as really getting serious about Christ, but many resist it because of what they understand getting serious means. They think of a very narrow "cookie cutter" life of Scripture memorization, half-days in prayer, analytical Bible study, door-to-door evangelism, and the forsaking of life's pleasures. They go on to declare that such elitism is fine for parachurch ministry, but not realistic for the workaday church member.

To cure such misconception, present the scriptural profile of a disciple (see chapter 3), which shows a positive life, full of creativity. The disciple's profile clearly communicates that the Christian must master certain basics. Once those are in place, then the spiritual gifts, life circumstances, and other particulars concerning the disciple come into play. The clear declaration that God wills every Christian to be a disciple is essential to overcoming this obstacle. This declaration, along with a clear profile of a disciple, should do the trick.

Other misconceptions, fully addressed later, are that discipleship is just skill training, one program of the church, or only for the young and the restless. "If you want to be a pastor, missionary, or serve full time," they say, "then discipleship is for you." Every disciple-making pastor encounters these long-held, aberrant views.

Weak Nonprofessional Leadership

Though many happy exceptions exist, and I hope you can confidently say that the leadership in your church is strong, in general evangelicalism is crippled at the leadership level. The lack of good lay leadership—people from the marketplace who are fruit-bearing believers, leaders who are disciples and disciple makers, men and women who model and reproduce themselves in the eager growers within their spheres of influence—debilitates the local church.

Here a pastor faces the obstacle of trying to work with unqualified people who have leadership positions. In many cases leaders who do not walk with God tell pastors how to spend their time and do their job. Such laymen don't pray, meditate on, study, or memorize Scripture. Many have never introduced a single person to Christ. How anyone could lead an organization that purposes to save the world and never lead one person to Christ is the enigma of the church. This kind of duplicity cannot exist even in the business community. Furthermore, such leaders possess no concept or experience in training, reproduction, or multiplication. The prospect that this pathology dominates the local church landscape is tragic. The fact that ungodly men dictate to godly men is one of the institutional church's greatest sins.

The disciple-making pastor is dedicated to placing disciple making at the very heart of the church. This requires three things:

1. Declare it from the pulpit, put it on the top of God's "to do" list.
2. Publish it in church literature and have written, measurable goals that can serve as an evaluator of church health.
3. Model disciple making at the leadership level. This means teaching and requiring the leaders to be disciple makers themselves.

This is a tall order, particularly in the established church.

The pastor doesn't know if the church leadership is open to learning. Are their hearts prepared to be accountable, to submit to learning skills in Bible study, prayer, evangelism, and so on? The entire restoration of church leadership is a "bloody battlefield." The disciple-making pastor will be resisted; a spiritual war will be waged.

In some cases, the pastor doesn't know his leaders' true attitudes about discipleship, because they don't know themselves. One pastor was recruited for his disciple-making theories. The board recognized that the church was at a stage where the people needed training in the work of ministry and called a man whose philosophy of ministry seemed to mesh perfectly with theirs. However, when the pastor opened his discipleship group, none of these people chose to join. They already saw themselves as responsible, God-fearing leaders, and all those other people needed discipleship. Things went fairly well until the old guard realized that new, spiritual leadership was emerging from these discipling ministries. Power struggles began, and accusations of favoritism and cliques followed. "Spies" were sent out to drop in unexpectedly at Bible studies to see what subversive things these people were cooking up to overthrow the leadership. Leaders unable to change with the new directions in which the disciples start taking the church will either move aside, join a group and begin to grow, or fight.

A pastor *can* restore integrity to church leadership and do it without demeaning the leaders or dividing the church. Never tell the church their leaders are not qualified; never demean or speak in a derogatory way about the church leaders. Don't announce that you will replace current leaders with new, more qualified leaders. The solution is to love them, teach them God's Word, and allow God to do His work.

The important thing here is to admit that the problem exists, then to meet this very difficult problem with determination and wisdom. In church planting, you can only start with qualified leaders. When I planted my church, I appointed the first pastoral team (our title for elders, those who lead and oversee) only when I had men who qualified in philosophy and ministry skills. In an established church, the process will take several years. Be prepared to stay a while.

Churches Have Not Taken the Great Commission Seriously

How many church boards agonize over their relationship to the Great Commission? How many even discuss it? How many understand it? Can state it? Even know what and where it is? What percentage of time do local church leaders spend thinking about and planning their church's obedience to its commands? I mention the church board because they dictate the direction and activity of the church.

If church leadership teams would devote as much time and energy to thinking through and implementing the Great Commission as they do to "housekeeping" issues, the church would be vital and effective. Most boards spend 95 percent of their time on in-house issues, much of which don't require leadership-level involvement. Analyzing financial statements, meditating on buildings and grounds, memorizing constitutional passages, plotting how to cover one's sanctified tail at the next congregational meeting—these are the grand themes of Churchianity.

The irony of this fool's comedy is that almost to a man, those involved in such nonsense detest it. They don't like to attend the meetings; they thought their lives would really count for something when they took leadership. Now to their disappointment, leadership has become dull and tasteless.

Average church leaders do not take the Great Commission seriously because they are not well taught. They have heard the commands to go and preach the gospel many times. They do not question the importance of world mission. But they do not know that the applications are for them. They have applied the Great Commission almost entirely to the church missionary force. By allowing the missions committee to allocate funds to mission projects, they believe they are doing right by the Commission.

They help the Great Commission by again giving permission for the missions conference to spend a great deal of money. Yes, these are important and vital to world mission. No, they have not taken the Commission seriously, because they have not applied it to their own lives and work. Oh, yes, they do have a visitation program that includes some evangelism training. In addition, they make sure the pastor throws out the fish net every Sunday morning to catch those who need the Savior.

Taking the Great Commission seriously means the church leaders themselves are evangelists. They share their faith; they make disciples. As a matter of fact, they were only considered for leadership because of their years of service as disciple makers. Their main ministry still is disciple making. They have placed it at the heart of the church and do the most important thing in communicating its value; they model it.

The major issue in taking the Great Commission seriously is the intentional guidance of the church leadership toward multiplication. A process must take people from conversion to trained disciple maker. This should occupy a great deal of the leadership's time and creative energy. They should lead the charge with respect to hands-on disciple making. Taking it seriously means that the church leaders focus most of their time and effort on making disciples.

The average church leadership team is a maintenance committee. Therefore, their understanding of their role, their training, their concept of the church all will serve as a great challenge to the disciple-making pastor. The mandate for the disciple-making pastor is to persuade church leadership to take the Commission seriously. That will be the beginning of obedience to Christ and fruitful ministry.

Clericalism

The pastor as a professional remains a serious threat to church health. Tony Walters writes, "A church dominated by its pastors, ministers and priests has no more chance of escaping from need than a child dominated by its mother, a health service dominated by doctors, or an economy dominated by a mass-consumer market."[3]

The fact that a congregation pays a professionally trained pastor for his work is not the danger. A legitimate difference in function exists between the professional pastor and the Christian layperson, and there is nothing wrong with a pastor-minister gap. The pastor as the professionally trained leader of the church trains the layperson, or minister, to fulfill a role in service to Christ. In short, there is nothing wrong with the pastor leading the people of the church into ministry. He has been trained to do so and that is his assigned task. That legitimate distinction will always remain.

The much discussed clergy-laity gap, however, does need fixing. Clericalism is the expectation that the professional clergy does the ministry. Though the teaching that the pastor is to equip the saints for the work of the ministry is widespread and well known, it is rarely practiced. There still is an iron-willed expectation that the pastor does three things:

1. He prepares and preaches sermons. This is a good expectation, solidly built on Scripture.
2. The pastor is expected to play the role of a manager. This covers the expectation that the pastor will be the main administrator for the church. He keeps the church machinery up and running. While leadership and administration are closely linked, too often the church unrealistically wants both a theologian and corporate executive.
3. The pastor should care for the flock. This means hospital visitation, home visitation, counseling, and officiating at weddings and funerals. In addition, the pastor has ribbon-cutting chores: attendance at committee meetings, fund-raising events, junior high pizza parties, and so on. The pastor preaches, administrates, visits, cares, and counsels.

While some of the above expectations have their roots in Scripture, most modern-day applications do not. The obstacle here is that the pastor is seen as a generalist. He does the ministry. The above list of expectations leaves little time for his main function: the preparation of God's people for the works of service. With so many expectations, there is no mandate or time for the disciple-making pastor.

There are solutions (see chapter 4), but you should be aware that the roadblocks are firmly in place. My best word of advice is to clearly describe your priorities to pulpit committees. Tell them what you perceive as your God-given assignment. Make sure you ask them to explain in their own words what they expect concerning these issues. If you are too far apart and flexibility is not possible on both parts, stay away.

Polity in Any Extreme

Any system for church organization that allows the unspiritual and disobedient to dictate is wrong. Any reasonable person would agree with these words, but very often exactly that happens: The unspiritual and disobedient do dictate the direction of churches by assuming leadership positions. Two extreme forms of this can occur in the church.

First, decision-making power may lie in the hands of a few. In and of itself this is not dangerous; in fact, the organization works better if a few people of ability and integrity lead the church. The danger appears when there is no check on or accountability of the few. If the wrong few get into position and become a self-perpetuating lifetime-elder system, then the church can be hurt.

In the other, much more common, extreme, large numbers of people are involved in a large number of decisions. This is a recipe for church fights. When people unqualified for leadership start making the decisions of spiritual leaders, they will make many bad decisions that will not take the church in the direction God would have it go. Such a system reduces the qualifications for participation to "a member in good standing," but many members in good standing are biblically illiterate, self-willed, pugnacious, and have factious spirits. When unqualified church members start dealing with complex spiritual matters, disaster is near. Add the American love for democracy, the petitions, the unexpected motions from the floor, the power plays, and so on, and you have a system where people can nominate the nominating committee from the floor. These often unqualified people in turn choose the leaders for the church. This, by far the most ludicrous means of selecting leaders ever invented, makes leading the church almost impossible.

In such circumstances, disciple making becomes difficult at best; at its worst, it's a mine field. The disciple-making pastor must be able to lead. Though he is to be account-able, the congregation must give him the freedom to take the church forward. Any polity that ties the pastor's hands by electing untrained and unspiritual leaders is a bad pol-ity. A balance between leadership and accountability must exist. The congregation has the duty to follow their leaders (see Heb. 13:17). The leaders are charged with the duty of leading and caring for the church (see 1 Peter 5:1–3). In the best of both worlds, the leaders lead with integrity, and the congregation follows with discernment. The happy result is an effective church.

Many churches' present polity extremes make effective-ness impossible. Disciple making requires an atmosphere of openness and freedom for leaders. The pastor needs the room to set the agenda, to implement the plan. Look for bal-anced polity; it should make disciple making possible.

Accommodation to Culture

By *culture* I mean "the belief systems of a society and its outworking of those beliefs through music, painting, writing, films, and television." Included are the powerful influences of technology, the social sciences, and the glo-rification of power through money, sports, and the spec-tacular. The ways culture militates against disciple making are complex and multifaceted. I will name a few.

The media and the mind. Next to sleeping and working, Americans devote more time to the media than to any other daily activity. In a typical day the average American spends eight hours on the job, seven hours sleeping, and nearly five hours absorbing media messages. Television has become a staple in the American diet, and Americans have a firm commitment to the media. Social analysts widely agree that media have a tremendous impact on our values, attitudes, behavior, and perceptions of the world.

If I were the enemy, I would challenge God's standards. I would use the most powerful forms of communication at my disposal: movies and television. I would want to impact you intellectually through your emotions. I would dramatize life, open you up emotionally, then drive my point home. I would use the thousands of murders, rapes, and bedroom scenes to keep pounding away at you until you were desensitized to certain forms of evil. If I were the enemy, I would want you to echo my words to Eve in the Garden of Eden, "Hath God said?" (Gen. 3:1 KJV). I want to confuse you; I want to fuzz the line between fantasy and reality.

Television is discipling America. When a disciple is fully taught, he will be like his teacher (see Luke 6:40). The media erode the moral base of our land, desensitizing you and me to evil and blurring the line between right and wrong.

The people sitting in the pew are products of television more than the Word of God. Their worldviews are not scripturally based; rather they are disciples of their culture. When the media mentions responsibility, they are not talking about moral responsibility, but about using contraceptives. Termination of pregnancy (murder) is the woman's right; being sexually active (fornication) is all right as long as you practice safe sex; having an affair (adultery) is expected sooner or later in normal, uninhibited people; narrow-minded extremists (Christians) are dangerous to have around schools and public buildings—and you wouldn't want one for a neighbor.

The people in the pew do not believe everything they hear, but the Christian community is slipping away from moral absolutes. What the pastor declares rubs against the cultural grain. The Word of God is abrasive when clearly presented in the present atmosphere. The American mind has become soft; it does not think critically. Therefore, many parishioners have self-contradictory belief systems.

The morality of need. The pastor preaches to minds that believe bigger is better; the more spectacular the more important; the most important thing about life is that it is enjoyed; basic needs are a nice home, two cars, a three-week paid vacation, several weekends away; life has cheated you unless you have a Caribbean cruise, a DVD player, and an iPod. People have a corrupted sense of need. Needs become values, they take on their own morality. The language of need has replaced the language of greed.

Attempting to extract commitment is difficult. When the disciple-making pastor asks for long-term commitments for long-term goals, he climbs a steep hill. The Christian message itself is abrasive enough, but when packaged in a disciple-making mode, the rub increases. The very nature of the disciple-making pastor's message requires long-term commitment. Americans' desire to have everything now, from a car to lawn furniture, militates against a meaningful Christian life. By their inability to keep commitments because of pressure to maintain a preferred standard of living, Christians evidence their dedication to materialism. The key to a disciple-making ministry is the willingness of the people to delay gratification. It takes five years to establish a discipleship flow and have it bear fruit within the church. Many pastors and parishioners simply don't possess the spiritual stomach for such a journey.

Accommodation to secular methodologies. The church should take advantage of advertising, the social sciences, and modern technology, when these methods and techniques assist the cause of Christ. The use of demographics, psychographics, telemarketing, and specialized marketing is fine. But when demographics become the determining factor in God's will for the location of my church planting, the demographics have replaced the Holy Spirit. When certain characteristics of growing churches become the "holy grail," simply because they work, not because they are biblically sound, then pragmatism has become an idol.

When psychographics determine the content and demeanor of my message, I have bowed my knee to the Baal of "button pushing." Secular methodologies have overrun too many church leaders' thinking. Evangelicals are too easily duped by the latest way to reach people, whether it be the Internet, nifty brochures, or musical extravaganzas. The entire approach puts more responsibility on the leadership to be creative and raise funds than it does on the members of the church to effectively penetrate their worlds for Christ.

We want it quick and easy: We hear story after story of the church that grew from zero to one thousand in eighteen months, through telemarketing, psychographically analyzed sermons, specially marketed music and drama. Entrepreneurial pastors who accomplish these Herculean feats parade before the wannabe pastors who listen with wonder, then promptly go out and try "what works." The present fervor for success has caused many a pastor to forsake his convictions for the sake of success.

The timeworn work of the pastor, such as solid exegetical preaching, prayer, and disciple making, have gone out of style. We determine a successful church by how many come to the Sunday morning performance. How good is the preacher, how talented are the musicians, how charged is the atmosphere, how big are the offerings, and how beautiful are the buildings? These things warm the heart. Many have stopped asking the right questions: *What are those gathered for the performance like? Are they penetrating their worlds for Christ? Are they walking in integrity before God? Are they placing Him first financially? Are they committed to world evangelism?* These are the right questions.

I have no argument with the use of secular methodologies. My argument is with what is being communicated as significant. The church has become more effective in gathering people, especially in church planting. But the real issue is, what do we do once people are there? This is the real work of the pastor, and no secular methodologies will help him do it. That calls for the supernatural work of God's Spirit, to interest people in being disciples, learning how to reproduce and reach the world for Christ.

Don't shy away from secular helps, but beware of the temptation to become a pragmatist. Commit yourself to your biblical convictions and refuse to budge. Christ desires that His church be composed of healthy, reproducing believers who penetrate the world for Christ.

Superficial Christianity. In a 1979 interview, the dean of Christian writers, the late Elton Trueblood, referred to evangelicalism's "cutflower commitment, which lacks any deep rootage. It costs less and less and less to wear the evangelical tag in our society."[4]

The great writer G. K. Chesterton described the works of science-fiction author H. G. Wells as a vast ocean two inches deep. If someone fell overboard into the modern evangelical sea, he would be in no danger of drowning. Like Wells's works, he would find himself standing ankle-deep in water. Today's Christians lack the spiritual depth of character from which to draw during difficult times.

The influence of the world's psychology has created a new cult of self-worship. People are preoccupied with themselves and how they might meet society's manufactured set of needs. Psychology exists by putting people in need; people have been told they have needs they never before knew existed. Just as the advertising industry creates false needs in people to go out and spend money on alleged need items, people scramble about trying to meet new strata of emotional needs manufactured by the psychological industry.

The newscaster gives us the awful truth, which is reality; the Bible gives us the revealed truth, which is revelation; psychology has given us the hidden truth, which is a rip-off. America is the psychological society, and the language and philosophy of need have seduced the church. Therefore, the people in the pew ask all the wrong questions, based on cultural programming: *What can the church do for me? Can I get my needs met here? Do I feel good when I leave here? Does the pastor make me feel guilty? Will I have to do what I don't feel like doing?* These questions and more reflect the corruption of self-idolatry primarily fostered in our society by the secular psychological community.

This has led to the development of a "need theology" that finds its roots in gratifying the desires of the flesh. Therefore, the most popular theologies of today are directed toward immediate need gratification. Television lends itself perfectly to the message, which is often called the healthy-wealthy heresy. The promise is that God wants to heal you; God wants to make you rich; all you need to do is believe. Not only will God give you health and wealth, He also wants to give you a variety of very exciting sensual spiritual experiences. In other words, following Christ is just one buzz after another. You have pain; He will take it away. Do you need money? He will provide it if you will plant a seed offering to that particular ministry. Do you need to overcome depression, anxiety, marital problems, and conflicts with others? Just close your eyes and believe, and you will have the victory.

Like a television show, God will make things better by the end of the program. Just as the detective catches the felon and the hero gets the girl, so everything will work out for you too. This trains Christians to think selfishly and superficially about their faith.

Another aspect of superficial Christianity that deserves a brief mention is the "aren't we special, neat, and full of potential, and needy for positive self-esteem" nonsense. This brand of teaching highlights the abilities and glory of man. While God values man, and man needs to think well of himself, this teaching simply does not tell the whole truth. The other side of the story, of course, is our sinful natures. We are special enough to God that He acted in His Son to save mankind, but we need to repent. We can feel good about ourselves after we start behaving in a manner pleasing to God, but all human potential is limited and must be carefully monitored by the Spirit of God and the accountability of the church.

The danger of superficial teaching is that it develops a manward instead of Godward focus. It lends itself to study of psychological literature and light devotional fare and directs itself toward the emotions more than the mind. Rarely do people of this ilk spend much time with the Scriptures, studying, memorizing, meditating on eternal truths that give the full story.

Someone said the difference between the men and the boys is that the boys want to be somebody, while the men want to do something. The superficial Christian wants to have all the benefits of a victorious Christian life without the commitment. He looks for an escape hatch from his problems and an easy, enjoyable life.

Sensual Christianity possesses an insatiable appetite. The populace will need more and more to keep the "spiritual buzz" alive. It's no different from drug addiction, because the tyranny of more and more eventually destroys the user. A spiritual life built on a sensual/experiential foundation is short-lived and dissipates in times of trouble.

The disciple-making pastor preaches for commitment, and without Spirit-engendered convictions, there can be no commitment. People need good spiritual experience built on a foundation of objective truth, which is found in Scripture. You face the challenge of deprogramming those under your teaching. They need to unlearn the superficial "gospels" of the later twentieth century and to be schooled in the first-century teachings of Jesus. The church must put off this tripe and commit to the commanded teachings of our Lord.

The disciple-making pastor fights a personal battle of self-doubt. Many will ask you to "lighten up" on your message. "You're asking too much," they will say. "If you really loved us, you would make it easier." The temptation is to give people dessert in your sermons instead of the main course, to skip the difficult passages, to eliminate the details of geography, history, culture, and language that bore the superficial attention span of today's Christian consumer.

You'll face the temptation to reduce your goals, to trim your sails. Don't ask people to be reproducing believers. They will run and hide; they won't want to pay the price. *Study the Bible, pray, memorize Scripture, witness to friends and neighbors: That is too much! Take care of us, be our shepherd!*

The same temptations will arise in qualifications for leaders, the length and rigor of discipleship groups, the insistence that all potential leaders exhibit experience and success in evangelism. Again and again the superficial consumer Christians in the congregation will challenge all these standards. The church never gets easy.

Traditionalism

Tradition is the living faith of godly progenitors, passed on from generation to generation. *Traditionalism* is the dead faith of living Christian leaders attempting to hold on to power. The word for -*ism* means a distinct doctrine, theory, or cause; it reflects a state of being. A communist recruits others, and it becomes *communism*, *liberal* to *liberalism*, *conservative* to *conservatism*, and so on. Tradition is a good thing. Families, churches, clubs, businesses, all practice traditions that form foundations for corporate values. Churches need tradition, not only in doctrine, but in many familial practices. Tradition runs into trouble when it sours and becomes traditionalism.

> Then some Pharisees and teachers of the law came to Jesus from Jerusalem and asked, "Why do your disciples break the tradition of the elders? They don't wash their hands before they eat!" Jesus replied, "And why do you break the command of God for the sake of your tradition?"
>
> Matthew 15:1–3

Traditionalism militates against doing God's will. In hundreds of ways local church leaders manifest it and unknowingly hinder the work of God. The church fathers try to keep the Wednesday-night prayer meeting alive by fighting a small group ministry. They resist innovative worship styles, new qualifications for leaders, constitutional rewrites, because they threaten the safe confines of the familiar. As a result, they hinder progress and create an atmosphere of conflict. The "founding fathers" of a particular church find themselves fighting to the death over unimportant issues. Many times they forget the reason for the battle, and the conflict takes on a life of its own. Too often, the entire church dons full mountain-climbing gear to ascend anthills.

Traditionalism is still very strong in many regions of the United States. It would be foolish for the disciple-making pastor to charge into an existing church without knowledge of church traditions and values. Work in a traditional atmosphere by riding piggyback on their dreams. Then ask them to add some of your own, without taking important things from them. This approach will do much to assuage the ire of "founding fathers." But prepare for conflict anyway; some will always fight any change. A freshman United States senator commented to a thirty-year veteran, "Senator, I bet you have seen hundreds of changes during your time in Congress." "Yes," said the seasoned senator, "and I've been against every one of them." Respect the traditions, use them to your advantage. Fight traditionalism for all you're worth.

Seminary Education

I am a seminary graduate and would not recommend that any person take on a preaching-pastor position in the United States without the advantages of solid seminary training. Supporting and maintaining theological seminaries is essential to protecting, revitalizing, and building healthy local churches. As stated earlier, the seminary determines what pastors believe and finally what the person in the pew believes.

Local church pragmatists regularly criticize seminaries. They are too academic, the critics claim, but they level a more serious charge when they say seminaries do not train students for the pastoral work. In addition few seminary professors have pastoral experience, therefore, students are being taught what to do by those who haven't, they protest.

I rush to the defense of these special servants of Christ. Seminary teaching is a special and needed calling. The seminary teacher undergoes rigors unmatched by the secular academic community. Not only does he spend three to four years on his basic theological degree, the master of divinity, an additional three years is required for professional teaching credentials, the ThD or PhD. Such academic rigor takes a person whose heart burns for Christ and one gifted by Christ with an enlarged intellectual capacity. Unlike other secular fields, where a PhD insures a handsome salary, the majority of seminary professors make less than pastors.

The seminary professor's role is not to provide students with the "nuts and bolts" of ministry. Those who criticize the nonpractical aspects of seminaries fail to recognize both the purpose and limitations of academia. The seminary provides the student with tools by which he can build a ministry: critical thinking, a working knowledge of fields of study that pertain to maintaining the integrity of the Word of God, and the tools for preaching and teaching the Scriptures. In the long run, there is nothing more practical than a solid doctrinal understanding along with a philosophical framework for worldview. On this foundation a pastor can build a lifelong ministry.

The seminary is not intended to fully equip a graduate for the pastorate. In conjunction with the local church, it is responsible to make it possible for a young man to begin pastoring the church. Seminary provides him with the basic tools for ministry; the church will be responsible to help equip the man in other areas. The typical seminary graduate knows about 50 percent of what is required to pastor. The other half must come from experience, the example of others, internships, and previous ministry experience.

Seminary professors are not on the front lines for Christ. True, they are not the typical troops in the trenches, and we should not expect them to be there. As the custodians of truth they protect the integrity of God's Word. How do you put a price tag on that? They are not the front lines; they are the last line of defense. They stand between the church and the abyss of subjectivism. If the enemy gets past the defenses of the local church, they still must fight to win the victory. Satan attacked the liberal church from the rear; when he attacked the seminaries, he brought down entire denominations. The enemy would love to convince pastors and laymen alike that seminaries are outdated, irrelevant, too academic, therefore, let's scrap the academic model. This belief is shortsighted, ignorant of what pastors really need, and doesn't help a bit. Some recommendations should be considered for improving the seminary. But in the meantime, we should esteem, pray for, and support these very special people on the last line of defense.

I believe the seminary should give the student three primary gifts: First, it should provide a scripturally based and challenging academic education, so that the foundations of the major theological disciplines are deeply rooted. Second, it should give exposure to the lives of older, seasoned faculty members. The exchange of lives and viewpoints the seminary environment provides has lifelong value. On these two issues, several seminaries do an outstanding job.

However, the third area is in my opinion the number one weakness of our evangelical seminaries. They do not provide students with a scripturally based philosophy of the church on which to build a ministry. The student learns what the church is, but not what the church does. Yes, what the church is determines what the church does. But does the graduate walk into the first pastoral assignment with a philosophical framework by which he can understand his work? Does he have the distinctives represented by the disciple-making pastor? I do not require that students possess the exact philosophy of this book, but they should possess convictions concerning a framework. Does the pastor understand who he is and what his job is? Does he have an objective with people seated before him in the pew? How does he motivate and move people through the discipling process without polarizing the congregation? These are but a few questions that graduates should have wrapped in their sheepskins.

I recommend an entire course of study, required in the master of divinity program, that exposes the students to such issues. In addition to the typical pastoral ministry and pastoral counseling courses, a minimum of three major courses would greatly benefit the students. First, a core course that would build a philosophical base from Scripture for the nature of the church and its task and the role of the pastor. The core course would be theoretical in nature. Two subsequent courses would focus on how to identify principles and how to put them to work in the local church structure. This is the "missing link" for our seminary graduates. Too many enter the church knowing how to give a sermon, marry, bury, counsel, and little else.

While I would not expect a person fresh out of seminary to work with the wisdom and effectiveness of a more seasoned man, I would like to see him with these additional principles and convictions added to his toolbox.

Seminary education without this third gift to its students will remain another obstacle to disciple making. It's not an obstacle in the same way as the other ones named. Without the seminary, the future of the church would be in peril. But we cannot remain satisfied with sending graduates into churches without convictions concerning disciple making.

Further Reflections

"Disciple making takes more faith than any other task of the church. Since it is top priority for God, it is top priority for Satan. No work of God's servant draws more resistance than disciple making" (see page 39).

Hmm, I had forgotten how much clarity I had two decades ago. No wonder it has been so hard to stay on topic, to have a disciple-making focus.

Precisely what do I mean by *disciple making*? What I *don't* mean is a well-organized program with a world-class curriculum. It may include that, but it's really about the heart of a church. Making disciples is much bigger, broader, and grander than a program, and it can't be domesticated. By *disciple making* I mean any good faith effort by leaders to provide an intentional environment with accountability on the basis of loving relationships.

Disciple making needs a nurturing and missional component. Its organizational level is determined by size, money, and culture. Satan can see disciple making in action, and he is ready to oppose it at every turn. But as he stands facing you, he often finds his hands empty, because he has already thrown everything he has at you. And still he tries to find more junk so he can ruin your life. First he accuses you that you are not a good, caring pastor because you can't and won't let people's whims and wishes create your agenda. What really frustrates him is that you go away and pray; you seek to hear what God is saying, instead of the chorus of voices in your head. Then he lies to you—usually through your insecurities, his congregational minions, and colleagues who lust after success—that disciple making doesn't work because your church is not growing and everybody is chasing after the "celebrity" pastor who lives down the street. Next he tries to kill you, but God won't let him, so he sets out to steal your sense of purpose and depress you so you might do something foolish like yell at your wife, neglect the kids, and indulge yourself in some unseemly way.

Satan would shred you if he could, but the accuser can't because your Father won't let him. Jesus alone stands between total defeat and us. Christ has come so that we could have a rich and satisfying life. Yes, it's a bloody war and the enemy is real, but we have armor, and we possess the same power that will destroy the would-be destroyer. We must be alert to how crafty the enemy can be. He and his system can be subtle.

Eugene Peterson has said, "American culture is stubbornly resistant to the way of Jesus."[5] The culture is strongly individualistic; the church is to be strongly communal. The culture is impatient; the church is to be persevering. The culture is celebrity-ridden; the church is to be a culture of humility. The culture celebrates competence; the church's first priority is dependence. The way of Jesus, then, is one of community, and submission, service, and patience in that community. Jesus' way is the road of humility, living in a state of brokenness before God. Jesus' way is a people anxious to depend on God rather than on competence alone.

Jesus' way is the vineyard in which we labor. Yes, the culture is resistant, and the real Jesus can make even the religious subculture nervous. But the most persistent and challenging conflicts are inside each of us, and it seems that the strongest adversary is impatience.

Impatience

I have always been in a hurry. I don't like loose ends, and I was trained to set goals and meet them. So naturally I turned making disciples into a project that had clear goals and timetables. My plans had symmetry: You should train six people the first year, twelve the second year, twenty-four the third year, and so on. But real life has little symmetry; it is very messy. For example, three of your first six trainees could move from the area, and one more could leave your church because his wife didn't like your sermon illustrations.

If your plan did work, it would likely lead to church growth most of the time, but not every time. If any group of people is aggressive in outreach, you will see new people come into your fold. But often the reason for growth is a creative and effective outreach program rather than people being formed in Christ. Still, these are not mutually exclusive; part of a person's formation involves reaching out to others.

I had been taught that every year a church should have a net gain in numerical growth so that leaders would have to keep going hard after it. When our church had a bad quarter, I would begin to lose sleep, to question if my work conditions were optimum for making disciples. I would say things like, "Aren't we all tired of playing church? Let's quit dinking around and get serious." This was my impatience at work.

Impatience can stem from a lot of things: a desire to control or anger that provides a rationale for lashing out at others. But at its root, impatience is due to a lack of trust in God. Eugene Peterson considers impatience the besetting sin of American pastors. *Besetting* means "it won't go away." Peterson says, "We're going to evangelize everybody, and we're going to do all this stuff and fill our churches. This is wonderful. All the goals are right. But this is slow, slow work, this is soul work, this bringing people into a life of obedience and love and joy before God."⁶ Impatience refuses to rest in God's care, God's plan, and God's timing. Impatience doesn't trust the idea that you pray, work hard, and leave the results in God's hands. It really won't accept that you are still valuable and important to God if your goals take longer to reach or if you don't even reach them.

The normal defense mechanism is to interpret impatience as the push of the Holy Spirit to fulfill the Great Commission, and impatience works better in the American Christian subculture than anywhere else. Any holy harangues or accusatory verbal onslaughts can masquerade as a needed blast from the Holy Ghost. They would never be seen as spiritual pollution spills from the unmet needs of a frustrated control freak. When we measure God's blessing primarily by productivity, we will always live in the irritating world of impatience.

I found the cure in rest—not primarily physical rest, but soul rest—in God's approval and His promise to give me fruit in His time. But His rest didn't just fall out of a tree; I had to invite Him into my inner world for fellowship. I had to learn to be quiet and listen to His whisper, to understand His hand in the circumstances of my life. I had to learn to hear Him in the beauty of the earth and in the pleasure of relationships. And so I started to understand my personal time with God as a conversation, and I sought to know Him in a relational way. I learned to let God love me. Over a period of years, impatience left me little by little.

Investing one's life in forming others in Christ is urgent, but it is a work for a patient person. God is patient with us; it makes sense that His leaders would be patient. Patience doesn't cancel out urgency, standards, enthusiasm, or hard work. Twenty years in pastoral work has yielded the truth that impatience is the most consistent barrier to making disciples. So don't throw yourself off the pinnacle of the temple in a grand effort to change the world. Do something courageous: Keep patiently moving forward with those God has entrusted to your care. I refer you to the words of Richard Neuhaus cited on page 41: "The key to the church's engagement with the world is the church's engagement with God."

The Product

George Orwell's statement "We now have sunk to such a depth that the restatement of the obvious is the first duty of intelligent men" deserves a second look. The obvious observation is that the church needs to upgrade its product. Call it renewal, revitalization, restoration, or getting with it: A recommitment to Christ's clear commands is the first order of business. The upgrading starts with establishment of the biblical foundations for the product.

Biblical Foundations for Disciple Making

Disciple making should be installed at the heart of the church, and the commanded product of the church is a fruit-bearing believer called a disciple. Christ's command to His church to make disciples provides the scriptural mandate. The text is the familiar words of Jesus found in Matthew 28:18–20.

This text brings needed clarity to the other four Great Commission texts. No evangelical has seriously challenged the status of the Great Commission. It represents the commanded work agenda for the church. There should be no confusion as to the Great Commission's bottom line. The objective is world evangelization, the population of heaven. These, the last and most important words of Christ with respect to the church's task, form the heart of what the church is and what the church does.

The postresurrection declarations are found in: (1) John 20:21 (RSV): "As the Father has sent me, even so I send you"; (2) Mark 16:15–17: "Go into all the world and preach the good news to all creation. Whoever believes and is baptized will be saved, but whoever does not believe will be condemned"; (3) Luke 24:47–48: "And repentance and forgiveness of sins will be preached in his name to all nations, beginning at Jerusalem. You are witnesses of these things"; and (4) Acts 1:8: "But you will receive power when the Holy Spirit comes on you; and you will be my witnesses in Jerusalem, and in all Judea and Samaria, and to the ends of the earth."

We could state a summary of the four commissions this way: "Go and preach the gospel all over the world to every person. Go in the power of the Spirit, with accompanying signs and wonders of God's power. Tell them what you have witnessed. Start at home, and work your way to the remaining world from there."

This would be very much like declaring to a crowd of novice contractors: "Go build houses; make them special, award-winning houses; here is the money; build them all over the world." The contractors do not know enough about the houses. They need a fuller description, a blueprint, if you will, that gives the specifications for the product. They also need a methodology for building their houses. This is why Matthew 28:18–20 is so vital to Great Commission comprehension. It gives the blueprint, the methods, and methodology for fulfilling Christ's command:

> All authority in heaven and on earth has been given to me. Therefore go and make disciples of all nations, baptizing

them in the name of the Father and of the Son and of the Holy Spirit, and teaching them to obey everything I have commanded you. And surely I am with you always, to the very end of the age.

Three important actions called for by the text are *going*, *baptizing*, and *teaching*. *Going* is a circumstantial participle that could be understood to mean "as you are going." The command of the text is not to go; Christ assumes and the disciples understood that reaching the world is not for the sedentary.

Therefore, as you are going through life, whether you travel or live a localized life, this work is for you. Note, however, when we factor in the strategy of Acts 1:8 (Jerusalem, Judea, Samaria, and the ends of the earth), travel is necessary.

While *going* is circumstantial, *baptizing* and *teaching* carry a bit more exegetical weight. They qualify the main commanded action of the text. The subsidiary and qualifying work associated with the commanded action is to baptize and teach. Baptizing converts requires that new believers make a public profession of faith. A public, formal, and dramatic testimony of a new life is the importance of baptism.

Teaching others to obey cuts a wide swath through Christian experience. For now let me say that teaching people to obey is the most important ongoing ingredient for a meaningful Christian life. Baptizing and teaching people to obey form a fuller description of the Great Commission work. More on this in due course.

The imperative command of the text is *make disciples*. This is the formula for evangelizing the world and the methodology required to bring reproduction and multiplication to world mission. *The Great Commission without multiplication is evangelism paralyzed from the neck down.* By specifically commanding the making of disciples, Jesus specified the work product of the church.

He did not say "Make converts" or "Make Christians." Being a convert or a Christian does not necessarily equal reproduction. Many Christians are spiritually sterile; many don't take the gospel forward. When a disciple is made, two good things happen: a disciple is healthy and godly; disciples reproduce themselves, and some become disciple makers, resulting in multiplication. Therefore, disciples solve the crisis at the heart of the church. Disciple making creates a quality product and an effective work force. This is God's plan for His church.

Disciples are the product; baptizing and teaching to obey are the qualifiers. At minimum, a disciple goes public in his witness, through baptism, and submits to the authority of others by being taught. He makes himself available for training; he understands the virtue of accountability. He devotes himself to a lifetime of learning. No disciple making occurs without accountability. Chapter 6 contains entire units on both multiplication and accountability, so I won't belabor the points here.

A progression toward disciple making cannot be ignored if we wish to obey the Great Commission. To get disciples, there must be accountability, otherwise, people will not be taught to obey. Only those who have placed themselves in an accountable learning mode will become reproducers. Out of this group will emerge those with leadership gifts and special abilities, who will form the disciple-making core of any church. They, in turn, create environments for disciple making and multiplication. This results in exponential growth of the church. Disciple making is the heart of the church, because it is the heart of the Great Commission.

The Obedient Church

"Teaching them to obey everything I have commanded you . . ." refers to the Great Commission itself. Teaching the church to obey the Great Commission is a vital, but neglected, work. The question arises, if a church does not obey the Great Commission, is that church obeying God; is it an obedient church? No, it is not. Determined dedication to the Great Commission lies at the heart of Christ's command. Of course we must also ask "What qualifies as obedience to the Great Commission?"

The bare bones of obedience is the *intentional effort* to define a disciple, then to produce disciples through various vehicles of the church. This book will show various ways to get the job done. But a nonnegotiable is the intentional effort. In addition obedience requires a *commitment to reproduction*. The evidence of such a commitment appears in training people to do evangelism: showing them how, doing it with them, then letting them do it. The creation of expectations and providing training to meet those expectations with accountability is a true commitment to reproduction.

A third component for bare bones of obedience is *a commitment to multiplication*. The evidence of such commitment can be seen in the selecting of those with leadership ability to be trained as disciple makers. This means special training that teaches leaders to create environments where they make disciples in batches. They learn how to train groups of people and how to teach other gifted disciples to become disciple makers. From this pool you draw elders, pastors, missionaries, church planters, and other key leaders.

Obedience to the Great Commission hinges on the three qualifiers: an intentional plan that defines and trains disciples, a commitment to reproduction by training in evangelism with accountability, and a commitment to multiplication by special training in order to produce disciple-making leaders. These are the bare bones of obedience to the Great Commission; anything less is sin.

Are Disciples More Than Converts?

Jesus ordered us to "make disciples." Disciples are both the people who please the Lord and the people who will reach the world. Therefore, a clear identification of a disciple is imperative. Understanding what a disciple is and what a disciple does are top priority for the church. The irony of the church is that we throw the word *disciple* around freely, but too often with no definition. Such a condition is like a shoe company trying to produce a product without specifications. The product coming off the end of the assembly line would be interesting.

The definition has proven elusive. Is a disciple a convert, one who has simply trusted in Christ alone for his salvation? Is it more, a fruit-bearing, reproducing believer described by Jesus in other passages? Or is it only for the totally committed person whom Jesus described in Luke 14:25–35, who puts Christ before possessions, self, and family?

Are Disciples Born or Made?

If disciples are born and not made, then they must, from the moment of spiritual birth, reflect the definitions and meet the requirements described by Jesus. These characteristics need not be fully matured, yet they should be present in embryo. They would look like abiding, obedient, fruit-bearing believers who glorify God, possess joy, and love one another (see John 15:7–17). They would have the priorities of the disciple described by Jesus in Luke 14:25–35 and the dedication of the follower who gives up everything for the gospel (see Luke 9:23–25).

If disciples are born and not made, while these characteristics would take time to develop, they would develop 100 percent of the time in the truly regenerate. Therefore, every single Christian would be a healthy, reproducing believer. If people did not reflect the disciple's profile, then they would not be Christians.

If disciples are born and not made, non-Christians dominate the evangelical church. A generous estimate would find no more than 25 percent of evangelicals meeting Christ's standard for a disciple. As stated earlier, only 7 percent have been trained in evangelism, and only 2 percent have introduced another to Christ. By Christ's definition, disciples reproduce themselves through evangelism. If one takes the "disciples are born and not made" theology and joins it to the definition of a disciple given by Jesus and then adds the objective facts concerning today's evangelical church, the results are alarming. At least 75 percent of evangelicals are not Christians, because they just don't measure up to Christ's standards of what it means to be a disciple.

The "disciples are born and not made" theology has many harmful effects. Some quarters accept it because they have not stood that theology toe to toe with Jesus' definitions. When it does stand toe to toe, it creates a gospel of works. It adds to the requirements for salvation. Not only does it require faith in Christ, but commitment to the disciple's profile is required. Unless you are willing to commit to world evangelism, labor in the harvest field, placing Christ before everything in your life, then in the words of Jesus, "you cannot be my disciple" (Luke 14:25–35); therefore, you are denied salvation.

While Scripture teaches definitive transformation subsequent to salvation, it does not teach that all believers will become reproducing disciples. Christian maturity is taught as a goal for every Christian but is not considered the evidence of regeneration. Paul's thirteen epistles sufficiently testify to the church being composed of immature Christians who should have done better. The existence of such texts as 1 Corinthians 3:1–3 and Hebrews 5:11–13 provide evidence that disobedient/carnal Christians were still considered Christians.

The confrontation between disciple as convert and disciple as mature, reproducing believer is like two bald men fighting over a hairbrush. The controversy is unnecessary and the product of a poor hermeneutic. The problem comes from composing definitions on lexical meaning alone, trying to define *disciple* by the word's etymology without consideration of more important data.

Another mistake is to argue from silence that Jesus never made a distinction between *disciple* and *believer* or *convert*. This falsely assumes that every time *disciple* is used it means the same thing. The word is much more fluid than such a hermeneutic allows.

A lexical definition of *mathetes* "always implies the existence of a personal attachment which shapes the whole life of the one described as *mathetes*, and which in its particularity, leaves no doubt as to who is deploying the formative power."[1] To summarize Kittel's article, a disciple is a follower, a student of a certain teacher; John the Baptist, Plato, Jesus had disciples. It always means a supremely personal union.

The article goes on to mention that *mathetes* is always associated with following. Disciples do more than simply believe; many believed in Christ, few followed Him. Few dropped their normal life routine to become followers. Note that up to five hundred followed Him during the height of His popularity. Disciples made sacrifices to adjust their lifestyles to obey Christ; they were a breed apart. A disciple was and is a person of concrete action and commitment.

Jesus characterized disciples as people of commitment and obedience. They also willingly suffered and shared in the work. The primary use of *mathetes* in the Gospels described the relationship between the earthly followers of Jesus during His earthly mission: the twelve, the seventy, and the five hundred. The contextual aspects, plus lexical definitions, require us to think of a disciple as a committed follower of Jesus Christ. It means more than just a believer, but a person who demonstrates belief by action.

Another use of *mathetes* is in the Acts of the Apostles. Kittel once again comments, "It is to be noted first that *mathetes* is used for Christians only in specific sections of Acts, namely Acts 6:1–21:6. Before chapter six, Christians are 'those believing' or 'the brothers.' The use of *mathetes* is unsystematic, it does not occur in the 'we' sections except 21:4, 16." "We" sections are those parts of the writing where the author Luke was present.[2]

In Acts the term *mathetes* is used for Christians in general, not just the personal followers of Christ. It includes those who did not know Jesus personally; for instance, Timothy was called a disciple. The mark of a disciple in Acts is found in 6:7, obedience of the faith. Paul, we are told in Acts 9:26, had disciples. On the first missionary journey Paul and Barnabas returned to the evangelized cities and strengthened the disciples and appointed elders (see Acts 14:21–24).

Jesus' Definition of Disciple

The most important factor in defining a disciple is the teachings of Jesus. He was the disciple maker; He was speaking to the disciples when the Great Commission was issued. Jesus' definitions are head and shoulders above any other. Jesus defined a *disciple*, and we will consider that profile in detail in the next few pages.

We can summarize Jesus' teaching on disciples as follows. A disciple:

Is willing to deny self, take up a cross daily, and follow Him (Luke 9:23).
Puts Christ before self, family, and possessions (Luke 14:25–35).
Is committed to Christ's teachings (John 8:31).
Is committed to world evangelism (Matthew 9:36–38).
Loves others as Christ loves (John 13:34–35).
Abides in Christ, is obedient, bears fruit, glorifies God, has joy, and loves the brethren (John 15:7–17).

If a person is not willing to make such commitments, Jesus declares emphatically three times, "He cannot be my disciple" (see Luke 14:26–27, 33).

To draw the conclusion that Jesus made no distinction between believing in Him and commitment to Him is to ignore the facts. Jesus spoke to many about the importance of eternal life. To Nicodemus, the woman at the well, and the thief on the cross, He did not mention the rigors of discipleship. He emphasized belief and trust; ". . . Whoever believes in him shall not perish but have eternal life" (John 3:16). John 6:25–29 and John 11:25 also provide Jesus' teaching on salvation as distinct from His teachings on the requirements of being His disciple. Jesus does make a distinction between the need for faith, leading to eternal life, and the need for commitment, leading to following Him and being His disciple. Therefore, I have drawn four conclusions concerning the definition of *disciple*.

1. Truly regenerate believers are technically disciples from the moment of spiritual birth. True believers are followers of Jesus; this does not mean that they will become mature followers of Jesus or they will make their lives count for Christ. They may live in spiritual slumber, their lives may waste God's gifts and talents. Therefore, the command to go and make disciples does include evangelism. Introducing people to Christ is the first step to the Great Commission.
2. Jesus meant more than "make converts." While every true believer is a disciple, Jesus meant more than just "go and do evangelism." Believers are to be baptized, openly identified with Christ, and taught to obey all that is commanded, that is, to be trained and built into mature, reproducing disciples.

   When Jesus said, "Make disciples," by necessity, the disciples understood it to mean much more than simply getting people to believe in Jesus. They had seen hundreds come and go; had witnessed the multitudes of the needy, the takers, and the superficial scramble after the spectacular; and knew that getting people to say, "Yes, I believe," was not enough.

They had to interpret it to mean to make out of others what Jesus had made out of them. The very fact that they had to count the cost, make sacrifices, and follow Him, meant that Jesus required a long and intentional process for people to become disciples. Their task began with evangelism, but that was just the start. They needed to produce people committed to reaching the world, those through whom the gospel could be multiplied. Making disciples includes winning them, but winning them is just the first step.

3. Making disciples of all nations is stated as a goal. The process would be to win as many as possible, to develop as many as possible, and multiply through as many as possible. "Make disciples" includes the entire disciple-making process, from conversion to trained disciple maker. Therefore, the process of disciple making is legitimate. Not only that, it is the very heart of what Christ expects of His church. Disciple making introduces people to the Savior, builds them to maturity, and trains them to reproduce and be effective for Christ. That is the work of the church and the commanded work of the pastor.

The belief that disciples are born, not made, leads one to conclude that disciple making is evangelism. The commanded work of the church, then, would be to evangelize at the expense of the general health of the church. The commanded work of the church would be to evangelize, the secondary work would be maturing the saints, if time permitted. Disciples are first born, then they are made. They are born by the Spirit of God, with the right factory-installed equipment. Then they must be built, trained, taught, and led to commitment to Jesus Christ. Therefore, Jesus commanded more than evangelism; He commanded taking all Christians to His definition of a mature disciple.

4. When Jesus commissioned the church to "make disciples," He charged the church with the responsibility to build reproducing disciples. He speaks to the quality of the product. The quality of the product is the key to world evangelism.

Disciple making triggers multiplication. As a strategy and process, multiplication is the key to world evangelization. Disciple making is more than a product; it is a methodology required to reach the world. To the degree the church dedicates itself to disciple making it is obedient to Christ. Now the mission is in trouble because the church has stopped at the first step to disciple making. Too often the church wins and baptizes, but does not teach and train. The sad result is a lack of reproduction and multiplication. God desires that every Christian be His disciple. He wills that every Christian become spiritually reproductive.

Christ commissioned His church to make disciples to insure that two things happen: that the church will produce a healthy product (a reproducing disciple) and that world evangelization will become a reality. But only disciples reproduce and multiply; there is no other way. Therefore, disciple making must be at the heart of the local church. The pastor must install disciple making as first priority.

The Disciple's Profile (John 15:7–17)

Jesus teaches that His relationship to the disciples is like that of a vine to the branches. The emphasis of this upper room teaching is a fourth phase of their relationship. The "come and see" phase was introductory and four months in length. The "come and follow Me" phase established the Twelve in the basics and lasted ten months. The "come and be with Me" stage was twenty months long and was the Twelve's specialized training in preparation for taking over ministry responsibility. The fourth phase, called "remain in Me," Jesus explained within the analogy of the vine and branches.

Jesus has told them of the change in their relationship. He is leaving and the Holy Spirit is coming. He will be with them in a different, completely fulfilling way. The absolute necessity for effective ministry is stated in 15:5, "I am the vine; you are the branches. If a man remains in me and I in him, he will bear much fruit; apart from me you can do nothing."

The nonnegotiable for the fruitful Christian is remaining in Christ. But Christ does not emphasize fruit bearing, but remaining in Him. By remaining in Christ, as a branch depends on the vine, the believer will bear fruit; indeed, he cannot avoid bearing fruit. This teaching is crucial to disciple making, because Jesus goes on to describe the fruit-bearing believer who pleases God. He identifies this person as a disciple. He is talking to disciples about disciples by describing the ideal disciple. In other words, Jesus describes the product of the Great Commission. A disciple's profile has six dimensions.

A Disciple Remains in Christ (15:7)

"If you *remain* in me and my words *remain* in you, ask whatever you wish, and it will be given you" (15:7, italics added).

"Remain" comes from the Greek word *mena*, meaning "to abide or maintain contact for a sustained time." Christ means that He and His followers must maintain an organic relationship. This will be an essential for fruitful service. But even before we define what it means to remain in Christ, we should consider the first word of the sentence.

The first word is *if*. In English the word implies a degree of doubt. There are four different forms in Greek for saying *if*. This particular form clearly communicates a degree of doubt. The choice will determine the possible future action. Each Christian makes the choice daily, "Will I follow Christ today?" "Will His Spirit guide me?" "Will His teaching instruct me?" Each person is required to respond to the call of Christ, "Follow Me, and I will make you become fishers of men" (Mark 1:17 NASB).

Too many think that once you become a Christian you turn on the spiritual autopilot. Christian growth is supernatural, not automatic. The important difference is the daily decision to follow Christ. Choice directly governs the degree to which one remains in Christ. By starting with the conditional *if*, Jesus clearly communicates an ongoing responsibility, on the part of the disciples, to maintain their relationship.

Sadly, many Christians have rejected discipleship based on a misconception. They wrongly think that serious allegiance means being a Green Beret for Christ or God's Delta Force, that unless you are willing to invade enemy territory, do hand-to-hand combat, and go door to door, you cannot be a disciple. Let's look at the facts. Saying yes to Christ requires two actions that make it possible for any person to remain in Christ.

Be rightly related to Christ's words. The disciple has a commitment to Scripture. Jesus stated earlier, "If you hold to my teaching, you are really my disciples" (John 8:31).

Clearly, Jesus refers to His oral teachings. Equally clearly, He built much of His teaching on the Old Testament; see, for example, the Sermon on the Mount. The distilled twentieth-century application says the disciple is committed to Christ's teachings as found in the New Testament. However, the complete canon of Scripture is considered God's Word; therefore, the disciple is committed to the authority of the entire Bible. The only way a disciple can rightly relate to Christ's Word is to demonstrate a commitment to it. This commitment demonstrates itself in the disciple's working knowledge of Scripture. Functionally, that working knowledge has several dimensions.

STUDY. "Do your best to present yourself to God as one approved, a workman who does not need to be ashamed and who correctly handles the word of truth" (2 Tim. 2:15).

"Do your best" means to be diligent, to make every effort to understand Scripture well enough that you can be a skilled craftsman and hold your head high when confronted as to your knowledge and ability to apply Scripture to life. This means that a disciple will read the Bible, study the Bible, memorize the Bible, and be able to teach and apply the Bible to life.

FIGHT. "For though we live in the world, we do not wage war as the world does. The weapons we fight with are not weapons of the world. On the contrary, they have divine power to demolish strongholds. We demolish arguments and every pretension that sets itself up against the knowledge of God, and we take captive every thought to make it obedient to Christ" (2 Cor. 10:3–5).

The disciple must know the Bible well enough, through study, to fight temptation and protect himself against the ideas and philosophies of the world. The disciple is confronted daily with thousands of messages and ideas. A biblical defense system must sort out the ideas, take what is obedient to Christ, and reject what is not. The average Christian's defense against the philosophies of the world is about as effective as using the lights in Boston's Old North Church that prompted the famous ride of Paul Revere, one if by land, two if by sea, to warn against a nuclear attack. Many Christians—no, I would say the majority of Christians—are helpless in the face of modern media messages.

When the teen asks, "Why is it wrong to read pornography?" many Christian parents cannot go to the Bible for an answer. They don't know where to find it. This reveals the biblical illiteracy among evangelicals. What does the Bible say about abortion, capital punishment, feeding the poor, loaning money to friends, teaching children, anxiety management, finances, marriage, and so on? If you haven't studied it, you won't know it; therefore, you must fight without any weapons. Every Christian must wage war with the world, the flesh, and the devil. The question is, are you equipped for the battle? The disciple is; the majority are not.

DEFEND. "Always be prepared to give an answer to everyone who asks you to give the reason for the hope that you have. But do this with gentleness and respect" (1 Peter 3:15).

The disciple studies Scripture to renew his mind and shape his own behavior, to have a working knowledge of God's principles as they apply to life, so he can fight temptation and take every thought captive to the obedience of Christ, and in order to defend the faith among those seeking to understand the Christian message.

Every disciple should understand what he believes well enough to spot counterfeit teaching. He should be able to answer the basic questions that people ask: "How do you know the Bible is reliable?" "Why does God allow suffering and evil?" "How can you say that Jesus is the only way to God?" The disciple must possess the knowledge and ability to answer such questions.

Study, fight, and defend; these three functional abilities result from demonstrated commitment to Scripture. The disciple has been transformed by the renewing of his mind. The information that renewed his mind and reprogrammed his behavior is the Word of God. God speaks to the disciple through His Word. This is the first and most important action in remaining in Christ.

The Bible is the starting point for any disciple. Many Christians lay "dead in the water," living in the spiritual doldrums. They desperately need to set their sails by making a commitment to study Scripture. When they try to skip this crucial step, they thereby pull away from the vine. The Christian's relationship to God's Word is the most critical issue in a vibrant walk. Everything about walking with Christ and living in the world is built on it.

Without a working knowledge of the Word, the Christian is weak. Paul does not extol that kind of weakness in 2 Corinthians 12:10, "when I am weak, then I am strong." Deliberate neglect of a commanded activity causes this weakness. Today's ineffective church product results from Christians not rightly relating to God's Word. Yes, many evangelicals will attend church and listen to a sermon. But it ends there. They must be spoon-fed. Disciples are self-feeding; they know how to take food and put it where it belongs. Little consternation seems to exist over the fact that the majority of Christians cannot feed themselves. Hearing and reading the Bible will not make you a self-feeding disciple, because they alone do not help you study, fight, and defend. There is just no way to get around this first step: "If you plan to remain in me, my words must remain in you."

A commitment to prayer. "Ask whatever you wish, and it will be given you" (John 15:7) speaks of effective prayer. A disciple who remains in Christ and understands His Word knows what and how to pray. He knows what to ask for and how to get it. He understands what not to ask for, as well. This verse does not give disciples carte blanche. It must be balanced with many other comments on prayer. Other qualifications for answered prayer include commandment keeping (see 1 John 3:22) and praying according to the will of God (see 1 John 5:14–15). The disciple is a person of informed and authoritative prayer.

Communication with God forms the basis of remaining and the root of living as a disciple. God talks to me through the Scriptures. I talk back to Him through prayer. Getting to know God, in some respects, is like getting to know any person. There is conversation, sharing of lives, the interchange of ideas and opinions. Talking to God is as vital as God talking to us. The disciple learns to talk to God by listening to what God says first. Prayer responds to what God has already said. Remaining in Christ requires both God's Word and prayer.

Most problems that come to the pastor's study find their root to the counselees' inadequate relationship with God. At the root lies the problem that they do not commune with God. They are not taking time to listen to His voice, to reveal their hearts, and to understand His Word. One of the most disturbing aspects to the common malady of Christians' lack of communion with God is that pastors suffer as much as the congregation.

Too many pastors study the Bible because it's their job: Study the Bible to preach and pray, in order to improve pastoral performance. They have professionalized Bible study and prayer. The utilitarian approach corrupts communion with God. God is being used in the same way I use my electric pencil sharpener. When I want it to write better, I just stick my pencil into the machine. When I want to preach a hot sermon or get more money raised for a project, I pray for God's help.

There is nothing immoral about asking God for help. In fact, He encourages us to do so. The immorality appears when we only give God attention to ask Him for something. He doesn't get any time to feed our souls, lift our spirits, or just allow us the pleasure of His company. How long would most of our earthly relationships last if we only took?

The other issue facing many Christian leaders is the life-long need for such communion. Christians never outgrow the need for basics. Quite often leaders started their Christian walks well. They had good disciplines of Bible study, prayer, Scripture memory, and personal evangelism. As time marched on, however, they neglected these basic skills for the esoteric, the elitism of Christian professionalism. Pastors and Christian leaders often burn out because they have left their first love. The spiritual flames flickered out because the fire wasn't kindled by constant communion with God.

Michael Jordan, the great basketball player for the Chicago Bulls, does spectacular things on the court. People "ooh" and "ah" repeatedly as he does superhuman feats. Yet unless Jordan learned and mastered the basics, he would have no foundation on which to build. If he could not dribble without kicking the ball, pivot without traveling, rebound without fouling others, pass without throwing the ball away, it would mean nothing that Jordan can jump out of the gym, run like a deer, and move quickly like a cat.

First Christians must master the basics that give them the spiritual foundation to maintain a lifelong commitment to Christ. The Christian can best utilize spiritual gifts, talents, and life circumstances when he has that foundation. The first mark of the disciple's profile is that he remains in Christ by communicating with God through the Word and prayer.

A Disciple Is Obedient (John 15:9; Matthew 28:20; John 14:21)

Jesus' qualifier to "making disciples" in Matthew was "teaching them to obey everything I have commanded you." People must be taught to obey, because it does not come naturally. "All men are ruined on the side of their natural propensities," wrote Edmund Burke. Strengths become weaknesses. Accountability is essential to successful disciple making, because it teaches people to live obedient lives for Christ. Jesus said a disciple obeys, therefore, there is no such thing as disciple making without accountability.

We practice accountability daily in our homes and places of business. The truth is that Christian growth is also nearly impossible and unbalanced, at best, without it. When I survey my Christian life, I see several people who have contributed, but the ones who helped me the most held me accountable for my actions.

Jesus links obedience to love. "As the Father has loved me, so have I loved you. Now remain in my love. If you obey my commands, you will remain in my love, just as I have obeyed my Father's commands and remain in his love" (John 15:9–10). A few minutes earlier Jesus said, "If you love me, you will obey what I command" (John 14:15), and, "Whoever has my commands and obeys them, he is the one who loves me. He who loves me will be loved by my Father, and I too will love him and show myself to him" (John 14:21).

Jesus requires loving obedience of His disciples. He taught that love equals obedience, that the very act of obedience is love. The uneducated Christian waits until he feels the prompting of the Spirit before he takes action. The Word-filled believer takes action based upon the facts of God's commands, regardless of how he feels about it. He prays out of obedience; he witnesses because God commanded it. He reaches out to those in need because it is clearly God's will. Many times the obedient disciple feels like doing all these wonderful things, but often he does not. The difference between the disciple and the unsuccessful Christian is the disciple's commitment to obey God regardless of circumstances, feelings, or other pressures.

The rewards of loving obedience are many. We can summarize the combined teaching of the above texts as follows: God loved us first. He started the process by sending His Son as a ransom for many. "For God so loved the world that he gave . . ." (John 3:16). God loved and therefore took action. "We love because he first loved us" (1 John 4:19).

The next step is that we respond in loving obedience to what God has done. "If you love Me," Jesus said, "you will keep My commandments" (John 14:15 NASB). We step out by faith in loving obedience, and the results are wonderful. "He who loves me will be loved by my Father, and I too will love him and show myself to him" (John 14:21).

God loves us back by teaching us more about Himself. Jesus teaches us the secrets of the Spirit by revealing the details of God's plan for our lives. The details and spiritual secrets of God are found on the path of obedience. Have you wondered why some people seem to know more about God and how He works than others? They have walked down the path of obedience for many years, and God has taught them much.

The majority of Christians, however, stand at the edge of the path of obedience, waiting for more information. "God, if You would give me more details about my future or what is out there for me, I would take a step of faith; I would be ready to go." God answers that request simply, "You don't get more information until you start walking down the path of obedience." The next step is yours, so start walking down the path. If you require all the facts before you step out in faith, you won't get anywhere. God wants you to walk by faith, not by sight. The Word of God is a light to your path and a lamp to your feet. It provides enough light to walk and see where you are going in the next step. If you could see the future, had all the information, you wouldn't go. If you could see the challenge, the trouble, the pain, if you had all the information, you would choose to stay, to avoid the pain. You have only one way to live the obedient Christian life: Walk by faith, step out in loving obedience, regardless of fears or feelings. If you do, God promises to love you in wonderful ways that you can experience by no other means.

Accountability stimulates stepping out in loving obedience. Disciple making would be impossible without it. Disciples keep their commitments to God by loving obedience. Disciple makers assist in the process by helping people keep their commitments to God through accountability. It all works together for making disciples. A disciple's life is one of close communion with God and walking in loving obedience, assisted by accountability.

A Disciple Bears Fruit (John 15:8, 16)

The mark of what a disciple produces comes next. "This is to my Father's glory, that you bear much fruit, showing yourselves to be my disciples" (John 15:8). In addition, "You did not choose me, but I chose you and

appointed you to go and bear fruit—fruit that will last"
(John 15:16).

Jesus expected His disciples to reproduce. That is what
fruit means—by their very nature, they by necessity produced fruit. If the branch remains connected to the vine
for a sufficient time, it will bear fruit.

If the disciple remains in Christ for a sufficient time,
the disciple will bear fruit. Fruit bearing does at least
three things: It glorifies God (see John 15:8), it meets
with the expectations that Christ had when He called the
disciples (v. 16), and there will be a lot of high-quality
fruit (vv. 8, 16).

There is some discussion as to the nature of the fruit. Is
the fruit that of personal evangelism, or is it simply generic?
This is not an either-or situation. Just as by its nature a
healthy branch connected to the vine will bear fruit, so a
healthy Christian will bear fruit. The healthy Christian's nature will reproduce the fruit of the Spirit: "love, joy, peace,
patience, kindness, goodness, faithfulness, gentleness and
self-control" (Gal. 5:22–23). This fruit is characteristically
active, not passive. Kindness is not a sickly smile; it takes
action, it does something. A simple act of kindness may be
picking up a dropped table utensil, or it may be introducing the person to Christ. The fruit of the Spirit is much
more than personal evangelism, but fruit bearing without
personal evangelism is unthinkable.

Therefore, we don't want to limit fruit bearing to evangelism, but all demonstration of the fruit of the Spirit touches
evangelism. No positive thing a believer does could be ex-
cluded from being a witness to someone for the authenticity of Jesus Christ. The one nonnegotiable we should
not overlook is that all Christians are responsible to share
their faith.

The church must guard against the belief that you can
bear fruit, be pleasing to God, but not share your faith. This
is impossible. No reproducing believer does not share his
faith. No disciple doesn't share his faith. There are Chris-

tians who do not share their faith, but no disciples who glorify God do not verbalize Christ to the world.

There is a hierarchy of fruit bearing and outreach. The objective of all outreach is to introduce others to the Savior. That a fruit-bearing disciple would not lead others to Christ is unthinkable. The top of the hierarchy of fruit bearing is personal evangelism. When Jesus said, "I chose you and appointed you to go and bear fruit," He surely meant to spread the Word of God throughout the world. Every disciple knows how to communicate the gospel. Not only that, he *does* communicate the gospel and leads others to Christ. Christ expected every disciple to reproduce.

Evangelism is vital to making disciples. Far too many people call themselves disciples but do not share their faith. Far too many churches claim they believe and practice disciple making, yet there is not training or accountability toward personal evangelism. There is no such thing as a sterile disciple. Disciples reproduce. This is why they are the commanded product of the church.

The evangelical church is packed with people who have been trained in a contorted manner. They have been taught how to study the Bible, how to pray, how to have good fellowship, but evangelism is left out. Those cases will result in people whose Bible study has become academic, their prayer life boring, their fellowship superficial—all because they have neglected the catalyst for the first three, namely personal evangelism.

God's plan for the church is that the discipled church membership is the outreach program. Their behavior and their ability to penetrate their world for Christ tests their relationship to Christ. What are they like on the playground, in the office, the teacher's lounge, the boardroom, and the courthouse? The fact is that a quality product will reproduce itself. A trained army of ministers deployed into the local community will bear much fruit—fruit that remains.

A Disciple Glorifies God (John 15:8)

The disciple glorifies God more as a general result than because of a specific skill or characteristic. I include it because it is so important to the total perspective. "This is to my Father's glory" (15:8). This first struck me when I was attempting to determine how I could best glorify God. No Christian would argue that the purpose of God's people throughout history has been to glorify God. No one questions that this is the purpose of the church.

At the close of his wonderful prayer in the Ephesian letter, Paul puts it perfectly, "Now to him who is able to do immeasurably more than all we ask or imagine, according to his power that is at work within us, to him be glory in the church and in Christ Jesus throughout all generations, for ever and ever! Amen" (Eph. 3:20–21).

The church best glorifies God by making disciples, simply because fruit-bearing believers glorify God. Fruit-bearing believers are called proven disciples (see John 15:8). Christ said to make disciples because they will reproduce, they will create multiplication, and that will lead to world evangelism.

In Matthew 28 Christ commanded the church to "make disciples." Now in John 15, He has told us how to measure disciples: Men and women who remain in Christ are obedient and bear fruit. They also do the best job of glorifying God. This kind of person is worth dedicating ourselves to producing. May the church be obedient and apply itself to its holy calling.

A Disciple Has Joy (John 15:11)

I don't know anyone who is against joy. Jesus was for it too: "I have told you this so that my joy may be in you and that your joy may be complete" (John 15:11). Only disciples are candidates for joy. Joy is distinct from happiness. I am all for happiness; however, it is more fleeting than joy. Happiness comes and goes with the conditions of life. Anyone who has a good life situation can experience happiness, and it does not require any action from God.

Joy, on the other hand, is a supernatural sense of well-being that comes from knowing that we are pleasing to God. People can take my happiness, but no one can touch my joy. Jesus had joy when He went to the cross. Paul sang for joy while in prison. Many martyrs and others who have suffered have told stories of unbounding, uncontrollable joy during times of great suffering. Jesus tells anyone who is willing to try, "You can have joy by being a disciple: I want you to have a full measure of joy. The way you do so is by applying the things I have just told you, namely the disciple's profile. If you will remain in Me through the Word and prayer, if you will obey Me by stepping out in loving obedience, if you will commit yourself to reproduce, you will glorify God and be the glad recipient of great joy."

The disciple-making pastor loves people so much that he will insist that all become disciples, because disciples' lives count for something and are lives of joy. It is a tremendous calling to help people develop lives of joy.

Disciples Love as Christ Loves (John 15:12–14, 17)

"My command is this: Love each other as I have loved you. Greater love has no one than this, that he lay down his life for his friends. . . . This is my command: Love each other" (John 15:12–13, 17).

I would think a person who communicates with God regularly, through the Word and prayer, who walks in loving obedience and has reproduced himself many times over, and who knows he is glorifying God, which gives him a deep sense of joy, would have a hard time not loving others. The standard Jesus raises is a high one: "as I have loved you." He doesn't expect perfection, but He does expect imitation.

All the disciples needed to do was remember. Remember His caring for them, His patience with them, the fact that

He met all their needs, that there was nothing He would not do, including washing their feet, raising family friends from the dead, and giving His own life so they might have eternal life. Regardless of the length of their lives, once Jesus qualified loving each other with "as I have loved you," they would have volumes of memories by which to define *love*. Those memories would guide them through the difficult times before them. Earlier Jesus gave this command an evangelistic twist when He claimed that the entire world would know they were His followers if they had love one for another (see John 13:34–35).

Modern-day disciples, of course, have the written record of Christ loving the disciples and others as well. In addition, we have the wonderful track record God has established in our lives. We have experienced His love many times over. The mark of a disciple is love. Love is preeminent in its ability to win others for the Savior. The distilled essence of Christ's ministry to mankind was motivated, sustained, and underlined by love.

Further Reflections

Disciples are born to be made. If only that clear thought would have descended on me before the 1988 publication of this book, I could have saved myself a lot of debate and discussion with critics. It did finally find its way into my brain, but, I must confess, under considerable duress.

I was interrogated—I mean, questioned—by seminary faculty members a couple of years after *The Disciple-Making Pastor* was published. I was confronted with questions such as, "What other kinds of adjectives could you have used to describe the work of a pastor? Why did you choose 'disciple-making'?" I thought a quip might work in response: "Is there any other kind of pastor?" They didn't seem to get my humor, so I forged ahead: "I know there are pastors who see their main function as something other than disciple making, but biblically, isn't disciple making the only important work of a pastor?"

I have always thought of the orders Christ gave His disciples as the central calling of every spiritual leader—the commission to disciple the nations, to baptize them, to teach them everything Christ commanded, and to encompass preaching, counseling, discipline, nurture, confrontation, exhortation, evangelism, and leadership training. What is there for a pastor to do other than to make disciples?

Then came the question, the kryptonite special, that threatened to stump me: "Are disciples born or made?"

(In those days the "lordship salvation" controversy was white-hot. John MacArthur, a well-known pastor, had published *The Gospel according to Jesus*, and several theologians had taken exception to his assertion that true belief includes obedience. I didn't allow myself to be sucked into the abyss of controversy then, and I will resist now except to say, "Attaboy, Johnny.")

The question stunned me; my brain froze in place. I can't describe the look on my face, but I must have appeared to be locked in a freeze-frame. Then it happened: the answer to my desperate prayer. The angels sang, the wind ruffled my hair, the oil of anointing ran down my neck, the bright blue sky opened, and a dove descended with the answer. I spoke ex cathedra: "Disciples are born to be made." The room was silent. The answer was eloquent but so simple that no one could disagree. I stood there knowing God had rescued me, proving once again that He is committed to taking the foolish things of this world to confound the wise.

The question the faculty should have asked me was, "Why does a book like *The Disciple-Making Pastor* need to be written?" The call to make disciples is as obvious to the work of a pastor as dancing is to a ballerina, as swimming is to a dolphin. It is not easy to explain why some pastors or leaders really understand and relate to the command to make disciples, while others do not. I think a major component is their cultural conditioning. Another is who mentored and influenced them and who trained them theologically. Yet another important factor is gifting. We all tend to gravitate to what we are good at and therefore enjoy.

There are more immediate rewards in preaching and numerical growth than in the slow, often difficult work of forming people in Christ (see Gal. 4:19). In the last twenty years I have interacted with and taught thousands of pastors around the globe. Almost all of them have believed in the inspiration and authority of Scripture. They all have had a passion to obey Christ and fulfill the Great Commission. Virtually all of them desire to make disciples, so the problem isn't intent or desire. The problem continues to be a lack of commitment to give time and energy to the creation of a disciple.

The reason I named this chapter "The Product" was not to extol a business model. Many took it as a crass term that implied a factory cranking out can openers. I am still a bit baffled by this objection. I chose the term to emphasize what kind of people we are to develop. The late Peter Drucker liked to ask, "What is your business?" *Business* refers to "one's work, occupation or profession or special task, duty or function."[3] And that "work" is to be a disciple and to make disciples.

In the many years since the first publication of *The Disciple-Making Pastor*, I have learned that being a disciple is a lot more important than a plan to make disciples. As I mentioned earlier, there should be a landfill somewhere where all the unused and disappointing discipleship programs are buried, primarily because we forgot to be disciples. It is the old problem of being Christian without being Christlike. In the second half of chapter 3, the profile of a disciple is drawn from John 15:7–17. Those six characteristics were:

a disciple remains in Christ through the Word and
   prayer;

a disciple is obedient;

a disciple bears fruit;

a disciple glorifies God;

a disciple has joy; and

a disciple loves as Christ loves.

It seems as if we have been in such a hurry to organize
our plan to reach others and get them growing in the faith
that we have not attended to our own lives in Christ. Life
in the fast lane has not worked. The faster we go, the less
we become.

"The product" is a person who is formed into the likeness
of our leader. Jesus was a man for others. He came to offer
Himself as a servant, and He sacrificed Himself. His disciples' first calling, then, is to choose the same life—a life of
humility, submission, sacrifice, and service. When we begin
to live for others, we will begin to have the same effect on
others as Jesus did. Living for others in brokenness is where
the power is. Our brokenness is God's special playground;
it is where He becomes mature in us (see 2 Cor. 12:9).

I have learned to slow down, to trust God to do a work
in me that then will be the key to those around me. What
gives me power and credibility is the fruit of the Spirit
being evident in my life. I am at peace with the future and
with what results come.

Nowadays when people ask me to sum up what it means
to be a disciple, I answer simply, "Rearrange your life around
the practices of Jesus." Live your life as though Jesus were
living it. If Jesus were a schoolteacher, what kind of teacher
would He be? If He were a husband, what kind of husband
would He be? If He were a pastor, what kind of pastor would
He be?

The kind of people we are determines what we do. I
don't believe you have to be a mature follower of Jesus

before you can serve Him. That is just an excuse not to obey. It is crucial, however, to know that Jesus' desire is for us to be mature disciples, because mature disciples are the key to giving the church the credibility it needs to get the world's attention. Then we will be willing to take up our cross daily and follow Him. The wonderful result is that His rule, His love, and His character will infiltrate every part of the culture, and His kingdom will grow. It will grow not just through churches but also through families, neighborhoods, businesses, clubs, recreation leagues, community services, and any other association of people. I like the statement I heard recently: "Get people outside their churches so they can become the church."

The Role of a Disciple-Making Pastor

Word Meanings and Observations

Want to start an argument? Ask pastors and church leaders to answer the following questions: What is the role of the senior or lead pastor? Are various biblical models equally valid? Is there a prescribed pastoral job description that emerges as top priority?

Want to escalate a proper theological debate into a shouting match? Then propose that the pastor is a specialist, primarily a teacher/equipper. Assert that he is called to work with the strong more than the weak, and that by training the well, he takes better care of and strengthens the weak. It is, in fact, true that the only real hope for the weak is the disciple-making pastor's multiplying his influence through the preparation of Christians for the work of service.

I have proposed that there is a crisis at the heart of the local church. The integrity of the church's product is in jeopardy, therefore, threatening the mission and turning the present church environment into a hotbed of weakness. I have also proposed that the top priority for corrective action is to rediscover and deploy the disciple-making pastor.

So what is a disciple-making pastor? What does he look like and act like? How is he different? The first part of the answer comes from an examination of Scripture.

The word *pastor*. The word *pastor* means "shepherd." No one will argue that the shepherding image was drawn from a common function in an agrarian society. It was an ideal illustration because everyone was familiar with the duties of a shepherd. This is no longer true. Therefore, it will be helpful to review the word history.

The Hebrew *roeh* and the Greek *poimen* have common meanings. *Roeh* means "to feed, to keep, to lead." From ancient times leaders were evaluated on their ability to "pastor" the people under their charge.[1]

Poimen as a noun means "shepherd," and as a verb, "to herd, tend, to pasture, to tend sheep."[2]

The contextual usage in both testaments refers to the leadership of God's people. In Old Testament passages such as Ezekiel 34:1–31 and Zechariah 11:4–14 God declares His disdain for selfish shepherds and His determination to replace their arrogance with His lovingkindness. Note that God considered prophets, priests, and kings shepherds. Kings of Assyria and Babylon were to shepherd their people, to protect and provide. The condemnation of "the shepherds of Israel" in Ezekiel 34 was directed against rulers. Other political, military, and spiritual leaders considered shepherds were Moses, David, and even King Cyrus of Persia.

The ancient use of *shepherd* was not employed as it is today. The average church member thinks of his pastor as a shepherd. That is correct, but the twentieth-century man's understanding of a shepherd is veiled by time and culture. He sees a man dressed in robe and sandals, leaning against a tree in a green pasture, strumming his harp. He is passive, gentle, nonconfrontational, and ready to answer every call of the sheep. That's why the elders bought him a cell phone.

But in antiquity shepherding reached into all of life. It meant to lead people in such a way as to meet an entire spectrum of real needs. Moses, David, and others were shepherds, yet were forceful leaders.

If we are to understand shepherding we must rid ourselves of the modern portrayal of shepherds as passive, weak, and unable to lead in the *real* world of politics, business, and world affairs. If this attitude isn't pervasive, why such an outcry when clergy enter the public square?

A common misreading of Old Testament roles is the case of Ezra and Nehemiah. People often say that Ezra was the spiritual leader and Nehemiah the civic leader. Ezra stuck to preaching, and Nehemiah concentrated on building. Ezra was the shepherd, Nehemiah the leader. While their role distinction was valid, restricting Nehemiah from being a shepherd is not. Nehemiah fits the Old Testament description of shepherd in every way. He led the people; he cared for them; he made spiritual renewal a reality through the task, while meeting their needs. Nehemiah was an outstanding shepherd.

Old Testament usage defines *shepherding* as "leading a people." This included all of life: commerce, education, foreign affairs, and providing the proper environment and instruction for spiritual life. The ancient understanding was multidimensional, more holistic than present usage.

The twofold task of the elder/bishop/pastor. The New Testament confirms the broader meaning of pastoring. Not so much lexically, but by two other words used synonymously. Many believe as I do, that *elder/bishop/pastor* are used synonymously.[3]

For example, take Paul's farewell to the Ephesian elders at Miletus. His final charge to church leaders reveals this trend: "Keep watch over yourselves and all the flock of which the Holy Spirit has made you *overseers*. Be *shepherds* of the church of God" (Acts 20:28, italics added).

Paul, an apostle, issues orders to elders. They are to oversee the church and shepherd the people. Their title is *elder*, their function is to oversee and shepherd. The following core data should help.

> *Elders* (from *presbuteros*) are the people to whom the care of the church is committed (see Acts 14:23). Their character qualifications are given in 1 Timothy 3:1–7 and Titus 1:5–9, and their importance is recorded in 1 Thessalonians 5:12; 1 Timothy 5:17; Hebrews 13:17; and 1 Peter 5:1–3.
>
> *Bishop* (from *episkopos*) is a function of elders to give oversight and leadership to the church (1 Tim. 3:1).
>
> *Pastors* (from *poimen*) are elders who pastor the church, feeding the flock by teaching the Word and protecting the church from various enemies both from within and without (1 Peter 5:1; Acts 20:28; Eph. 4:11).

Therefore, elders have two major functions:

OVERSIGHT

To rule (1 Tim. 5:17, *proistemi*, "to stand before the church"). In 1 Thessalonians 5:12 (NASB) the same word is translated "have charge over." Elders are given authority in order to manage church affairs. Though churches give authority in different ways, according to their polity, the point is that elders *are* to have authority.

To labor (1 Thess. 5:12, "respect those who work hard"). The responsibility requires work. Elders are expected to give their best.

To lead (Heb. 13:7, 17, 24, *hegeomai*, "to lead"). The description of leadership responsibility, particularly the mention of "watch[ing] over your souls" in 13:17 (NASB), leaves little doubt this refers to elders. Elders are to provide leadership, vision, and direction for the church. Elders should be proactive, rather than reactive.

PASTORING

To care (Acts 20:28; 1 Peter 5:1–3). Pastoral care is entrusted to the elders. They are responsible to be good examples of caring people. Elders must see to the care of the people, especially during difficult times.

To protect (Acts 20:28; 2 Tim. 2:24; 1 Thess. 5:14). Elders are to protect from wolves in sheep clothing in doctrine, lifestyle, and harmful attitudes.

To teach (2 Tim. 2:22). Paul wrote that Timothy, an elder/ pastor, should find others through whom to multiply himself ("able to teach"). First Thessalonians 5:12–13, and 1 Timothy 5:17 indicate a teaching responsibility. Not every elder needs to be gifted as a teacher in the formal sense, but each should be able to communicate the important truths of Christ to others.

What, then, are the implications for modern-day pastoring? First, it should be said that the modern-day version of the pastor is not found in Scripture. The position we call senior pastor of a local church is not clearly presented but is there by implication.

Reasons for the modern-day pastor. It is clear from Paul's early church planting that he delegated the oversight and pastoring of the churches to a group of leaders called elders (see Acts 14:23). This trend continued, because churches established later, such as Ephesus, also had elders. Regardless of what polity conclusions one draws, the leadership structure of the local church placed authority in the hands of a small group of men, not just one man. Whether that authority came from the apostles, or in modern times, from the congregation or the structure above the local church, accountability should exist as a principle.

The plurality of elders in the local church is solidly built on biblical example. This provided accountability for the one man who usually emerges as the dominant figure. Three fundamental observations lead me to believe that the modern-day pastor's existence is necessary.

First, throughout human history, the truism "leadership is vital to successful venture" has remained constant. For good or ill, leadership has spelled the difference. Consider the biblical examples. Why didn't God form a committee with Noah as chairman and ask them to do a feasibility study on the possibility of worldwide flooding and man-hours to build an ark? Why didn't God tell Abraham to ask around to see if others thought it would be a good idea to sell everything and go to a deserted, barren land? Moses and the Exodus, Joshua and conquering the Promised Land, there are many examples. God didn't ask, because His plans for rescuing the world were too important to get stuck in committee. God didn't ask, because He believes in leadership. God, by His actions, uses a key figure to lead His people. It was true then; it is true now.

Some churches claim to have a plurality of elders, with no single leader. But objective observation clearly demonstrates one person stands head and shoulders above the rest. While there may be accountability, debate, give and take on issues, the leader remains.

The societal structures of modern America make a full-time pastor essential for a church to grow and develop. I may be the master of the obvious, but the working man does not have the time or energy to do what is required. The working person can fit into and be an important part of the ministry, if the church staff can set the stage, define the task, provide the training, and assist in the work.

A second reason that the full-time pastor is essential is the biblical example. On the day of Pentecost God sent in His first team, namely the apostles. When God launched an aggressive evangelistic thrust to the Gentile world, the Antioch church sent their best, the apostle Paul. After three missionary journeys, many new churches had been established. The apostolic authority was then delegated to elders on the local church level.

Along with this arrangement came the first inklings of a full-time pastor. For three years Paul served as a pastor to the Ephesian church and another eighteen months in Corinth. The evidence that there was a pastor who gave his full time to the work of the church and had special authority in the office are Paul's letters to Timothy and Titus. Paul's writings reveal that both Timothy and Titus needed advice and encouragement with respect to their duties in leading the church.

Beginning with Jesus himself, the apostles, the elders, Timothy, and Titus, the church has required leadership. Not only that, but each local assembly requires that one person emerge as the key leader. In contemporary culture, as in the first century, that person has been called the pastor.

A third reason to believe that the full-time pastor is necessary to the modern church is history. Church historian Bruce Shelley writes: "After the turn of the century Ignatius, the pastor of the church at Antioch, wrote a series of letters. In these he speaks habitually of a single bishop or pastor in each church. . . . No one seems to know just how the single pastor, assisted by the elders and deacons became the widespread pattern within the churches, but we know it did."[4]

The local church pastor has emerged as the key player in setting the course for the church. He is the key both to revitalization of existing churches and to the priorities and look of new churches. Like any other, the above biblical imperatives and descriptions require the disciple-making pastor to engage in both oversight and pastoring. He is different, however, in the way he gets it done.

Now that we have erected the biblical framework for the elder/bishop/pastor function, let's become more pragmatic. From this point forward, I will use the term *pastor* to mean the senior pastor who is called by a local church. Assume from this point forward that the pastor is working with some sort of accountability with elders or congregational checks and balances. Let us also assume that the pastor is one of several elders, but by virtue of his office, has been given greater liberty to lead, to design, to shape the life of the church.

It is time to get more specific in answer to the question, Is there a specific job description for the pastor? I believe so. Too often thinking about pastoral function stops with the general framework described above. This incomplete and unfinished thinking has led to the existence of a Frankenstein monster: the generic pastor. The Frankenstein image works because the generic pastor has become the major contributor to the weakness of the Western church. What the church has created is in the process of destroying the church.

The Generic Pastor. By *generic* I mean "general, nonspecific, or plain." Not plain in style or look, rather, general and plain in purpose and goal. The generic pastor is in many ways the exact opposite of the disciple-making pastor.

First it is important to understand that the generic pastor and the disciple-making pastor agree more than they disagree. Ironically, often they agree on what they should do, but differ radically in work behavior. They might agree on all cardinal doctrines, but differ in theology of the church. Commonly they agree about functional matters of teaching and training, yet the generic pastor has not thought it through. The following are some marks of the generic pastor:

1. He considers himself the servant of the people. Therefore, he stands before them and says, "I am here to serve you." I believe this is a big mistake, because a pastor serves Christ, not people (see 1 Cor. 4:1). People taken in isolation are not worth serving. God alone is worth my worship and my service. When the pastor serves people, he serves their interests. When He serves Christ, he doesn't serve their interests, but rather their best interests. Only when we serve Christ can we serve the best interests of people. Otherwise we will burn out from the frustration of trying to please their whims and desires.

   People's interests are often in direct conflict with God's desire for them. A common example is the evangelical proclivity to withdraw from unbelievers and insulate themselves from the ones God calls them to reach. This is usually done under the guise of good Christian education programming. The servant of Christ is dedicated to making people do what they don't want to do so they can become what they have always wanted to be. Otherwise the pastor creates weak Christians. Instead of making disciples, the pastor produces dependent, parasitic believers.

2. He lets the church set the agenda, under the guise of being sensitive to their needs. Somewhere, someone taught pastors to enter an existing church with no plan. Just spend the first year getting to know people, finding out what they are interested in doing, and then design a plan around their dreams. While this might work 10 percent of the time, the other 90 percent it's a disaster. The pastoral body count is extremely high in this area.

   The generic pastor has fallen under the dictatorship of the disobedient. The church can become a crazy place where immature, unskilled believers set the agenda for a highly motivated pastor. It can be a place where men and women who don't walk with God tell a pastor who does how he should spend his time. Examples of this approach working do exist, but they are outnumbered many times over by the brokenhearted pastors who ran into a carnal buzz saw called the church.

3. He accepts the church's role expectations concerning his time and activities. Churches should write a job description explaining what they want in a pastor. Yes, there are nonnegotiables that a pastor must accept. If the church is inflexible with its demands and it doesn't fit the potential pastor, he should not accept a call.

   Too often the generic pastor does not have a specific understanding of himself and his role. As a sad result he finds himself in an ecclesiological straitjacket. He finds himself running from committee meetings to hospital rooms to rewiring the sound system. He finds time for almost everything except what God called him to.

4. His ministry strategy is circumstantial; it reacts to church conditions. He responds to the environment rather than creating it. He does not possess the philosophical gridwork needed to filter and focus. He can't filter out the demands on his time, energies, and direction in order to focus on reaching the commanded objective for the church. He finds himself in the woods, so preoccupied with individual trees that he loses his way. Once he has lost the objective, the details of ministry will begin to erode both positive outlook and productivity.

While many factors have contributed to the creation of the generic pastor, I believe the generic pastor himself to be a faithful, hardworking man of God. In fact many generic pastors have excellent ministries. God mightily uses them, and my comments are not meant to discount their work. God wires around pastors' imperfections on a regular basis, including the disciple-making pastor's weaknesses.

The pressure point is the difference between good and best. The present conditions are tolerable, but unacceptable in light of the Great Commission. The sin of omission is at work. The qualifier for "make disciples" is "teaching them to observe all that I have commanded you." With people attending church more and having it mean less, Christianity suffers from a debilitating duplicity. Therefore, the church must repent and change course. The key figure to that change is the disciple-making pastor. He is to play a specific role. In our progression from general to specific, Paul's Ephesians passage begins to piece together the disciple-making pastor's profile.

The Disciple-Making Pastor's Functional Role

The plain meaning of Ephesians 4:11–16 stands in stark contrast to general pastoral practice. It presents the church with a simple but effective plan for corporate maturity. Instead of pouring energy into the clear formula for effectiveness, the church has chosen to worship this text rather than obey it. It has been treated like other holy shrines of Christendom, such as the Lord's Prayer, the Sermon on the Mount, and 1 Corinthians 13. Shellac it, encase it in glass, hang it over the fireplace, or mount it on the wall, but most people don't expect you to practice it.

If applied, this text's principles unlock the key to corporate maturity, effective evangelism, and a self-perpetuating growth. One fact must not be ignored: *The disciple-making pastor is the trigger mechanism that sets the process into motion.* Let's look at the text: "It was he who gave some to be apostles, some to be prophets, some to be evangelists, and some to be pastors and teachers, to prepare God's people for works of service" (Eph. 4:11–12).

The passage names four gifted functions: apostles, prophets, evangelists, and pastors/teachers. The reason for the slash between pastors and teachers is the Granville Sharpe rule of Greek syntax. Pastors/teachers refers to one function, not two.

The first two gifted functions are unique from the second two. Apostles and prophets were foundational to the establishment of the church. Paul explains this, "built on the foundation of the apostles and prophets, with Christ Jesus himself as the chief cornerstone" (Eph. 2:20). The apostles and prophets played a vital role to ground the church in two ways. Apostles were the authority base in the first century. That authority is now based in the priesthood of all believers. Today the authority base is delegated either to elders or to other corporate structure.

Prophets were the custodians of revelation from God to the church. Now that revelation is found in the New Testament. The apostles planted and shaped the new churches, and the prophets taught the word that was given. In most cases the apostles also functioned as prophets.

Today the apostles and prophets find their subsidiary functions in evangelists and pastors/teachers. The apostles planted and shaped the early church and today the work of outreach is done by evangelists. The prophets taught the word, and now that is done by the pastors/teachers. While these divisions of labor are not absolute, they are needed functions, and the people who fill them are leaders.

I will not engage in a debate as to the validity of all four functions in today's church. My purpose is to focus on the one function at the center of the local parish, that of the pastors/teachers. The necessary principle is leadership. In order to please God and fulfill the commanded mission, the body must be led. What leadership is called is less important than what it does.

Some misconceptions about "the pastor." Scripture speaks of pastors and teachers in the plural. This is obvious, yet commonly overlooked because most people think of one lead pastor per church. One paid lead pastor per church is the norm, but the text does not work with that cultural model. One elder/bishop/pastor per local church did emerge by the second century, as was quoted earlier from Shelley's church history. Later we will return to and work with this present reality. But the text's main thrust is a plural leadership with respect to authority. Paul does recognize the necessity for leadership of a man by personality and passion. But he also teaches the permission for that person to lead comes from a plurality of leaders.

The pastoral/teaching function is not a one-person job. The notion of "the pastor" of a church is a major contributor to weak churches. The only person known as "the pastor" is Jesus Himself. Jesus is called "Good Shepherd" or "Chief Shepherd," which is another way of saying the "Good Pastor" or the "Chief Pastor" (John 10:11; 1 Peter 5:4).

The pastor, singular, implies that one person is equipped to meet the needs of the entire flock. This simply is not true. The origin of such an idea baffles us because it is not found in Scripture.

The pastor of the church is the combined gifts, wisdom, and faith of a pastoral team, namely the elders. In most churches a full-time, paid pastor and several ministers known as laymen would compose this group. Larger churches would combine several full-time staff with the ministers, to form a pastoral team. The plural use of pastors/teachers indicates several leaders per local church, engaged in pastoring the flock. This does not preclude the role of professional clergy; in fact, it enlarges their importance and removes a great deal of triviality from their lives.

The emphasis on plurality of authority and giftedness on one hand and the necessity of strong leadership from one person on the other appears contradictory. The dual emphasis is no contradiction, but rather a call to balance—the balance of a group of gifted leaders called to pastor the church and the leader of the gifted leaders to set the pace.

The expectation that one person can pastor the church is both a mistake and tragedy. It's a mistake because no one person has the time, energy, or gifts to pastor a church and do it right. Doing it right is explained in Ephesians 4:11–16, not only in process, but in product. A talented few have built big, successful, praiseworthy works. But the litmus test is not Christendom's evaluation; it's the standard set by Scripture. What appears successful could be cultural success masquerading as God's success.

Tragically, pastoral bodies are strewn about outside the back doors of local churches. The high casualties exist because of unrealistic expectations. When one man tries to meet the needs of the entire flock, he will fail. The majority of broken pastors leave the ministry due to the misconceived expectation of congregations.

The answer is not to form pastoral teams without strong leadership or to find outstanding talents and expect more than is possible or biblical. It is to reshape the face of pastoral ministry by following the clear directions of Ephesians 4:11–16.

Let's move from the role of an entire pastoral team engaged in pastoring the flock to the function of the modern-day, full-time professional clergy, called pastor. If there are several paid staff, then by *pastor* I mean "the lead or senior pastor."

What titles teach. Titles reveal expectations. The most common title given full-time paid clergy is *minister*. There is something trite in saying, "Fred is our minister over at First Church." It implies not only that the church has only one minister, but that the church members are something other than ministers. They could be passengers, an audience, consumers, supporters, but not ministers.

Dr. Fred is another option. This is derived from the professional model. Seminaries are designed along the same lines as medical and law schools, where people train for a specific profession. People go to a lawyer, and he provides a service; the same is true of a physician. The pastor as doctor functions as the professional medicine man who provides a service to the Christian consumer. The major difference between physicians, attorneys, and pastors is that the first two would not train others to be physicians and attorneys. But the pastor's job is to train others to become ministers, that is, to do what he does.

Elder is another option, but it won't do. It sounds too stuffy and is inappropriate for young people in leadership. The worst title is *reverend*; almost no one likes *reverend*, especially reverends.

The subject of titles should not be left without mention of the most demeaning title of all, *preacher*. Not only is this a regional title for *pastor*, it describes one thing a pastor does, not what he is.

There we have them: *minister, doctor, elder, reverend,* and *preacher.* While all apply to Christians and are occasionally on target, none properly describes the modern-day lead pastor's work.

Paul employs the title *pastor/teacher.* His title is *pastor,* what he does is teach. *Pastor* is appropriate, because it emphasizes the relationship with those being taught. While *pastor* should not be discarded, there are difficulties with it as well. *Pastor* implies sheep, and there is much regarding shepherds and sheep that is unknown to the majority of Christians.

The office of pastor as distinct from the word *pastor*. We should make a clear distinction between the office of pastor and the word *pastor.* The office is a pragmatic reality; the word describes a leadership function much larger than one man's work. *Pastor* has developed in contemporary society to mean "a person with professional training who devotes his full time to leading a church." This person filling the office may not be strong in pastoral-care areas such as counseling, visitation, and so on. Other members of the pastoral team would move in to fill in the needed areas within the exercise of their gifts.

The modern church makes false assumptions that have created and continue to create havoc. They confuse the office of pastor with the meaning of the word. They confuse them by their synonymous use. People commonly discover the richness inherent in the word *pastor* and then expect the local church pastor to be like and act out the word.

As stated earlier, in both Old and New Testaments the word for "pastor/shepherd" meant "to lead, oversee, feed, discipline, teach, and equip the people of God." It was not limited to the passive, gentle, pastoral image that has corrupted the fuller meaning.

This has led the church populace to think of a pastor in a limited way. He has become a passive person whose main job is to service the needs of the congregation. If he places their felt needs first, he is considered caring; if he puts their real needs first, often conflicting with felt needs, he is considered noncaring. He is not to be controversial, strong willed, or to challenge the church to world mission. He is considered the spiritual leader of the church, but not the leader of all the church. Finances, buildings and grounds, and other "nonspiritual" areas are considered outside of his calling.

The church can't have it both ways. If finances, buildings, and grounds are outside the pastor's areas of leadership, by necessity, those areas must be labeled nonspiritual. Does the church really want to make this kind of division, which leads to spiritual and nonspiritual departments of the church? Do churches want all leaders who handle money, buildings, and grounds to be considered working in nonministry, nonspiritual areas? If the pastor is limited to "spiritual issues," then laypeople are limited to "nonspiritual issues." Exactly this dichotomy debilitates the church. It gives life to the clergy-laity gap, which creates burned-out pastors and spiritually weak laypersons.

This kind of thinking is biblically indefensible. Often presented under the guise of protecting the pastor, I am convinced congregations use this division to keep the pastor in his place. "Now, pastor, you stick to preaching, counseling, praying, and caring for the flock. Let the board run the church." While common, it is dead wrong to lock out the pastor from total leadership. He needs to give leadership to the total program and direction of the church. This can be done without his having his hand in every pie or keeping the checkbook. The office of pastor calls for strong leadership, much the way the word was used of leaders such as Moses, Joshua, and David.

To shepherd is a function of the pastoral team. The person filling the office of pastor may not be involved in shepherding the flock if his gifts are not oriented to pastoral care. This is not an issue of strengths and weaknesses, but a matter of proper use of spiritual gifts. Confusion over it has led to many a case of a church asking a man to fill an impossible role.

The reformation of professional pastoral work begins with the pastor's viewing himself as a specialist. His top priority as teacher/equipper is to get the work of ministry done through others. Doing it right means multiplication of ministry through every member.

The office of pastor functions best with strong leadership—the pastor as teacher, trainer, shaper of the vision. It is better for the shepherding or caring ministries to be decentralized throughout the entire body. In other words, pastoral care as traditionally understood is not a primary hands-on responsibility of the lead pastor. More on this later.

The work of pastors/teachers is "to prepare God's people for works of service" (Eph. 4:12). Simply stated, the preparation is designed to "build up" (vv. 12–14) the body so it may "grow up" (vv. 15–16).

The leadership task is to bring the body of Christ to full operational efficiency through training. The word *katartizo*, translated "prepare," has many dimensions. It can mean "to set a broken bone," "to mend a frayed fishing net," "to furnish a house," "to restore something to original condition," or "to condition an athlete."

It's used of the Scripture in 2 Timothy 3:17, "so that the man of God may be thoroughly *equipped* for every good work" (italics added). Jesus used it with respect to individual discipling: "Every one when he is *fully taught* will be like his teacher" (Luke 6:40 RSV, italics added). In the Ephesians text Paul uses *katartizo* as the primary task of the leadership to bring about corporate maturity. *This text presents the only methodology that guarantees corporate maturity.* The prescribed means to maturity is the lead pastor's dedication to preparation of people for deployment into ministry. To ignore this is tantamount to disobedience.

The problem with this passage is not that the main facts have been ignored; the exact opposite is true. It is widely taught and highly revered by serious-minded pastors, but ignorance of the text's implications in practice remains. The applications have not been thought through; therefore, few have fully executed the teachings.

Preparing people for work of service means more than teaching the Bible and meeting one on one with interested growers. Too many young men exit seminary thinking that preparing people for the work of service happens through outstanding preaching. While effective preaching is an important first step, in isolation preaching can do more harm than good.

The multifaceted meaning of *katartizo* demands more of pastors. Setting a broken bone implies helping broken people put their lives back together. Restoring some item to mint condition means helping the languishing to get back on track. Furnishing a house communicates the development of people, providing the information and skills needed to live effective Christian lives. Training an athlete means providing the necessary challenges to prepare someone to effectively compete in the front lines of ministry.

The pastoral task is one of multidimensional restoration. That is why one person cannot do it. The broken need to be put back together, the unruly corrected, the weak strengthened, and the young nourished. There is an element of truth in the axiom "start where people are, at the point of their need." This is a needful idea and important to the overall task.

The church's pastoral team makes sure this full-orbed ministry takes place. The pastoral team working in concert makes a great pastor.

All the above are important to the preparation of people for works of service. If people are not cared for, they will not feel loved and therefore will not allow the Word of God to enter their lives. While the pastoral team or elders are responsible to see that people are cared for, it is not required that they are the primary people doing it. Working in their proper role, they identify the properly gifted members of the body to minister in caring work. In this way, the needs, even felt needs, of the congregation are handled more effectively. I must stress that even though the disciple-making pastor may not engage in a great deal of hands-on pastoral care, under his effective leadership the pastoral care is in better hands. The church must decide what it wants: effective pastoral care or the lead pastor doing pastoral care. You can't have both and have quality.

Introducing the pastor as coach. The confusion over the words *shepherd* and *pastor* has motivated me to seek a modern equivalent, a word widely understood by contemporary society that fits the job description of Ephesians 4. That word is *coach*. The pastor-as-coach image is not due to my personal bias as a former athlete. In fact, the idea has been around for many years. The dean of Christian writers, Elton Trueblood, taught the pastor as coach thirty years ago. A Harvard PhD and brilliant thinker, Trueblood considered coaching the best modern analogy to pastoring.

The coaching profession is widely understood. Most American children participate in sports. You would be hard pressed to find people who had no idea as to the work of a coach. However, scores of individuals do not have the foggiest understanding of the work of a shepherd.

The second reason I have adopted the pastor-as-coach model is that it accurately describes the pastoral task. The similarities are striking. People understand that a team's performance is linked to the quality of the coaching staff. With no major changes in personnel, a team's performance can improve. Vince Lombardi and the Green Bay Packers make the point. During the fifties the Packers were the laughingstock of the NFL. Lombardi took the same losing team and within four years won the NFL championship. The Packers went on to win several NFL titles and the first two Super Bowls.

The late Tom Landry, the coach of the Dallas Cowboys, defined *coaching* as "making men do what they don't want, so they can become what they want to be." An apt description of the pastoral task is to call people to do what they don't want so they can become what they want to be.

The coach doesn't play the game. He has played the game, but his purpose is to teach others to play. When the whistle blows and the game begins, the coach stands on the sidelines. His work is not to play, but to manage those who do. He demonstrates skills, develops team philosophy, and designs plays. He motivates, disciplines, aggravates, and whatever else is needed to prepare the team to play.

All the greats—John Wooden, Bobby Knight, Vince Lombardi, Paul "Bear" Bryant—translated theory into action and got top performance from their players. The pastor is a player-coach; he never stops playing entirely. He discovers the vast potential inherent in regenerate people. He views people as gifts from the Holy Spirit to His church. The pastor as coach is in the business of opening packages and taking out the gifts. Then he encourages people to grow and develop.

The reason for the term *disciple-making pastor* is the text's prescribed end product, namely the mature believer. The mature believer who does his part in the body and in the world is equivalent to what Jesus called a disciple: one who abides in Christ, obeys, bears fruit, glorifies God, and has joy (John 15:7–11). In addition a disciple loves others (see John 13:34–35). The qualifying statement for "making disciples" is "teaching them to obey everything I have commanded you" (Matt. 28:20). Jesus and Paul call for the same results. In order for that desired end product to become a reality, the pastor must be a disciple maker. He is dedicated to the process that prepares people to be mature, self-feeding, reproducing Christians.

A later section will develop the principles of the pastor as coach in greater depth. The immediate task is now to move through the text and determine the course that the disciple-making pastor takes.

PREPARATION AS TOP PRIORITY. The pastor is "to prepare God's people for works of service" (Eph. 4:12). Conditioning for ministry is the real need of God's people. This is God's priority for His people, but it often conflicts with the desires of His people. The battle begins here: What will the pastor choose, which way does he go? Does he submit to the desires and pressures of God's people, if they oppose God's stated purpose? The disciple-making pastor has the courage of his convictions, digs in his heels, and stays the course. He commits himself to motivating people to do what they don't want so they can become what God wants them to be.

Christians behave very much like wannabe athletes. When the lights are turned on and the stands are filled with screaming fans, the frustrated athlete says, "I could be out there; I'm as good as those guys." He might possess the proper talent to be a team member, but if he is not willing to prepare to play, his desires and opinions only become a means to frustration. Long before the lights went on and the fans filled the stadium, the athletes engaged in a grueling preparation that tested their inner resources.

Wayman Tisdale, the great All-American basketball player from Oklahoma University and member of the 1984 Olympic basketball team, was asked what winning the gold medal meant to him. With his winsome smile and quick wit, Tisdale said, "This medal isn't for winning the basketball tournament; it's for surviving Bobby Knight." Bobby Knight, the Olympic coach, was tough on his team. His philosophy tells us why: "The will to win is not most important; it is the will to prepare to win."

All Christians have a desire to grow, please God, and make their lives count. The desire surfaces periodically; the pastor/coach looks for those teachable moments and claims them as precious jewels of opportunity. The Christian becomes inspired by a sermon, reading Scripture, or a conversation. The event causes him to renew his commitment to grow. But desire without discipline derails good intentions. This discipline and accountability come from the environment created by the disciple-making pastor. He translates desire into the disciplined practice the Christian needs for preparation.

PROPER IDENTIFICATION OF GOD'S PEOPLE. Near the top of the disciple-making pastor's "to do" list is to tell the people of God who they are and what their purpose is: "Prepare *God's people for works of service*" (Eph. 4:12, italics added). Proper identification is vital. *God's people* is a loose translation for "saints." The English word *saint* is *hagios* in the Greek; it means "to be set apart." The priesthood of all believers teaches that all Christians are saints, set apart for service, and that all saints are ministers (see 1 Peter 2:9; Rom. 1:1–7; 1 Cor. 1:26). Being called to ministry is not for a few, but the heritage of every Christian (see 2 Cor. 5:18–21).

Some have attempted to separate the common saint from works of service. This practice is the aforementioned clergy-laity gap. There is a legitimate pastor-minister gap, because the office of pastor is for a few. The proper title for God's people is *minister*. The word *minister* and the word *service* are both derived from *diakonios*, meaning "to serve." It is translated *minister, serve,* and *deacon.* The key idea is that God's people (or saints) are to engage in works of service; therefore, they are ministers.

The disciple-making pastor, through the vehicle of public address, stirs the fire that flickers in every regenerate soul. As he stands in the pulpit, he does more than dispense information, inspire the spirit, or teach doctrine. He strings together a series of pictures of the Christian life and its meaning. He tries to interest the people of God in the work of God.

Former Oklahoma University football coach Bud Wilkenson once described the physical state of the American public: "America's physical condition is akin to the situation on any given Sunday in football stadiums throughout the

NFL: twenty-two men on the field desperately in need of rest and eighty thousand in the stands desperately in need of exercise." The disciple-making pastor calls willing spirits into action. The cry of the pastor/coach to the congregation is "get out of the stands and onto the field and into action."

The pastor as coach tells God's people they are called to ministry, set apart for the service of Christ. His job is to prepare them to do this work. In addition, they must submit themselves to training in order to play their part in the body and for the kingdom. The disciple-making pastor communicates clearly to God's people who he is, who they are, and what their relationship is. He inspires them to believe the wonderful truth that by playing their respective roles, they will be strong, fulfilled Christians, and the church will effectively penetrate the world.

PASTOR/TEACHER, NOT PASTOR/TELLER. After the pastor/coach has called God's people to action and they have left the stadium bleachers and reported to the field, then what? For a pastor, this could be both the fulfillment of a dream and the sobering thud of reality. He has always dreamed of eager and willing spirits. But now that they are poised before him, the reality hits: *What do I do now?* If the pastor has been trained in most evangelical schools, he will continue to give great "chalk talks." He will inspire the spirit, warm the heart, fill the mind, but the team will never leave the huddle. Although the team doesn't leave the huddle together and approach the scrimmage line with a play in mind, a few highly motivated mavericks will leave the huddle and try to go it alone. They join parachurch organizations or try to work out their own ministry without training from the church. Pastors/tellers always use a talented few as examples to justify their existence.

How long would a football coach last if his team never left the huddle? Many pastors do nothing more than give "chalk talks," and people think they are doing their job.

The American church is so easily duped that the pastor/ teller has become the most highly esteemed member of the religious establishment. He tells people what and why, but that is where it stops. Those who think of themselves as pastors/teachers normally consider their main task giving "chalk talks." Others revere them as great speakers; many become evangelical luminaries; yet I submit they are not pastors/teachers; they are pastors/tellers.

Pastors/tellers do not prepare God's people for works of service; they talk to people about works of service. Pastors/ tellers encourage people to do works of service, but they do not fulfill their God-given responsibility. Please do not misinterpret my words. I believe the effective telling of God's people is a first and crucial step to their preparation. I work hard at communicating the Word of God to the congregation. But if I stop at telling, I am not teaching. In the church, preaching is the first and most important step in the disciple-making process.

It would be most natural for you, the reader, to jump to the false conclusion that I am referring to highly gifted pastors of the superchurches. Not necessarily. Most highly gifted pastors who excel at telling also possess large pastoral staffs who prepare people for works of service. While one cannot determine their pastoral behavior if they were to go it alone, the superpastor and the superchurch usually do a good job of training.

The problem of the superpastor and superchurch is that it is abnormal. When we use the ministry style of the superpastor as a model (and he is), it proves debilitating to the average church and for the average pastor. It creates unrealistic expectations that are both unfulfilled and un-biblical. *The most common myth is that effective preaching leads to effective ministry.* Effective preaching is a good start to the process, but falls far short of effective ministry.

Over 90 percent of pastors must face the reality that preaching is not enough. It is not enough for the top 10 percent either, but they usually aren't required to confront their reality. Many pastors will agree that preaching is not enough, but they do not consider it their responsibility to fill in the gaps. They have been thoroughly schooled in the erroneous belief that their main role is to preach. This false notion is a clear example of reading cultural trends into Scripture.

The pastor/teacher has the responsibility to work hard at and effectively communicate the Scriptures. He is equally charged to prepare God's people by providing training vehicles. In most cases he must lead the charge and be the model for what he wants people to do. Training vehicles are required, not just home Bible studies or unstructured options that lack accountability, skill development, and goals.

Telling people what to do without providing the means to do it is cruel and defrauding. It creates spiritual schizophrenia, Christians who are experts on what they are not experiencing. Not only does it leave people unprepared for ministry, they become guilty and frustrated with the Christian life. This also gives the devil a choice opportunity to create problems inside the church. When an army never goes to war, it by necessity focuses on shining boots, making beds, and marching in a straight line. The church that does not move to action by necessity must focus on *Roberts Rules of Order*, committee rules, and acquisition of pulpit furniture.

The pastor as teacher is the pastor as coach. Teaching means more than telling people what and telling them why. It progresses to showing them how, doing it with them, letting them do it, and deploying them into the harvest field. This six-step teaching method was employed by Jesus and hallmarks the disciple-making pastor. The disciple-making pastor is a true pastor/teacher; he coaches God's people by taking them through the six-step process that leads to real learning. More on the six-step teaching method in chapter 8, "The Pastor as Coach."

GOAL-ORIENTED LEADERSHIP. In the broadest of terms, the text has described characteristics of the pastor/teacher's role. He is committed to the preparation of God's people as top priority and the identification of God's people as called ministers. The pastor as coach is the pastor as teacher. Now added to the list of characteristics is goal orientation.

The true test of goal orientation ability is not the original charting of the vision, but the management of the process over an extended period. The ability to keep the details of the process on course over a long duration is goal-oriented leadership. Like the hurdler, the disciple-making pastor keeps one eye on the process and the other on the finish line.

Once again, *the goal* is a mature, trained army of ministers who penetrate the world. The text defines the *process* as well: "So that the body of Christ may be built up" (Eph. 4:12). The reason for building the body is the effective ministry of the body: "Until we all reach unity in the faith and in the knowledge of the Son of God and become mature, attaining to the whole measure of the fullness of Christ" (v. 13).

The process is being built up "until we all reach unity." Another way of saying until we all reach unity is "until we all arrive at the goal." Every good coach has a process that parallels his goals. He can lay the vision before the team and then put the plan or process into practice. The great Vince Lombardi told his players that their goal was to win games. The process was that they would block better, tackle harder, and run faster than the other teams.

The pastor as coach gives the vision, then says, "We will engage in the process until we arrive at the goal." The goal of "attaining to the whole measure of the fullness of Christ" is not fully achievable in this life. Paul becomes a bit more precise when he defines the fullness of Christ as unity of faith and knowledge of the Son of God. Like other unreachable biblical aspirations, the church dedicates itself to reaching these goals until Christ returns.

The disciple-building process is to be ongoing. The stopping point is identified by the word "until." *Until what?* is the logical question. In the sense mentioned above, the process doesn't end until the return of Christ. However, the text does give a pragmatic, measurable indicator, stated in the negative—until "no longer": "Then we will *no longer be infants*, tossed back and forth by the waves, and blown here and there by every wind of teaching and by the cunning and craftiness of men in their deceitful scheming" (Eph. 4:14, italics added).

On a positive note, Ephesians 4:13 defines maturity beautifully and considers it a reachable corporate goal. On the negative side, maturity will elude us until we stop being what verse 14 graphically describes as children lost at sea, victimized by every ideological wind, trickery, craftiness, and deceitful scheme.

Exactly this trendy subjectivism makes goal-oriented leadership such a challenge. The majority of Christians are immature and untrained. They tend to be unstable, victimized, and whirled around by philosophical winds, until they lose their sense of direction. Two wise men, Solomon and Isaiah, speak to the wayward nature of God's people. "Where there is no revelation, the people cast off restraint" (Prov. 29:18). Without a vision of the greater corporate good, people scatter to their own agendas. Isaiah adds, "We all, like sheep, have gone astray, each of us has turned to his own way" (Isa. 53:6). The human condition is such that without strong, directive leadership from God's representative, people will lock in on personal priorities. The enemy desires that leaders be reactive, nondirective men pleasers, who strive for peace at any cost, even at the cost of disobedience to the Great Commission.

The challenges to stated biblical corporate goals are many. Myriad distractions so common to the immature slow progress toward biblically shaped corporate goals.

An immature body is riddled with personal agendas that supersede the larger corporate plan. The ability to delay gratification and to submit personal desire to the greater good are all but lost.

Two forces that come against the immature, when faced with ministry responsibility, are *intimidation* and *deception*. Intimidation is pictured in the roaring sea, and deception in the words *cunning* and *craftiness*.

Given such circumstances, it is imperative for the pastor to help people focus on the one common denominator: the journey to maturity. If the pastor does not pull the factions together and lubricate friction by pointing people to a common cause, the disobedient will dictate his life. It is too common to find a well-meaning pastor buried under a heavy pile of personal agendas. The infighting, the waste of time and labor, the throwing away of gifts, the disenchantment of the seeker, all occur due to losing sight of the goal. More than that, when they have no sense of progress toward the goal, people lose enthusiasm.

Goal-oriented leadership requires a strong philosophical grid, a deeply embedded conviction, and skills to mobilize people toward the goal. The philosophy, convictions, and skills are fundamental to the disciple-making pastor's makeup. The key tool is a strong, biblically based philosophy of ministry and mission that he passionately presents over and over again. I will elaborate later.

The need to move people toward the goal is not a cultural manifestation of twentieth-century management principles. It is the God-given responsibility of local church leadership and, to be more precise, the lead pastor. He must keep the body moving.

CREATION OF A GROWING ENVIRONMENT. Effective coaches create a winning environment. The players think positive; they expect to win. The team environment must be one of dedication to hard work and sacrificing personal goals for team goals. The players must believe they can get better and that the coach has confidence in them. Good coaches point out progress, even in moments of defeat. You can learn a great deal about the success or failure of a team by watching them practice. If the coach is consistently negative, browbeating his players and punishing them for every mistake, he will get tentative play, based on fear. While pointing out mistakes is integral to good coaching, pointing out good points and progress is more important.

We can learn a great deal by listening to the way the pastor/coach talks to his team. He can create an atmosphere of guilt and fear or love and acceptance. He can point out progress, even when things go wrong, or point out weakness when things go right. He can preach to the "empty seats" or motivate those present. To a great degree the attitude of the pastor will determine the attitude of the church.

Like the coach, the pastor must point out the weaknesses of people, the negatives of culture, and the need for repentance. But he must balance it with the gracious alternative of forgiveness, restoration, and a vision for personal achievement.

The text implies three marks of the right environment: The first is a strong sense of progress. We see this in the statement "speaking the truth in love, we will in all things *grow up* into him who is the Head, that is, Christ" (Eph. 4:15, italics added). If they are to make progress, people must well understand that it is all right to make mistakes. A growing atmosphere is an accepting atmosphere.

Tom Peters's fine work *A Passion for Excellence* introduces the now famous "skunk works" approach to innovation and efficiency. The large corporation cuts through the debilitating red tape and forms small teams that can create and act quickly. This kind of daring should be encouraged by churches. Yes, it is risky; yes, it is hard to control; yes, they will make mistakes, but since when is the church charged to major on playing it safe, administrative control, and being perfect?

Peters recently published a new work that extols the virtue and necessity for business to manage chaos. Flexibility and adapting to the fast-changing nature of consumer needs is his new call. Peters recognizes the nature of humans and culture. The business or church that protects the basic beliefs, but allows members to cut a wide swath, will find greater progress, faster growth, and more creativity.

Church heroes should be those who try the hardest, who take the greatest risks, and who make the most mistakes. Mistakes are a necessary part of growth. When the creative risk taker falls flat on his face, the church should pick him up, dust him off, applaud, and say, "Go get 'em."

The pastor as coach creates the environment by what he says and does. He celebrates progress and parlays mistakes into positive motivation.

There is a second aspect to creating environment. The individual believer is to demonstrate commitment by "speaking the truth in love" (Eph. 4:15). The literal rendering is "truthing it," a kindred translation is "stick to, adhere to." Like a bronco rider who sticks with the twists and turns of the wild animal beneath him, the growing Christian sticks to the way of Christ. The faithful consistency of walking in obedience is the key to growth. First, the pastor as coach esteems growth and progress corporately; then he coaches people toward the goal by teaching the necessity for individual consistency.

A cause-and-effect relationship exists between truthing it and growth. As we stick with it, "we are to grow up," becoming more like Christ Himself. The proof of individual maturity is adhering to the truth; the path of obedience leads to the objective called maturity. Political leaders are limited in their ability to bring about world peace. The primary limiting factor is the spiritual character of the individual. While the world can reach periods and degrees of peace, total peace is not possible without a spiritual change in individuals.

As mentioned earlier, the church is only as good as its product. The individual walk with Christ determines the quality of person. Church leaders are hamstrung if they do not have the individual maturity to form the basis for corporate maturity.

The third dimension to creating environment is cooperation. The proof of individual maturity is adhering to the truth or consistency. The proof of corporate maturity is cooperation, the symphonic working together of its members.

Ultimately individuals express maturity by the ability to work with those whom they would not choose as friends. The church is not for clones. God's genius has been to throw together a hodgepodge of called-out believers and require them to love one another and do the impossible together. The only way such an enterprise could work is through supernatural enablement. That is why Paul said, "Grow up into him who is the Head, that is, Christ" (Eph. 4:15). Christ is the head. He is the source and the sustainer of body life. "From him the whole body [is] joined and held together" (v. 16). Christ gives the growth, Christ holds the body together. If all body members obey the head, they work in concert for effective action.

Every member plays a vital role. The terms in verse 16, "every supporting ligament" and "as each part does its work," mean that every member gives something necessary to the other members. Each member supplies a product for the good of other body members. For this reason Paul sharply rebuked the Corinthian Christians: "The eye cannot say to the hand, 'I have no need of you,' and the head cannot say to the feet, 'I have no need of you'" (see 1 Cor. 12:21). The body operates best when all systems are go and each member does its work.

Each part doing its work is teamwork. People lay aside personal agendas to team up in obedience to a group direction. This is as rare as it is vital.

The 1984 United States Olympic basketball coach Bobby Knight made this point before a group of reporters. The reporters had praised Knight's ability to get near-perfect teamwork from great individual stars in winning the first three games. "Yeah, I'd like to see ten of you egomaniacs write a column together," said the coach.

A basketball team must submit to the will of the coach and the team plan. Likewise, body members must submit in loving obedience to the head, who is Christ. Satan opposes the pastor as coach and the laity players because they will accomplish a great deal together.

The greatest threat to Satan's kingdom is not the American megachurch. It is whenever and wherever a motivated disciple-making pastor coaches an awakened laity to work together. When they do, multiplication is near. To Satan the most frightening thought is that pastors and leaders would take seriously the commands of making disciples and multiplying themselves. The exponential growth of the church, through its members, is the most dynamic force possible to man.

Paul describes the effect on the body when everyone does his or her part; it "grows and builds itself up in love" (Eph. 4:16). Dr. Paul Brand describes a physical phenomenon that applies to the spiritual body as well. He explains that although it has nerves specifically for pain, cold, heat, and touch, the body has no pleasure nerves. However, when the organs work together, one of the by-products is an enzyme that bathes the nerves and causes what Brand calls "the ecstasy of community."[5] When the body functions as a team, a group ecstasy manifests itself in growing and building itself up in love.

The phrase "building itself up" is essential to our understanding. When the proper foundation has been laid, a self-perpetuating flow is established. Paul's mixed metaphors of body and building combine to teach the importance of the foundation of a building and the growth and teamwork of the body. The proper foundation is laid by the pastor/teacher. Then he coaches the body to work together, and the result is a quality product of mature Christians and effective mission through trained ministers.

When the proper environment is created, there is growth, and that growth multiplies. The ministry and the mission of the church feed on and improve each other. Once set into motion, this creates a spiritual juggernaut that penetrates the world like nothing else. There is no segment of society left untouched. When passive Christian residents in the harvest field are transformed into motivated, skilled ministers in that same field, they penetrate every nook and cranny for Christ. This is God's plan for His church. The key to a mature, penetrating church is the disciple-making pastor. The disciple-making pastor is the pastor as coach.

In defining the disciple-making pastor and his biblical role, I have drawn broad categories. They form a foundation, but they are no more than a start. Now, I will move to filling in the empty spaces with further details that distinguish the disciple-making pastor from others. But it must be said that following the role described in this chapter would make a pastor a breed apart.

Further Reflections

As I reread this chapter, I was encouraged that I still believe it. Yes, I could change a few words, but I don't think I could improve much on the content. Yet there is a dimension missing: The most important role of a disciple-making pastor is to develop his or her relationship with Christ. In light of that, I would retitle chapter 4 "Important Roles of a Disciple-Making Pastor."

The danger is to focus first on being successful in leading others, and if you have any time left, you can attend to your own soul. Yet there never seems to be any time left to do that. The poet T. S. Eliot said it well: "I had the meaning but missed the experience."[6] Being in love with God is like being swept off your feet by a great symphony or standing before a painting like Rembrandt's *Return of the Prodigal Son*. It is an experience; it is to dwell in His presence, listen to His voice, and taste His goodness. Getting to know God this way takes some time and effort. It means opening the door on which Jesus knocks and inviting Him in to have fellowship. It means putting yourself in a position to hear Him, to listen, to contemplate. It begins with our relationship to the Bible, which is the basis for our communication with God. We read the Bible to submit to God, to know God, to confess our sins, and to strengthen our hearts.

The late-twentieth-century evangelical culture taught us to lead for impact and to study for presentation. I would advocate that we should lead from a satisfied soul and study to submit. I love the way Eugene Peterson puts it in *Eat This Book*. He says God tells John to put down his pen and "eat this book," meaning the scroll that was both bitter and sweet (see Rev. 10:9–10).

I was taught to study Scripture to master the text. But we should study it to submit to the text. Figuratively speaking, we should put down our pens, pick up our forks and knives, and eat the book. I must allow Scripture to read me and to lead me into a life of humility, because then the floodgates will be open for God's grace to come pouring into my life. As a leader, I will touch others out of my experience. The character of Christ in me as a leader will be the basis on which people will follow.

The disciple-making pastor's most daunting task is to get the Bible into the minds, hearts, and mouths of men and women. The basis for a lifetime of discipleship, of following Christ, is a passion for and ongoing relationship with God. If you, the disciple-making leader, have little experience in this matter, you are just skating over the top of transformation. Your only real hope is a deep well from which to draw. You must operate from a restored soul that comes from resting beside still waters, partaking of the nourishment of the green pastures. It comes from the taking on of Christ's character—humility, submission, sacrifice, and the commitment to live for others.

Create a Symphony

If our prayers and God's dream for the church were fulfilled, the church would look and sound like a symphony. Paul's picturesque language in this respect has stood the test of time: "Under his direction, the whole body is fitted together perfectly. As each part does its own special work, it helps the other parts grow, so that the whole body is healthy and growing and full of love" (Eph. 4:16 NLT). This is a symphony indeed. Each part is orchestrated by the Spirit of God, but the pastor is the conductor. He or she is charged with the responsibility to nurture and train each member to play his or her instrument. The pastor is commissioned to "equip God's people to do his work and build up the church, the body of Christ" (v. 12 NLT).

One of my first lessons as a pastor was that people didn't care very much about my ideas unless they thought I cared about them. One of my sons summed up a feeling he had about me as a father: "Dad, a lot of the time when I was a kid I felt coached more than nurtured." That wasn't easy to hear, but I'm glad he could say it. As fathers and leaders, we must be willing to align our lives with the truth. We must own up to our influence, no matter how difficult it is to do so. Angry leaders make people angry, self-indulgent leaders encourage self-indulgence in others, and so on. The wrong environment can destroy the most brilliant plans. What kind of effect do we have on others? How are they experiencing us? The pastor's most basic power is his expressed love to those in his community.

This ability to show love to others is the second most important role of the disciple-making pastor. I suppose the subject of this chapter now finds itself in third place. You can see how skill, competence, plans, and strategy keep getting shoved aside. This symphony is really about love. If its product is love, its source is also love. I still believe in what I wrote in this chapter nearly twenty years ago, but as Paul said, without love it is just noise. It may make you want to stick your fingers in your ears. But with love, you can take your fingers out and listen to the beautiful music.

The Understanding of a Disciple-Making Pastor

What makes the disciple-making pastor different? In the broadest of terms, he has committed time and resources to the job of making disciples who can do ministry. On the other hand, the generic pastor has committed time and resources to doing ministry rather than reproducing it.

Three distinctives make the disciple-making pastor stand out from the rest: his understanding, his commitment, and his practices. We'll look into them in the next three chapters and then will consider the method Jesus modeled, a six-step way for the pastor to become a coach.

Let's start with a look at his understanding.

He Understands the Big Picture

The disciple-making pastor is a biblical ideologue. The word *ideology* was first used during the French Revolution. It means "revolution for structural change." Disciple making at the heart of the local church is revolutionary ideology that calls for fundamental change within the church. While he makes no plans to storm the Bastille, the pastor does call into question the structures and priorities of the modern church.

The ideology is simple, obvious, and treacherous. The Orwell statement used earlier tells why: "We have now sunk to a depth at which the restatement of the obvious is the first duty of intelligent men." The church has stumbled so far from the prescribed purpose and methods that people consider restating the obvious revolutionary ideology. Like Christ calling the religious establishment to live their faith, the disciple-making pastor asks the church to return to her first calling.

His theology of the church is clear. He looks at both the universal and local church through a discerning scriptural lens. Because he thinks systematically concerning objectives and methods, he is able to place people in the best vehicles for their growth. He has the big picture.

Too many pastors have a microtheology of the church. They understand the church in bits and pieces. Because they have not pieced together the larger picture, their goals and programs are short-term and shortsighted. In a 1981 speech at the University of Illinois, Dr. Francis Schaeffer lamented concerning the micromanaging of the Christian faith, "Christians have understood the truth of Christianity in bits and pieces."

The local church piece, the personal salvation piece, the social action piece, the cross, discipleship, evangelism, the family, the gifts of the Spirit are all like parts of a puzzle, strewn about in our minds. So few Christians have the big picture as to God's objective. Just as Christians commit themselves to pieces of the puzzle rather than the big picture, pastors fall into the same trap.

Pastors need to concentrate on specific areas of their giftedness and calling. But in order to take the church to full maturity in ministry and mission, they must also communicate the big picture. The failure to understand and place the church into the larger redemptive drama has made the church less than it was meant to be.

Without the larger picture, pastors think of the church existing for itself. The church becomes an idol. Commit yourself to it, build it up, make it the focal point of Christian experience. The focus is the ministry of the church to the church. Such pastors achieve success when the church populace is satisfied, their felt needs met, and they enjoy a good reputation with other churches.

Therefore, the highest calling is to be all you can in the church. This has caused leaders to challenge the church populace to pieces of the puzzle, rather than to the larger vision. The reason commitment is rare is that the challenge is too small. Without the big picture, leaders cannot present the big challenge. They have offered eager Christians fragments rather than the whole, and that is not enough.

The mundane, the easy, and the ordinary do not set people's hearts aflame. Most Christians are challenged to make it big in the church. If you try hard, work diligently, and keep your nose clean, you can work your way up to deacon, trustee, or even (dare we mention it?) elder. Break out the hats and horns! Is this the great challenge to which we ask people to give their lives: to attend committee meetings and shuffle papers?

While no one teaches the above ideas verbally, corporate church behavior powerfully communicates it. The esteemed members of the congregation serve within the four walls. It *is* important to have dedicated servants and leaders within the church structure, but let us not mistake that for the reason the church exists.

This is an indictment as to the limitations of local church thinkers. Dedication to the church itself is not enough. Whether we make it the development of a model ministry, disciple making at the heart of the church, the Great Commission, or church planting around the world, none of these by themselves is big enough. What is? I will now propose the larger philosophical gridwork that the disciple-making pastor uses to filter his thinking and focus his work.

Jesus employed four major hooks onto which we could hang the big picture. They are the essentials for building convictions in disciples. For the disciple-making pastor, Jesus modeled how to motivate and teach people by the use of the larger objective.

Jesus provided His followers with an objective that would require all they had for as long as they had. But even then they would not have reached the finish line. His larger objective would require the repeated passing of the baton from generation to generation. The four hooks are:

The kingdom is the model.
The cross is the means.
The commission is the method.
The coming is the motive.

The Kingdom Is the Model

Jesus taught that where the king was there was the kingdom (see Matt. 12:28; Luke 17:20–21). But He said much more. Christ clearly communicated His objective. Immediately following His temptation, Jesus announced this objective. "From that time on Jesus began to preach, 'Repent, for the kingdom of heaven is near'" (Matt. 4:17). Several times the Gospels mention this as His message (Matt. 4:17; Mark 1:14). Immediately after the selection of the Twelve, Jesus delivered the kingdom manifesto called the Sermon on the Mount. He explained who was great in the kingdom and who could get into the kingdom, and later He offered the kingdom and taught parables about it.

He told the disciples to pray for the kingdom, and when He sent them out, He told them to preach, "Repent, for the kingdom of God is at hand" (see Mark 6:12). He said where He was, there was the kingdom. He promised the disciples privileged status in the kingdom. He wept over Jerusalem because it had rejected his offer of the kingdom. He told the disciples that the kingdom would come when the gospel of the kingdom was preached to all nations. At His ascension, they asked if this would be the time He would establish the kingdom.

Christ's objective was and is to establish His kingdom among men. The kingdom of God is nothing less than the absolute eternal rule of God in the new heavens and the new earth. The objective was clear: a perfect society where peace and justice would rule. This is big enough for the most talented person's total commitment; it is something to live for, to die for, to work toward.

Regardless of your view of the kingdom, whether it be a literal, millennial reign of Christ or the manifestation of Christ through His people, I am sure you are in favor of it. The pastor must communicate the same vision for people today. First, the kingdom means Christ's rule in individual Christian experience; second, Christ's rule in the corporate body of the church; and third, it is mature Christians taking the rule of Christ into the home, workplace, classroom, courthouse, and all facets of life and business. The people of the church are the salt that preserves society and the light that penetrates the darkened minds of unbelievers.

The disciple-making pastor is a kingdom thinker, which is much broader in scope than a mere local-church thinker. The local-church thinker says, "We are building a great church." The kingdom thinker says, "We are taking the rule of Christ to the world." The local-church thinker says, "What you are in the church is most important." The kingdom thinker says, "What you are in the world for Christ is most important."

The kingdom thinker enlarges the scope of the church's influence. It takes much of the triviality out of the local church and enhances its purpose and redefines its goals.

Think of the positive changes that could be made by taking Christ's rule to the world arena. The home could be a stronger place of love and nurture, where husbands would love their wives and parents their children, where there was a real commitment to the values and priorities of Scripture, and where, before their children, parents truly modeled the life of Christ with integrity.

Imagine public schools that would teach traditional moral values and allow the existence of prayer that acknowledges God, where our children would be presented with balanced teaching concerning origins and the role of religion in history, where a child could not get an abortion without parents' knowledge.

Think of courts that would once again practice justice and that would restore religious liberty to public life; where Christian judges, attorneys, and police could fairly do their work; where pornography would be regulated, and the war on drugs escalated.

Think of a music industry that would curtail the music contributing to the corruption of our youth and of media that would report news fairly.

Courageous Christians would intentionally reach out in love to the homeless, the single parent, the hungry, the poor, the drug addict, the AIDS patient. They would protest and work to stop the slaughter of millions of unborn children. Christians would be honest, people of integrity, and would verbalize their faith.

Why would any of these segments of society change? Because dedicated disciples of Jesus Christ, effectively deployed by the church, would not rest until it happened.

The model for the church is to take the rule of Christ to the world. The church can change society. But it will take the disciple-making pastor, following the plan prescribed for him, to prepare people for such a task. Just as five-year-olds cannot be expected to get a job and make a living, the church cannot expect its untrained members to influence society.

This is where the church fits. It is the vehicle to take Christ's rule to all of life. This is big enough to motivate me for a lifetime; we have the responsibility to take His righteousness to the earth. We are His representatives.

The disciple-making pastor gets strong commitments from strong people because he has a big enough vision: nothing less than taking the rule of Christ to all of life. He also understands this will take courage, convictions, and sacrifice from God's people. Therefore, he needs to employ more than just the kingdom as the model. The kingdom is the model, but the cross is the means.

The Cross Is the Means

Ten months before the crucifixion Jesus told the disciples about the cross. It was so radical, so shocking, so demeaning, that to tell them earlier would have meant their defection. But Jesus waited and told them at the right time. Timely instruction concerning the cross resulted in the taking of the rule of God to the world. I use the term *means* with respect to resource and character, not methodology.

The cross provides the means for the rule of God on earth through God's people in two ways. First, the cross, along with the resurrection, provided the supernatural resources needed to get the job done. It brought about the regeneration of people and their divine enablement to live daily in the power of the Spirit. Jesus said that He came to give His life as a ransom for many (see Mark 10:45). Christ's life paid for the release of the human race from the penalty for sin.

Second, the lessons of the cross, such as dedication and self-sacrifice, gave people reasons to commit to the cause. The cross teaches that there are certain responsibilities we cannot delegate: "He then began to teach them that the *Son of Man must* suffer many things and be rejected by the elders, chief priests and teachers of the law, and that *he must* be killed . . ." (Mark 8:31, italics added).

Life is crammed with things we must do. Working, going to school, cleaning the house, and visiting the dentist are among scores of other unavoidable tasks. The first lesson of the cross is that we must face certain difficulties. Difficulties require sacrifice, some simple, like missing a meal or favorite television program, or more costly actions, such as separation from family or imprisonment. Regardless, we must do it.

Immediately following Jesus' announcement concerning the cross, Peter took Jesus aside in order to rebuke Him for such nonsense. Jesus' reply was precise and cut deep into Peter's heart: "'Get behind me, Satan!' he said. 'You do not have in mind the things of God, but the things of men'" (Mark 8:33).

The major obstacle pastors face in motivating people to make commitments is the classic struggle between God's interests and man's interests. First, point them to the larger vision of taking the kingdom to the world. A big vision garners a big effort.

Second, convince them that it will take sacrifice and that the sacrifice is worth it. Jesus demonstrated His commitment to the cross by not turning away from it. He communicated its importance as a principle in calling upon all who would follow Him to take up their own crosses. "Then he called the crowd to him along with his disciples and said: 'If anyone would come after me, he must deny himself and take up his cross and follow me'" (Mark 8:34).

This call to discipleship is not for an elite corps of God's Green Berets. Jesus intentionally called together the entire crowd before issuing the requirements. Clearly, the calling together of the larger group mandates discipleship for every Christian. Two actions are necessary to meet the requirements.

First, there is self-denial. Many associate self-denial with such trivial exercises as denying oneself desserts, a second piece of candy, or a glass of wine. Another extreme is to take it to mean renouncing self or ignoring real personal needs.

It really means to cease to make myself the center of my life and actions. I relinquish the right to call all the shots; it is no longer my body, my career, my money, my time.

In our self-hyphenated society of self-assertiveness, self-actualization, self-image, self-love, and looking out for number one, self-denial is not a hot item.

Self-denial means the sustained willingness to say no to self so I can say yes to God. Self-denial simply eliminates the obstacles, or man's interests, that get in the way of God's interests. If following Christ gives me a life of opulence, I will enjoy it. If it gives me a life of hardship, I will endure it. The successful completion of the first action makes possible the second necessary action.

The second action is to take up my cross. If a Jew saw a man with a cross on his shoulder he knew the man was soon to die. Most of us have rarely heard the phrase except in a joking way. A bossy in-law, a ding-a-ling neighbor, crabgrass, or a chronic oil leak prompts the response, "I guess it's just my cross to bear!" While life has its little irritants, the cross is much more than inconvenience.

The cross is the essence of mission. It is the mission that God has given me. For Jesus the cross was "what I must do." My cross is "what I must do." Whatever mission God has given me is my cross. I may enjoy it; I may need to endure it.

I will pick it up daily and follow after Him, not turning back. Jesus taught the virtues of duty, commitment, and willingness to face even death in order to please God. He stayed the course, and when He breathed His last and said, "It is finished," He had lived the truth.

Leadership means helping people say no to self so they can say yes to God. Not much will be accomplished unless Christians understand and apply the cross. They must appropriate the resources made available through the finished work of Christ on the cross. They must then practice the lessons of the cross: dedication, self-denial, and willingness to take up their crosses every day to follow Christ.

The kingdom as the model, the idea of taking Christ's rule to all of life, is nothing more than an unfulfilled frustration without the means of the cross. Therefore, the disciple-making pastor must keep the big picture in focus. Point people toward the goal, then teach them how to get there.

The Commission Is the Method

If the disciple-making pastor intends to get commitment from Christians, he must build convictions. A clearly understood objective produces sustained conviction. Leaders must clearly communicate the objective. The objective of God's action in history, through His individual servants—the nation of Israel and now the church—is to take His rule to the world, that is, His kingdom. The bottom line of history is Christ's rule over all creation.

Once the Christian has the big picture, he will need resources to join the cause. Christ provided the means in the cross: both the supernatural resources and the character derived from the lessons of the cross.

Another way of saying it is the kingdom provides the dream and the cross provides the resources for the kingdom. But then we must ask, "What is the plan and how do we get there?" This is where the church comes in. The church in this context is the only way to really understand it.

The church exists for mission. The church exists for mission and lives by it as fire lives by oxygen. Common metaphors used for the church teach its aggressive role: *salt* preserves food, *light* illuminates the darkness, *leaven* influences the entire loaf, an *army* breaks through enemy lines. The common descriptions of Christians as aliens from a different world, as ambassadors from a foreign country, and as pilgrims just traveling through all teach the temporary status and mission orientation of God's people.

How can we measure the effectiveness of the church? By the ability of its members to penetrate their world for Christ. The best way and the right way to grow a church is to improve the members' penetration ability.

The church is the family of God, a kingdom of priests, a building, a body, and a temple. What it is, though, we cannot excise from what it does. The church is a vehicle for the Great Commission. It is God's tool for reaching the world. I can't say it too much: The church exists for mission, not for itself. The church legitimatizes itself by prioritizing mission. Doing otherwise prostitutes the mandate.

Jesus built convictions concerning the dream of the kingdom. He demonstrated that conviction by commitment to the cross. He was equally committed to the importance of a special methodology. Here the disciple-making pastor and the disciple-making church part ways with the generic pastor and the generic church.

The disciple-making pastor sees the Great Commission's imperative to "make disciples" as the methodology for reaching the world. Disciple making is the trigger to multiplication and the key to world evangelism. Without multiplication, world evangelization is nothing more than an evangelical mind toy. Disciple making is more than a product; it is a methodology required to reach the world.

The disciple-making pastor spends the majority of his time with those willing to be trained to reproduce themselves, those who share the dream of the kingdom, who have the commitment of the cross, and who believe in multiplication as the commissioned methodology to reach the world. Let us never forget that the purpose of disciple making is not disciple making for its own sake. We aim to populate heaven, to reach the most people possible with the life-saving, life-changing message of Jesus Christ.

The biblically prescribed pastor is the disciple-making pastor. I believe God wants all pastors to be disciple makers. In order for this to become reality, pastors must willingly focus on making disciples who will multiply themselves. They can defend their position only when they possess the big picture. They need a biblically based philosophical gridwork by which they can field competing ideologies. The big picture enables the pastor to filter out competing ideologies and to maintain a focus on his specialized work.

The Coming Is the Motive

For the disciple-making pastor, accountability is a treasured way of life. Therefore, he diligently reminds the church that the return of Jesus Christ brings the possibility of reward and the reality of accountability.

Once the dream is established, namely the kingdom of God, the resources and lessons of the cross create the commitment to work for it, regardless of the difficulty. This is followed by putting the methodology in place, the work plan for fulfilling the Great Commission by making disciples. The final challenge is to sustain the commitment by consistent motivation and proper management.

The coming of Jesus Christ provides several helpful pieces to the big picture that assist all Christians in their work. First, the signs of Christ's coming strengthen already-placed convictions. When Christians see various prophetic events become reality, it perks their spirits.

Second, knowing that Christ is coming and when He does the struggle will be over sustains convictions. The world groans for deliverance; the hostility, despair, greed, and dishonesty rampant in society tend to discourage. The prospect that someday things will get better and the struggle will end helps one hang on a little longer.

The third and most important dimension of Christ's return is that it will bring both personal reward and accountability. Jesus promised the twelve disciples prestigious positions in the kingdom: They would sit on special seats next to Him, from which they would rule.

Personal reward. While Jesus never promised common saints special seats, He did say they will receive rewards. The parable of the talents (see Matthew 25) teaches that God will evaluate the believer by what he did with what he was given. Paul utilizes the imagery of elements tested by fire to communicate that Christians will be judged according to the quality of their work (see 1 Cor. 3:12–15).

People respond positively to the prospect of reward. The athlete strives for the ribbon, the trophy, money, or fame. The child works hard to get a pat on the back from Dad. Everyone likes to hear, "That's great!" "Good job!" "Way to go!" The promise that one day there will be an opportunity to receive kudos from Christ Himself and tangible rewards to boot highly motivates serious Christians.

Personal reward appeals to the better side of man's nature, the part of man that makes sense, the part that says, "If I do good and work hard, my life will be happy, and I will get many rewards." This kind of motivation appeals to Christians and very often works.

There is, however, the reality of the darker side or the propensity to depart from God's desire and disobey. This occurs at the point when possibility of reward fails, and accountability to the return of Christ does not.

Personal accountability. Paul's imagery of a person's works being tested by fire has both positives and negatives. The positive, already mentioned above, is the possibility of the work passing the test and receiving great rewards. The negative is the possibility that the work could be destroyed. The prospect of a life's work dissolving before one's eyes is frightening. This provides the Christian with enough accountability to hasten a more serious effort. All Christians need this element in order to keep life's mission "on its toes."

What would students learn without exams? What work would get done without deadlines? What teen would clean his room without his parents threatening life and limb? Why does behavior change when the teacher leaves the room, the coach the field, the parent the house? The answer is simple: It's the nature of human nature. Yes, even regenerate human nature is not perfect or always mature human nature. Report forms, report cards, authority figures and systems are essential to good human performance.

The Great Commission's qualifier surfaces again, ". . . teaching them to obey everything I have commanded you. . . ." Spiritual maturity without accountability is a canard. Those who refuse spiritual authority when they need it but don't want it are doomed to spiritual mediocrity.

Too often the church encourages people to disobey by teaching certain actions and morality as right, but ignoring clear violations of them. Regardless of the church dogma, what the church practices wins hands down. The message to the congregation couldn't come across more clearly: "We don't really mean it." This is teaching people to disobey.

The return of Christ works as a motive, both in the possibility of reward and the reality of giving an accounting for life's behavior. It works because, unlike flawed humans, God will perfectly keep His word. Don't expect Jesus to return and say, "Hey, guys, I was just kidding about hell, about the necessity of making your life count. All is forgiven; let's party!" God will not—indeed, cannot—do this. God cannot violate His own promises or depart from His commitment to justice and truth. He keeps His standard with no apologies.

The Christian is called upon to hold on, work hard, and look up. Work hard for your convictions and expect to hear Him say, "Well done, My good and faithful servant."

The big picture pulls all the pieces of the puzzle together and provides the disciple-making pastor with a clear vision. The kingdom is the model, the cross is the means, the commission is the method, and the coming is the motive. From this larger frame of reference, the pastor can focus on the critical issues for his time and his place. That clear focus is the role of the church and the commission as the method. This leads us to the second characteristic of the disciple-making pastor: his commitment.

Further Reflections

What is the difference between leaders who can stay on topic and those who are easily distracted? Possible answers include intelligence, philosophical training, a consultant who keeps whispering the right answers in their ears, or just plain grit. I would have preferred a giant neon sign in my head, blinking "make disciples" 24-7 to keep me on course.

Being a pastoral leader is very much like being a politician. You have a message, and daily your advisors set up situations so you can relay your message. But your opponent brings up your mistakes and any dirt from your past. Even if it wasn't really dirt, they make it so by taking it out of context. The opponent's goal is simple: Plant a seed of doubt about your character in the voters' minds. If your adversary is successful, you can't talk about your issues, you can't stay on topic, and the press peppers you endlessly about the dirty accusations.

Distraction from your original goal or message is the number one challenge to a pastoral leader. Satan and his gang are busy distracting you, throwing one obstacle after another in your path and draining the joy from your life. There must be a trick, a method, something that will keep the leader from the endless rabbit trails. Or is this the unavoidable plight of pastoral work?

The solution is to be able to hold a simple philosophy in your mind that can be repeatedly communicated to the members. In this chapter, I cited the words of the late scholar and apologist Francis Schaeffer: "Christians have understood the truth of Christianity in bits and pieces" (see page 134). It is a sad fact that the continuing crisis of Christians is that they don't read their Bibles or pray very much. Therefore, they have a religious scrapbook understanding of their faith. This heightens the need for pastors to have a comprehensive understanding of the gospel. They need the ability to hold it in their own minds and also get the core of it into the minds of their congregations.

The paradigm I presented on page 136 was:

The kingdom is the model.
The cross is the means.
The commission is the method.
The coming is the motive.

In other words, we as disciples are to take the rule of Christ to the world in which we live. We are to do this until Christ returns.

The Kingdom Mentality

The idea of a kingdom is simple. There is a realm—usually a piece of land that has a name. There is someone of special lineage who rules the realm—a king or, in some cases, a queen. Christ came speaking of the kingdom of God. The realm is heaven and earth, and as the Son of God, He is the King. He told us that because He lives in us, His children, the kingdom is within each of us. And wherever we go, the kingdom goes with us. The kingdom is bigger than the church, but God invented the church to enlarge His kingdom—in fact, to help create His kingdom. There is a tendency for those whose understanding of God's work is limited to think that what God is doing is just saving people and getting them to attend church.

The church is a sending center, an outpost, to take the kingdom to every part of life. When a disciple walks through the door to his or her office, the kingdom has arrived. And if there are other obedient disciples working at that office, they are like shoots of wheat among the tares. The call for each disciple is to infiltrate and take Christ's rule to the government, tourism, schools, sports, business, recreation, the media, journalism, and the entertainment industry. The church can't go there officially or in large groups with placards held high. History has proven that doesn't work, and it leads to unnecessary ridicule, because it isn't Jesus' way. The challenge remains to get the people outside the church so they can be the church.

So the kingdom mentality must be front and center in the thoughts and work of the disciple-making pastor. The ordinary disciples must have the clear vision that the real action is where they spend 97 percent of their time—outside the safe confines of the local church. The pastor leads the congregation in engagement with God because that is the key to engagement with the world. Being a disciple is the necessary prerequisite to making disciples. The understanding of disciple-making pastors, then, is to lay the vision before their people in a very personal way. They are the leaders and communicate through their own examples. They tell stories of success—how they have seen lives touched by Christ because of the living out of the vision.

This leads to my closing thought: Pastors too often get stuck in their spirits with the idea that if the vision is fulfilled in the lives of the people, the church will grow large. When that doesn't happen, they might conclude that the plan is not working. Therefore, a new plan, very much like all the other plans for church growth, must be engineered and executed. This is a devilish temptation and deception. *The kingdom may grow while a local church that is faithfully participating may not.* The kingdom grows organically through friendships and families, as well as through associations such as recreational leagues, golf foursomes, reading clubs, and so on. The best talks I have are with neighbors on summer nights while our children play across our collective yards.

It can be that many will find Christ and begin to follow Him but never come to our church. The disjointed society in which we live doesn't lend itself to neighborhood churches. If a large percentage of a congregation is planting the seeds of the kingdom daily and broadly, then yes, there should be new souls entering into the congregational life of that church. But there will not be enough by that method to create a very large church. If the church does become large, it will be due to a combination of factors broader than simply disciples who are obedient. This is very hard for some to accept, but a spiritually mature congregation may not be a large one or even exciting by contemporary standards. The healthiest frame of mind for pastors is to forget numerical church growth and to concentrate instead on advancing the kingdom through the members, letting the growth issues take care of themselves. We must break free of the strong grip of consumerism.

The Commitment of a Disciple-Making Pastor

The disciple-making pastor has four commitments:

He is committed to placing disciple making at the heart of the church.

He commits himself to the clear identification and communication of the roles of the pastor, the people, and the discipling process.

He is committed to the priesthood of all believers.

He has a commitment to multiplication.

Without this kind of commitment, he will not move his people toward disciple making, much less lead them to become reproducing believers.

It all starts at the heart of the matter—where he places disciple making in relation to the church.

Placing Disciple Making at the Heart of the Church

Through Isaiah God once lamented, "These people come near to me with their mouth and honor me with their lips, but their hearts are far from me" (Isa. 29:13). Many pastors

151

and church leaders give lip service to disciple making. To be against it is akin to denying a cardinal doctrine of the faith. But when it comes to demonstrating the courage of their alleged allegiance, their actions demonstrate that their hearts are not in it.

There are reasons for this duplicity. First is the false belief that discipleship is a program that fits into a department of the church, that it should be made available for those interested, but is not what drives the main engines of the church.

Second, while the pastor considers discipleship an important contributor to overall church health, he does not make it his personal responsibility. He thinks of hiring staff to man the program or bringing in outside consultants to begin and monitor lay leadership. But he sees his job as preaching, counseling, and administering the staff. He cannot get focused too closely on just a few people; that would not be a good use of his time.

This neglect stems more from inability than disobedience. Pastors think of themselves as pastors/teachers, when in reality they behave as pastors/tellers. They falsely consider themselves to be teaching and equipping when they are doing no more than informing. They think they are fulfilling the Great Commission and doing their job when they engage only in the introductory elements of disciple making.

A third reason for the difference between words and actions is that many pastors think of discipleship as being too narrow for the local church. To them, discipleship is a small group of ultracommitted soldiers of the cross who carry Scripture memory packets and are destined for full-time Christian service. They spend long hours in Bible study, witness door to door, and have made sacrifices to serve Christ. This is great for a select few, but not for the general church population. Pastors love to be around such people, because most pastors fit this mold themselves. But they don't think of it as the Christian norm.

The above-described troopers are not the Christian norm. But this belief has caused many pastors to downplay disciple making in favor of more palatable concepts. A strong emphasis on disciple making will be too narrow for the church, too hard for most Christians, just not practical. *It will polarize the congregation between the "haves" and the "have nots." Either people will leave the church or it will cost me my job, or both.*

Without doubt, the main reason for such duplicity among pastors is not knowing how to make disciple making the heart of the church. Three main actions will make it the heart.

Proclaim It from the Pulpit

The disciple-making pastor declares his beliefs concerning discipleship from the pulpit. He proclaims the purpose and goals of the church. In order for disciple making to become the heart of the church, the pastor must teach it as such. He justifies his claims with solid biblical exposition. He employs all the advantages available through his teaching gift to persuade the church populace of this objective. Scriptural convictions concerning disciple making must be proclaimed again and again. The effective disciple-making pastor never allows the vision to slip from the people's minds.

Many pastors fear this will polarize the congregation. There are traps to avoid. (I should know; I've fallen into most of them.) But it must be done anyway, for without the exposition and conviction from the pulpit, disciple making will not survive as a marquee ministry. The overriding factor is this: Disciple making is the heart of the church, and it is God's will for every believer to be a disciple. Say it often, loud, and with clear, passionate conviction.

Write It Down and Make It Church Dogma

When people see it in writing, they start taking it seriously. Put it into the church constitution. Clearly state it in other publications. When people see it consistently proclaimed from the pulpit, written into the constitution, and appearing in church brochures, it becomes accepted dogma.

Write it in a way that will motivate people to aspire to the goal, both individually, by becoming a disciple, and corporately, by working together to be a dynamic disciple-making church.

Write it in such a way as to require regular evaluation of goals and objectives: "The elders will annually evaluate all programs and activities of the church in light of the stated goals." If the goals are making disciples, introducing others to Christ, and multiplication, the church populace will know you are serious. This insures that future board members and pastors will be required to continue the same priorities.

Model Disciple Making at the Elder Level

The pastor can proclaim it and write it down, but if he doesn't practice it at the leadership level, it won't make it to the heart of the church. It is foolish to proclaim one thing as truth and yet do another in practice. To sell church members on discipleship, let them see it modeled in microcosm.

The elders should prove their disciple-making ability before they receive such a position. Develop an established process by which to train prospective elders. The duplicity between proclaimed priorities and leadership practices is the greatest debilitator of local churches.

Sadly, many church problems find their origin in the immaturity and selfish agendas of church leaders. Commonly, the hardest group to get along with in the entire church is the leaders. They often are argumentative, closed minded, power hungry, and dedicated to keeping a firm hold on their territory.

Once the church's core becomes corrupt, you have almost no chance for renewal. By *corrupt* I mean that the leadership core doesn't live out their stated biblical goals. They insulate themselves from important aspects of accountability such as personal evangelism, prayer, Bible study, reaching out to others in need. Sinful attitudes destroy their influence. Once again this teaches people to disobey. "The purpose of our church is to make disciples, but this does not apply to our leadership." Again leaders have said, "It's only talk, we don't really mean it."

Before discipleship can become the heart of the church, elders must exemplify the objective. How to do this will come later, but long-term revitalization of existing churches and the establishment of right priorities in new churches will not happen without it.

Revitalization must come from the top down, not the bottom up. "Grass-roots" renewal has its limits. There are many examples of church members becoming disciples and starting to make other disciples. The members' excitement charges the church atmosphere with new energy. The problems start when the grassroots energy slams into the church's leadership core. The leaders will give lip service to the positive aspects of renewal but will not move to change structures and priorities to facilitate total renewal.

Until the energy of renewal makes its way into the leadership core, it will not be the heart of the church. Therefore, it is crucial to place disciple making at the heart of the church, so the life and vigor that are part and parcel of a disciple-making church will live in its leaders. If it lives in its leaders, they will pass it on from generation to generation. It will grow and multiply in the establishment of new churches. But it must come from the top down, not from the bottom up.

Clear Identification and Communication

The disciple-making pastor combines clear vision with deep conviction. He lays out his scriptural convictions without apology. He tells God's people who he is, who they are, and where they are going. The result is passionate leadership. A deeply rooted ideology that demands obedience to the Great Commission drives him to action. Instead of waiting for people to decide to move toward the obedient action of making disciples, he points the way and says, "Follow me." This passionate drive to lead the church to obedience sets him apart. He avoids fuzzy thinking by clearly communicating three basics. By these, he avoids confusion and proves his consistency.

The Pastor: Who He or She Is

The disciple-making pastor tells God's people he is their spiritual leader, their coach, if you will. He has the responsibility to prepare them for the work God has called them to do. Emphasizing that this declaration has deep roots in Scripture, he teaches what his job is and details it for their understanding. He makes it clear that his energies, his allotment of time, his priorities are ordered by the Word of God. The disciple-making pastor's work is shaped by convictions, not by church tradition.

He establishes the priorities of his work and tells the congregation where he will work and why. He tells them where he will spend time and why. He tells them he has come to serve their best interests by obeying God rather than man. Therefore, he will not react to whims and desires of selfish agendas, but will stay the course on the critical issues that determine church health.

The cardiovascular concept. If the church is the body of Christ, the key to health is a good cardiovascular system. The pastor, therefore, positions himself as a heart specialist. If disciple making makes up the heart of the Great Commission and God's plan for reaching the world, then he must give his best time and effort to it. He identifies the tasks essential to a healthy cardiovascular system, then declares, "This is my area of focus, this is my calling, this will get the lion's share of my effort."

A cardiovascular system is composed of two elements. First are the principles that govern disciple making. Derive any methodology from biblical principles. Identify the principles that must be at work to produce healthy Christians, and you have your cardiovascular principles. One example is the need for accountability. Without direction, mentoring, and correction, Christians run aground on their natural propensities. Therefore, they must submit to some form of monitoring.

The second element that makes for a cardiovascular system is a vehicle to facilitate the principle. You may do this several ways: the small group, a one-on-one relationship, or a written reporting system. The best one combines other desirable elements such as training, Bible study, and ongoing relationships. To follow through on our example, the disciple-making pastor would focus on making sure that accountability is present in the small groups. In the initial stages he would lead the group himself. As the groups multiplied and leaders were trained, he would focus on the group leaders. This is what I mean by focusing on the well and the eager. The disciple-making pastor takes positive action by personal involvement in training and monitoring training vehicles rather than more traditional roles.

He might propose that pulpit teaching, training small group leaders, administering the professional staff, recruiting church planters, writing materials, and leading the church board through a training program will consume most of his time. This will establish a healthy cardiovascular system that will enable the rest of the body to function effectively.

Therefore, except for dire emergency, he would eliminate attendance at most committee meetings, home visitation, hospital calls, and obligatory socializing. Even a standard expectation such as counseling could be curtailed. In fact, if a pastor does what he should and creates a healthy cardiovascular system, much of the counseling will be eliminated.

What is left can be handled by gifted, trained members of the body. While I do not wish to get into a protracted statement concerning counseling, it makes no sense for pastors to spend a lot of time doing it. The pastor serving primarily as counselor is a flip-flop from his biblical role. The counseling pastor spends 50 to 75 percent of his time with the spiritually sick. This creates further weakness and keeps the pastor from the solution to the problems, the giftedness of the spiritually well. By spending most of his time with the well, the pastor can better help the weak. He should work on a cure, not treat the symptoms.

There is a need for counseling, but both the trained laity and the counseling professional do a better job than the pastor. The exception would be crisis counseling, which we might better name *crisis intervention*. In such cases, the pastor plays an important role.

The disciple-making pastor is a specialist who concentrates on tasks that make the heart and cardiovascular system work better: teaching, training, taking people through the six-step training process that will be detailed later. He defines who he is and what his responsibilities are and sticks with them.

The people. The second of the five principles that broadly govern the role of the pastor, stated in Ephesians 4, calls for the proper identification of God's people. Therefore, the disciple-making pastor clearly communicates the objective. Corporate and individual goals are well known. He has identified his role as preparing them to do the works of service. He is a pastor leading a group of ministers, not a minister leading a group of spectators. When the congregation understands the pastor's role, their responsibility becomes more defined. Until the church populace is properly identified, they will languish in their misconceived emotional notions.

He tells them that they are all ordained ministers of God. Every Christian is called to ministry. Seeing themselves as responsible for the ministry and mission of the church brings an entirely new perspective to their lives. The pastor's work, then, is to convince the congregation through scriptural teaching, effective storytelling, and "nuts and bolts" programming, that they are essential to the success of the church.

The process. The process is where the pastor must make it work. Once he has stated the goals and identified the roles, the process makes it a reality. Many pastors are experts at telling people who they are and what they should do, but teaching how to get it done is their Achilles' heel.

The pastor has told them they are ministers, that it is his job to prepare them to do ministry; now he must show them. He points them to specially designed vehicles that will yield the desired results. "A disciple knows the Word," says the pastor, "now join one of our small groups that teach you how to study Scripture." Unless the church provides vehicles for members to apply the teaching, you perform an abortion on new and eager spiritual life. One of the deepest rooted church pathologies is exhortation to action without a means to action. The ugly results are frustrated, guilty, angry Christians who give up on making their lives count for Christ.

Potential ministers need to be pointed to the first step of application as well as subsequent steps. There need to be clearly defined stages of development. My youngest son recently started karate lessons. His eagerness is matched only by his determined work ethic. He is hungry for accomplishment, to reach certain goals. He recites with unusual accuracy the many degrees of the karate hierarchy. Within each color belt, there are degrees of progress, as well. Part of the program's genius is that from the very first lesson, the student can achieve, make progress, and be rewarded. My son knows where he stands and how he is doing. He knows what the goal is and is given assignments and routines to get there.

Jesus let His disciples know where they stood as well. He extended simple invitations: "come and see," "come and follow Me," "come and be with Me," and "remain in Me."[1] These invitations comprise the training phases of Jesus for His men.

The four-part philosophical grid above gives church members a place to gauge their progress. I teach that Jesus never made people follow Him; He simply extended invitations. The congregation knows the difference between these phases and where they are within them. "Come and see" is where we welcome, interest and care for you. In "come and follow Me" we establish you. "Come and be with Me" is where we teach you to teach others. In "remain in Me" we deploy you. Later I will say much concerning these phases, but for now you need only to understand the importance of having a phased process. Just as important as having the phases is helping people understand where they are and motivating them to move ahead.

Another hallmark of the disciple-making pastor mentioned earlier was goal-oriented leadership. Not only does the pastor need to be goal oriented in his work, he must convince the congregation to be the same. Christians set goals in most areas of their lives: business, family, retirement, travel, hobbies, and so on. But ask the same goal-oriented Christians to identify spiritual goals, and the majority are stumped.

The disciple-making pastor transforms the church populace into an army of ministers who know who they are, where they are in their progress, and where they are going.

The Priesthood of All Believers

I choose to describe the disciple maker's belief as a commitment because there is nothing unusual about being in favor of the priesthood of the believer. *Commitment* means he practices his beliefs. The disciple-making pastor's ministry reflects this priority. His time involvement, decision making, and training programs all bank on the proposition that God has called every believer to ministry. He not only preaches this doctrine, his entire ministry rests on its truthfulness.

Abolition of a class of people called laity should be a priority for the church. Out of the ashes of the laity's demise will arise the church's renewal. The disciple-making pastor is determined to lead a second reformation. The first reformation took the Word of God exclusively out of the hands of the clergy and put it into the hands of the people. The second reformation is to get the ministry exclusively out of the hands of the clergy and into the hands of the people, where it rightly belongs.

Both Peter and John spoke of Christians as priests (see 1 Peter 2:5, 9; Rev. 5:10). The Old Testament ministry of the high priest was to represent the interests and needs of people to God. The letter to the Hebrews extensively describes Jesus as the perfect and eternal High Priest. Christ is the intercessor for the saints at the right hand of God. Through the work of Christ, the believer now has access to the throne of God and every Christian presently enjoys this authority and privilege. The corporate community of believers is known as a kingdom of priests (see 1 Peter 2:5; Rev. 5:10).

The priesthood of the believer implies that Christians have the authority and responsibility to minister for Christ as the priesthood traditionally did. If you join the priesthood of the believer with the common believer's call to ministry, you have the reasons for teaching that every Christian is called to Christian service.

Let's take a look at the word *called* as it relates to ministry. The Greek root is *kletos*, and lexicons define it as "called" or "vocation." Paul wrote, "Think of what you were when you were called" (1 Cor. 1:26) and "Live a life worthy of the calling you have received" (Eph. 4:1).

Paul makes no mention of a professional elite. The context clearly refers to all members in the body of Christ. Paul strung the same kind of thoughts together in Romans 1:1–8. Paul considered himself in a special category, since he referred to himself as an apostle. More important, he said he was "called" (Rom. 1:1). But Paul's teaching did not stop with himself: "You also are among those who are called. . . . To all in Rome who are loved by God and called to be saints" (Rom. 1:6–7).

"Among those" referred to Gentiles, and the Christians in Rome were included in the redeemed community. Paul emphatically stated it again in verse seven, "called to be saints." The entire family of God is a called community, called as holy ones or saints.

The next logical step is to identify what the called saints are to do. It already has been well developed that the saints are to be trained in order to do the work of service (see Eph. 4:11–12). Everyone is called to ministry, not just a few. One more passage will enhance our understanding. In his second letter to the Corinthians, Paul identified the possessors of ministry: "All this is from God, who reconciled us to himself through Christ and gave us the ministry of reconciliation: that God was reconciling the world to himself in Christ, not counting men's sins against them. And he has committed to us the message of reconciliation" (2 Cor. 5:18–19).

"Us" refers to members of the church, those reconciled by the work of Christ. The two important statements are "gave us the ministry of reconciliation" and "committed to us the message of reconciliation." The ministry responsibility has not been given to a group of less than 1 percent of the body, named *clergy*; it is the right and call to 100 percent of church membership, named *saints*.

So What?

So what does it mean on a practical basis? The priesthood of the believer is popular in theory: it is widely believed but rarely practiced. It comes up most often in sermons and church business meetings. Pastors preach it to get more people involved; laymen mention it to check the authority of pastors. One of the great pathologies of churches is the silly notion that since every Christian believer is a priest, every Christian's opinion is of equal value. This leads to a series of disasters such as disobedient, biblically illiterate Christians demonstrating their sinful attitudes and ignorance by sabotaging God's plan for His church. A cynical critique? Indeed, but a fair one. The priesthood of the believer must mean more than that everyone gets a job and everyone has a say.

The disciple-making pastor commits himself to the priesthood of all believers. He believes each possesses a spiritual gift, a special call, and should be serving Christ in some concrete work. How then does the disciple-making pastor demonstrate his commitment?

He gives permission. Most Christians simply don't believe it. The average Christian finds the notion that he is an ordained minister of the gospel both funny and frightening. He has always accepted the dedication of others—more than that, it inspires him. But the idea that he could be a minister seems surreal.

If I am a minister, reasons the layman, *then I am to do what a minister does. A minister teaches the Scriptures, he serves communion, performs weddings, counsels the hurting, and buries the dead. I have no interest in those activities, and in addition, I have no training.*

Another valid misgiving concerning entering the ministry is that someone has changed the rules. "For years," the layman could protest, "I have been told that being holy meant church attendance, serving on the Christian education board, and singing in the choir. Now I am told that to be okay with God I have to go into the ministry."

Misconceptions and misgivings are real obstacles to full employment of members in ministry. The disciple-making pastor demonstrates his commitment by giving people permission to enter into ministry. He tells them they are ministers; he addresses the misconceptions and misgivings by sound teaching.

Pastors too often stand in the way of the practice of the priesthood of believers. They teach it with gusto, but taking their teaching to its logical conclusion seems far too threatening. Many pastors, with the best of intentions, don't expect members to rise above the "helper" status. Not only haven't they seen it happen, they don't really believe it can happen. The populace is meant to fill in the many jobs of the church. If they give their money, in turn they receive good preaching and a full-service program from the staff.

The pastor who insists that people live up to their God-given calling often gets labeled *insensitive, noncaring,* or *too task oriented.* The exact opposite is true. The pastor who views Christians as good helpers, but not on his level, has a low and unloving view of people. The loving and high view means believing the average Christian is a gifted minister of the gospel and can be trusted with important spiritual ministry responsibility.

The pastor who does the ministry rather than training the people to do it, behaves in an unloving and noncaring fashion. Please note that I did not say he was unloving and noncaring. I said with respect to this area, he behaves like a parent who will not allow his child to mature. This style of pastoring perpetuates the present environmental weakness found in the church. When the pastor must control the ministry and save the best parts of it for the professional staff, people will continue to be weak and parasitic. The pastorate will continue to be unrealistic, and churches will remain environments for the weak and dependent. Not to train and unleash all willing members is the greatest pastoral sin.

The high view honors the average Christian. John Q. Christian can visit the hospital, pray for the sick, baptize his children, serve communion, and train discipleship group leaders. He can do these things better than the pastor, and he feels the freedom to do so. In fact, the disciple-making pastor taught him how.

The pastor gives permission by telling the congregation that he is not threatened by their increased involvement. In fact, their becoming more involved and effective will make him successful. When the body members minister, the body is better off and so is the clergy.

He becomes successful when there is full employment in the body; when people believe in their ability through Christ and their skills through training; when they effectively penetrate their harvest fields where they live, work, and play; when church members introduce people to Christ, establish them in the basics, and fold them into the church without direct pastoral involvement; when the ministries of the church are created, started, and administered without direct pastoral involvement. In short, when the members are as effective in practice during the week as they look and talk on Sundays, the pastor has reached peak performance.

He gives direction. Another way the disciple-making pastor demonstrates his commitment to the priesthood of all believers is by giving direction. He has redefined *minister*; next he must redefine *ministry*, so the church populace can get over the "going into the ministry" obstacle. There are three broad ministry categories.

RECONCILIATION (2 CORINTHIANS 5:18–21). This is the individual and corporate outreach of Christians to those in need of Christ. This is missions and evangelism.

EDIFICATION (EPHESIANS 4:11–16). This is the building up of the body of Christ. The saints are called to love one another. Romans 12 puts feet on ministry to one another by directing us to recognize that we are members of one another: Paul directs us to be devoted to one another, give preference to, honor, be of the same mind, exhort, comfort, and greet one another. Peter directs us to use our spiritual gifts to serve one another (1 Peter 4:10–11).

The expressions of serving one another are as numerous as Christians themselves. The healthy local body enjoys a reciprocal, self-perpetuating, and life-giving interplay between members. The ministry of reconciliation is a mission to the world; the ministry of edification is a ministry to the body.

PHYSICAL NEED. A cursory reading of Jesus' statement of purpose in His hometown synagogue confronts all believers with this responsibility. "The Spirit of the Lord is upon Me, because He anointed Me to preach the gospel to the poor. He has sent Me to proclaim release to the captives, and recovery of sight to the blind, to set free those who are oppressed, to proclaim the favorable year of the Lord" (Luke 4:18–19 NASB).

Jesus linked preaching, the poor, and those oppressed by circumstances such as imprisonment, hunger, and physical distress. Evangelicals have tended to emphasize the ministries of reconciliation and edification at the expense of ministry to physical needs. There is a valid hierarchy of outreach, and the verbalization of the gospel is at the top of the list. Still evangelicals need to correct their neglect of physical needs. The trend of the eighties indicates that evangelicals have begun to move into that area.

Too many Christians who have a heart for helping those in physical distress sit on the sidelines. They should be unleashed to utilize their gifts of showing mercy, helps, and encouragement, along with the gifts of healings. Cities have great needs in the areas such as the homeless, those addicted to alcohol, drugs, prostitution, along with battered wives and abused children.

Thousands of unexpected and unwanted pregnancies cause the needless slaughter of the innocent unborn, while the waiting lines for adoptions grow longer. Christians whom God has gifted in these areas have been on the shelf far too long. The redefined ministry for the saints is reconciliation to the world, edification to the church and to physical need, wherever it is found.

The disciple-making pastor demonstrates his commitment to the priesthood of all believers by redefining ministry itself and freeing people to explore and create.

He gives training. Without training, Christians experience nothing but frustration. The disciple-making pastor's training vehicles are consistent with his beliefs. The most effective way to abort the future of eager believers is to inspire them without training them. Tell them they are priests of God, gifted ministers of the gospel, then don't show them how to make it happen. Satan has honed this into one of his best weapons for brutalizing Christians.

The secret to spiritual maturity is the application of the truth over a sustained period. Paul claimed he experienced the peace of God because he had learned the secret that gave him contentment in every circumstance and the confidence that through Christ he could do anything (see Phil. 4:11–13). The word translated "learn" is *mathetes* and is employed in other places for "disciple." The word denotes a process practiced over a sustained period of time. The secret that served Paul so well was that change begins with the truth, but truth's importance depends on its consistent application.

The New Testament teaches two kinds of truth. First are the propositional statements of Scripture that are true regardless of experience. For example, the deity of Christ. The second kind of truth is what Paul terms "real knowledge" (based on Col. 1:9, the use of *epiginosko*), knowledge based on experience: "to know exactly or completely or learn to know."[2] "Real knowledge" of the deity of Christ would mean experiencing Christ's power in one's life. Then Jesus is Lord not only in theory but also in practice.

The translation of well-taught theory into "real knowledge" is the greatest challenge a pastor faces. The priesthood of believers demands that the disciple-making pastor develop ways of helping people apply what they have been motivated to do, through vehicles that provide them a safe place to practice new beliefs and skills.

The disciple-making pastor demonstrates his commitment to the priesthood of the believer in three primary ways: He gives *permission*, he gives *direction*, and he gives *training*. He lives out the courage of his convictions that every Christian is an ordained, called minister of Christ. He commits himself to it, because without the priesthood of the believer, no reproduction or multiplication can take place, making the Great Commission impossible. If the Great Commission is not possible, world evangelization becomes a fantasy. Then the concept of the disciple-making pastor becomes a moot point, a useless discussion. The disciple-making pastor without the priesthood of all believers is a pastor without portfolio. He's a soldier without a weapon, a rebel with a lost cause.

Multiplication

The successful completion of the Great Commission depends on multiplication. Disciple making results in reproduction; the result of reproduction among several people is multiplication. Jesus stated the Great Commission the way He did, because "make disciples of all nations" means much more than "make converts of all nations." Only healthy disciples reproduce. If the church fails to make disciples, it fails to multiply. If the church fails to multiply, it fails.

The command was not "make converts" or "make Christians" or "make church members." "Make disciples" is loaded with implications based on Jesus' definitions: "This is to my Father's glory, *that you bear much fruit*, showing yourselves to be my disciples. . . . You did not choose me, but I chose you . . . *to go and bear fruit—fruit that will last*" (John 15:8, 16, italics added).

The commission's command to make disciples is the imperative for the church to produce a quality product. The church must produce people who reproduce themselves; any other kind of Christian is spiritually sterile.

Reproduction is different from multiplication. Reproduction of a single disciple is wonderful, but it is no more than spiritual addition. In theory one disciple may lead many to Christ, but if none of the converts pass it on, there is reproduction, but no multiplication.

To illustrate multiplication, would you rather have a million dollars today or a penny today, two cents tomorrow, and four cents the day after that, doubling daily for thirty days? I'm no mathematician, but those who are assure me that taking the penny would give you many times the $1 million. In fact it would be $10,737,418.24. Who wouldn't prefer well over $10 million instead of the $1 million? While it seems unimpressive at first, multiplication later yields the greater results. Jesus called us to make disciples because only disciples make other disciples who in turn reproduce, which sets multiplication into motion.

Fifty percent of the world's population has not heard the gospel. Without multiplication, world evangelization will continue to limp along behind the population growth. It takes 1,000 Christians 365 days to introduce one person to Christ. At this rate, reaching the world is a fantasy.

A major reason for the rarity of multiplication is the unwillingness of the church to make disciples. It takes too long and calls for major restructuring of existing churches. It's much easier to maintain the status quo. Everyone experiences the powerful temptation to cave in to conventional measurements for success. Bodies, bucks, and buildings are the contemporary standards for having the "right stuff." I contend that measuring a church by bodies, bucks, and buildings means nothing more than having "the right fluff."

World evangelization languishes because sufficient multiplication does not take place. The lure and the lust of conventional success in American culture make it difficult to get the church's attention. Too many churches have become hollow shells, with sick or nonexistent cardiovascular systems, but they look so good. On the surface many churches appear healthy, but in reality, they are factories that produce weakness. If you demand little and put on a good show, you can always get a crowd. Large crowds don't prove anything other than that some talented people can gather large crowds. It doesn't mean discipleship; it doesn't mean obedience to the Great Commission; it doesn't mean multiplication.

Obedience to the Great Commission means determined dedication to disciple making. The disciple-making pastor dedicates himself to the multiplication task because it is the right thing to do. He will swim upstream, but he dedicates himself because Scripture clearly commands it. Now is the time to consider some relevant biblical data that reveals principles that will insure multiplication.

Prioritizing Disciple Making (Matthew 28:18–20)

"Make disciples of all nations, baptizing them . . . and teaching them to obey everything I have commanded you" (Matt. 28:19–20).

The disciple-making pastor may commit himself to making disciples so that multiplication can take place; he may make it number-one on his priority list; he may establish an environment for disciple making, alive with the well-known, often-communicated expectation that every member is to be a reproducing disciple. But only the rare church publicizes and proclaims this expectation from the pulpit. Even more scarce is the congregation where the pastor's and church leaders' behavior are consistent with this objective.

John's Gospel shows that fruit bearing is both the expectation and the natural result of abiding in Christ (see John 15:8, 16). Clearly a disciple reproduces, therefore, disciple making makes multiplication possible.

When a local church has priorities and training vehicles with accountability to back up the priorities, you can make disciples in batches. The church machinery can consistently pump them out. The church that has established a disciple-making flow will be healthy and will grow, and God wants this for both His church and a lost world. The end result of disciple making, which creates multiplication, is the population of heaven. Shortcuts don't work, so don't take them. Demonstrate the courage of your convictions; be a plodder, train people, make disciples, please God.

Proper Selection of Personnel (2 Timothy 2:2)

"And the things you have heard me say in the presence of many witnesses entrust to reliable men who will also be qualified to teach others" (2 Tim. 2:2).

I intend to speak in general terms here and in more specific ones later. Paul lays out four principles that will make multiplication work.

Multiplication requires several passes of the baton. Four generations are mentioned: Paul, Timothy, reliable men, and others. Paul sets the philosophy that for the gospel to be preached widely, its message must be broadly entrusted to others. The job is too large for a few and too long for a single generation. Paul's statement gives substantial credence to the fact that the belief in multiplication itself was passed from Jesus to the disciples to Paul and then Timothy.

Multiplication requires that those who have it must pass it on. The previous principle highlights the need for the multiplicity of passes; this point focuses on the pass itself. Most breakdowns in the multiplication take place when the time comes for passing it on.

The major hurdle for most pastors and leaders is the firm conviction that they should entrust the ministry to others. Almost all leaders see the need for the next generation to carry on. There is wide agreement that serious young people need training to go into ministry and to the mission field. But most of this takes place by divine accident. An oxymoron? Yes. A fair description? Yes, again.

A divine accident is when God's faithfulness compensates for our disobedience. When the church does not make disciples, God makes sure there are enough to keep the ship afloat. We see this demonstrated in the existence of the church itself. If God wasn't totally committed to building His church, it would have gone under long ago. To be fair, the church has done an adequate job of preparing professional leaders to fill pastoral vacancies. The passing on of the faith from professionals to professionals has been good and will continue to be so.

We must jump the hurdle of convincing professionals that the ministry should be passed on to the laity, that a fully serviced, highly prioritized effort should be made to train the common believer to pass on the gospel.

Multiplication means passing it on to the right people. Tom Peters, author of the bestselling books *In Search of Excellence* and *A Passion for Excellence*, claims that delegation remains the number one challenge to modern management. Peters says that, clearly, passing on work to others is the greatest challenge in the business community.

It would be senseless to continue to pass on something valuable to unreliable people. Who do we allow to drive our cars, stay in our homes, babysit our children, and manage our money? Those things we love the most, we pass on to others with the greatest of care. When I give something I treasure to someone else for safekeeping, I look for reliability. *Reliability* means "trustworthiness." You can count on the person. Paul teaches the necessity of reliability to multiplication, and he doesn't teach it in a vacuum. He defines it for future generations.

"Whoever can be trusted with very little can also be trusted with much" (Luke 16:10). "Now it is required that those who have been given a trust must prove faithful" (1 Cor. 4:2).

Paul carried on Jesus' teaching on the importance of faithfulness. They both agree that the right people to give responsibility to are those who have proven reliable. The frequency with which the church breaks this simple yet profound principle is shameful. How many times have you heard, "Joe is bored by ushering, but if we make him an elder, he would be much more reliable"? Paul and Jesus would call this nonsense! They taught the opposite. Don't dare give important work to people who treat God's work as unimportant by their lack of enthusiasm, diligence, and reliability.

Reliability is to God's work what a foundation is to a building. Without it, the weight of ministry responsibility will crush the faithful few holding it. When the faithful few pass on ministry to the untested and unfaithful, it works for a while, but those entrusted in the second and third generations break down because of character flaws. Multiplication breaks down because responsibility is given to the unreliable.

The church has disregarded the clearly presented imperative to train and equip faithful leaders. Twice Paul wrote to young pastors exhorting them to teach and practice qualifications for leadership. First Timothy 3 and Titus 1 detail the qualifications for local church leadership. Paul also admonished, "They must first be tested; and then if there is nothing against them, let them serve as deacons" (1 Tim. 3:10).

This certainly applied to elders as well. Add to the Timothy passage the Titus information, and you have a strong definition of *reliable*. Paul emphasized the commitment to impartially choose these kinds of leaders: "I charge you, in the sight of God and Christ Jesus and the elect angels, to keep these instructions without partiality, and to do nothing out of favoritism" (1 Tim. 5:21).

Giving power to unreliable leaders becomes a two-edged sword. First it cuts because the church lacks a commitment to train and equip leaders, therefore, it has no reliable people available to take on responsibility. Since there are not enough faithful available, the work of ministry is either left undone or done poorly. Negative defeatism and erroneous clichés such as "people don't want to serve," "no one wants to lead," and "people don't take pride in their work" riddle the church's atmosphere.

The second cut of the sword is that multiplication has no chance in such an environment. When the unfaithful do the ministry, the work becomes drudgery, inconsistent, dull, and poor. Who would want to export such an undesirable product? In such an environment, when work is delegated, the quality suffers, and eventually the work is returned to the delegator for retooling or burial.

To make multiplication effective, make reliable character the nonnegotiable test. Reliable character is the product of disciple making. When reliable character is esteemed from the pulpit, when the pastor and church leaders model it, it will make its way into the pew. Various principles govern such a process; for now, however, it is enough to say that multiplication is a product of building a solid foundation of reliability. When a church has reliable people to whom the ministry can be passed, the work will multiply.

Multiplication means passing it on to qualified people. The right people are reliable ministers who can be trusted. They have the character and have proven it by doing a good job with previous tasks. Whereas the right people are foundational, they also must possess the right skills for successful function. Paul clearly described the importance of skill when he told Timothy they "will also be qualified to teach others" (2 Tim. 2:2).

If I started a baseball team, I would first get all interested parties into condition. General characteristics such as strong bodies, endurance, a work ethic, and a positive attitude would be foundational. But when it came to playing, I would need people with specific baseball skills.

We build a ministry of multiplication upon the foundation of reliable character. But when it comes to passing on ministry responsibility, gifts and skills come into play. Common sense says that if the work is teaching, we require a person with the gift of teaching and teaching experience. If it be administration, an administrator; if hospital visitation or working with the terminally ill, the gift of showing mercy. This kind of matching gifts and bents to assignments is natural. Good materials on this matching are available. The church, however, has suffered a dual breakdown in this most natural responsibility.

First, it has broken down in giving training concerning spiritual gifts. Most churches do not inform the congregations that each person is a gifted and called minister of Christ. I define *inform* as teaching it as a cardinal doctrine of the faith equal to and part of the priesthood of all believers. After informing believers, the church must reach them concerning the nature of gifts and follow it with an assessment of their gifts. Then they need guidance to apply their giftedness.

Another serious training error is to treat the spiritual gifts teaching and assessment as the finish line, rather than the starting line. The congregation gets the uneasy feeling that once they have finished the training program they have broken the tape and are finished. Like graduation from the university, now they are on their own. Independence is good when held in balance with dependence on God and the local church. The Christian never outgrows the need for training, encouragement, and accountability. The most vital leader requires the creativity and honing that only the body can provide. It is vital to teach this at the beginning of a truly effective ministry; the best is yet to come.

The second breakdown lies in the failure to build leadership skills into those so inclined. This is why Paul described those "who will also be qualified to teach others" (2 Tim. 2:2). The breakdown in training in gifts occurs in the general populace; this step focuses on leaders. Character, reliability, and spiritual giftedness are the foundation for any good ministry. Many need skill development. Leaders need to communicate. Whether it be to evangelize, teach the Bible, motivate others, or administer a program, communication is a key skill. According to Paul, if they can't communicate, they don't pass the responsibility test.

Teaching others is a loaded term. It means to teach others in such a way that they can pass on the ability. It means to teach only those who can teach others. In other words, a certain package of skills is required in order for a person to have *transferable ability*. Not every believer is a multiplier.

Some won't possess the transferability. The most common reason is disobedience. Many could be, but won't be because they are unwilling. Never consider the first reason acceptable, but it is a reality. The second reason should be accepted, it is also a reality. *God doesn't give everyone the needed gifts and abilities to have that transferable quality.* There are two reasons why Paul instructed Timothy to use discernment in selecting multipliers. The first is sin and the lack of reliable character. The second is the giftedness and calling of the person.

The second reason is not a matter of spirituality, but suitability. For this reason church leaders must assess their congregation, filtering out those specially gifted for multiplication. They should provide training and fine-tuning of skills in preparation for greater ministry responsibility. Only by taking qualification seriously can any ministry expect effective multiplication. The ability to communicate or teach is one basic of transferability. This is consistent with Paul's phrase "qualified to teach others" and is a first priority skill. In addition a leader needs the ability to manage people, delegate, follow up, create corporate environment, and so on. Third, the leader must have the ability to motivate and inspire. The multiplier is a person of conviction; he has fire in his bones.

In addition he can address himself to common problems people experience; he has a basic counseling skill to treat the people he works with.

Finally, he has the basic skill of correcting those who are in error. He can hold people accountable without losing them. He understands the balance between correction and restoration.

To work, multiplication requires several passes of the ministry baton. Those to whom it is passed must pass it on. Leaders must pass it on to the right people, reliable in character, qualified properly gifted multipliers.

Reasons to Multiply (Matthew 9:36–38)

Reasons are critical to long-term commitment. Here are three rationales for making multiplication a commitment. Already we've established the priority of disciple making, for without the end product, there is no one to multiply. The second principle was the proper selection of personnel from among the reliable group of disciples. Now we turn to a third area, the general dynamics that work to call people to a lifetime of multiplication.

Compassion and multiplication. Disciple-making pastors often receive criticism for advocating the multiplication of ministry, because it requires a shared ministry. A shared ministry means that the pastor must give away parts of his traditional role. Traditionalists consider him unloving or say he tries to avoid his work.

Contrary to such belief, through His example, Jesus teaches that multiplication is the natural expression of compassion. In fact, a pastor shows no greater long-term act of love than that of multiplying his work through others.

"When he saw the crowds, he had compassion on them, because they were harassed and helpless, like sheep without a shepherd. Then he said to his disciples, 'The harvest is plentiful but the workers are few. Ask the Lord of the harvest, therefore, to send out workers into his harvest field.' He called his twelve disciples to him and gave them authority to drive out evil spirits and to heal every disease and sickness" (Matt. 9:36–10:1). The gospel of Mark adds, "Calling the Twelve to him, he sent them out two by two" (Mark 6:7).

An unmet need triggered the official multiplication of Jesus' ministry. That principle underlies the entire thesis of this book. The disciple-making pastor makes disciples so the corporate church will produce healthy reproducing Christians. These healthy Christians then will fulfill their responsibility to the world and evangelize. The result is the increased population of heaven. The unmet need in the world caused Jesus to issue the Great Commission. The same unmet need causes the disciple-making pastor to continue to move the church in the same obedient direction.

Jesus realized that if the unmet needs before Him were to be met, thirteen men working twelve-hour days would produce more than one man working an eighteen-hour day.

This is precisely why multiplication is so loving: The seekers are taught, the sick are treated, the discouraged are lifted. People's real needs are better cared for. The church's great mysteries have been its disaffection with multiplication and its avoidance of disciple making.

Too many people interpret love to mean direct involvement on the part of the senior pastor. This is clearly cultural in origin and debilitating to the church. Disciple-making pastors must take courageous action by moving the church toward decentralization of ministry. Offer Jesus' example as the scriptural justification. It will be resisted, but given enough time, it will work. In the end both those helped by positive residue from doing ministry and those helped by receiving ministry will thank you. Compassion as motive for multiplication is too powerful to resist.

Prayer and multiplication. Jesus described a troubling situation when He said there was too much work and too few workers. The need outnumbered the workers: workers for evangelism, to meet physical needs, to support those in emotional turmoil, and many more. What concerned leader hasn't been troubled by the hurting people who have no one to help them and the large number of willing people ready to be harvested who lack harvesters?

Not much has changed in this regard since Jesus spoke those words. The world's present needs far outweigh the workers to meet them. This is frustrating and perplexing. Karl Barth wrote, "Perplexity comes to us simply because we are ministers." Jesus voiced a simple solution: pray for workers to enter the harvest.

In the face of vast unmet need, compassion forces the concerned Christian to make choices. Jesus advocates a twofold choice: First, make yourself available for work in the harvest field; second, pray for God to send others into the harvest. Pray, because it's God's harvest field. Pray, because only God can convince someone to work in His field. Pray, because no one can recruit enough personnel from his sphere of influence alone. Pray for workers to enter the harvest field from all over the world.

Jesus said, "Make disciples" but "pray for workers." The difference is that God desires every Christian to be a reproducing disciple. But for a disciple to determine that he will give a lifetime of labor takes a divine tap on the shoulder. I am not saying a disciple is less serious than a worker; I am saying there are some differences of degree rather than kind.

The differences between a disciple and a laborer are experience and conviction. A laborer may or may not possess the experience, skill, and bone-deep conviction that will make possible a serious commitment to reach and minister to others. When Jesus commissioned the Twelve, He did so with high expectations. But He waited two years before challenging the Twelve to go out and labor without His direct involvement. Prayer is the most effective recruiting tool that leaders possess. Jesus encourages us to ask, to petition our Father to send more laborers.

Leaders can employ various recruiting tools: entertainment followed by an appeal; guilt stimulation followed by an appeal; calling in favors followed by an appeal; arm twisting followed by an appeal; and old reliable, the tearjerker film or story followed by a tear-jerker appeal. These are common, but not commanded recruiting techniques. The various appeals mentioned above are prefaced or followed by the obligatory prayer. But how common is the organization that uses prayer as their primary recruiting method? Honestly, I don't want to know; I would find it too discouraging.

I do not argue against the use of other methods in addition to prayer, but against the use of other methods as primary means of recruiting. To make prayer primary, issue a general call of the congregation to prayer. This means putting forth effort to organize prayer groups or meetings that are specifically tied to a need. Thoroughly school the church populace in why you have chosen the prayer method over others.

A plan for multiplication. Good leaders know how to frame an issue. Look at how Jesus framed the need for multiplication of ministry. Compassion for unmet need was the prime motive. He painted a picture of a world of hurt people languishing without someone to help. The objective for multiplication was extending God's love and care on a wider basis through a wider work force. Prayer was the primary tool for recruiting workers to fill the vacant work force.

He didn't stop there; Jesus had a work plan for the disciples. He took immediate action by commissioning the Twelve to go out in twos. Matthew 10 is entirely devoted to Jesus' detailed instructions concerning their first independent ministry tour. Not only had Jesus spent two years modeling ministry, He reviewed the details once more, just prior to their departure. He gave specific instructions, designed to insure maximum success. By severely limiting their message, their target group, even their travel schedule and amount of luggage, Jesus narrowed the objective for their benefit.

The disciple-making pastor has much to learn and apply from this example. He demonstrates his commitment to multiplication by preaching the reasons and praying for workers. But like Jesus, he doesn't stop there. He then has a specific plan to mobilize willing workers into the actual multiplication of ministry.

One of the best ways to kill the goose you want to lay the golden egg is to motivate people to ministry but not mobilize them to the actual work. Instead train them to do the work and then give them the opportunity to apply their training. I use a two-year training program that equips people in the basics of the Christian life. This is what I referred to earlier as getting potential baseball players into condition. Toward the end of the two-year period, we assess the gifts and abilities of each group member. This takes into account their impressions and leanings concerning God's leading in their lives. The purpose of the assessment is to launch them into further ministry. Here we match specific skills to specific ministry. This is like the coach looking for players who have specific baseball skills. Here multiplication takes place. The group members spread out and minister as couples or in twos, rather than remaining a group.

Not only do we present members with an assessment of who they are, they also receive a list of in-house ministry opportunities they are welcome to fill. We also encourage many kinds of outreach ministries; we want them to dream, to be creative, to allow God to lead them to their most effective ministry. The key ingredient overlooked in deploying people into the harvest field is the important two years of training that precede the deployment. Without the training, there would be far more casualties, and multiplication would break down.

The church needs a plan for multiplication. A plan means you have every intention of following through on your beliefs. The disciple-making pastor points people to training for ministry, then provides a plan for turning that training into multiplication.

Further Reflections

Commitment is "the act of binding yourself intellectually and emotionally to a course of action."[3] The four commitments of the disciple-making pastor that I identified in this chapter require a sincere and steadfast investment. They call upon a person to marshal all of his or her gifts and abilities for an extended time. I still believe the four commitments are crucial to the implementation and successful fulfillment of a disciple-making ministry.

However, you may find some of my thoughts disturbing. If you do, then we're getting someplace. The first thought that may come to mind when you are asked to commit is *sacrifice*. The call to donate money, to volunteer in a service project, or to enroll in a disciplined study group will require a decision to change. Then you think, *Okay, Christ made sacrifices, so I should as well.* To move ahead with this understanding has intrinsic value. When you give a hungry person a hot meal, it is an act of love without ambiguity, regardless of how you feel. However, this is not the best or most powerful basis for a sustained commitment to a sacrificial life.

If someone had asked the early disciples what the most important trait of a true Christian was, they would not have said sacrifice. They would have said love. This comes from the example of Jesus: "For God so loved the world that he gave his one and only Son" (John 3:16). I am not against service to others when we don't feel like it, because Jesus went to the cross when He didn't feel like it. What overpowered his human tendency to avoid suffering, what overcame the fear and the agony of becoming sin, was love.

I know I have sacrificed more for my wife and sons than anyone else. That doesn't make me a sacrificial person, but it does reveal that love is a powerful force. Love is invisible if not attached to an action. In fact, I am willing to opine that love requires action to be real; otherwise it is merely good intention.

What I have learned about commitment in the last twenty years is that I have been very committed to myself. I hesitated to commit to a church I was pastoring as much as I was asking those in the church to commit. When it came right down to it, if the church was not advancing my religious career, I wanted out. (I have written plenty about this struggle in articles and in my book *Choose the Life*.[4]) I didn't recognize this inability to commit my all to the cause. I was always holding back; I wanted to keep my options open, in case things didn't work out. It was my form of risk management so that I would not get caught in a situation I disliked. This was caused by doubt and fear—doubt that God would bless me as I desired, and fear that I would be average. My most frightening thought was that I would fully surrender to serve in a situation that would lead to obscurity. No one would really notice my work. I wouldn't be asked to opine, speak at events, or be recognized as a go-to guy in the church. Commitment is about trust, the belief that God truly loves me and will guide me in the best plan.

I *appeared* committed: My words, my hard work, and my vision for the church and others were all there. I even wrote a book on commitment that I still believe in, and what I said in it is true. But I had to admit that I was primarily committed to getting my way.

I changed, though the change was gradual and painful. It came in the startling fact that I did not love others as Christ loved me. I had always believed and taught that loving as Christ loved is the standard of one's discipleship—the evidence of faith. Christ lived for others, so as his follower, I am called to live for others. My commitment, then, was to live my life as though Jesus were living it. If He were a pastor, what kind of pastor would He be? He surrendered everything for people who showed Him little respect or interest. So I decided I must give up the right to run my own life. I would surrender the control of outcomes, time-tables, and projects. I would commit to love God every day and let Him control the results.

This change has allowed me to take up my cross every day and lose myself in the mission of serving others. When I sit down to write, when I pack my bag for a trip, or when I can't sleep in a land far away, I think of giving a gift that is about others, not me. Doing those things is sacrificial for me. When I travel internationally, I often find myself away from hot water and good medical facilities, and I realize I'm not in control. If I am home and near a good health facility, I have some control over when I get sick, and where and how I die. As you can tell, I am still working on "For to me, living is for Christ, and dying is even better." (Phil. 1:21 NLT).

So it comes down to this: If the pastor can submit his or her will and plan to God's for a specific ministry setting, then the commitment will be there. It will be the kind of commitment Jesus has for us. Jesus was a man for others. His mission was born in love and worked out in obedience, and even though He was tempted to quit, he hung tough. How liberating it is to be able to freely give ourselves to others without regret, to live a life unencumbered by personal goals that keep us from loving others as Christ loved.

The Practices of a Disciple-Making Pastor

You can identify the disciple-making pastor by his practices. As we've already begun to see, he:

practices the principle of selectivity;
teaches and practices philosophical purity at the leadership level;
believes in and practices accountability;
effectively uses the small group for disciple making; and
believes in and practices the decentralization of pastoral care.

The Principle of Selectivity

This could be the disciple-making pastor's greatest test. Though many give the doctrine of selectivity intellectual assent, in practice it is a firestorm. "It's all right for Jesus to practice," the founding church member bellows, "but don't try it here. Our system for choosing leaders works just fine! Thanks, but no thanks!" What is it about the doctrine of selectivity that draws so much flak?

First let's identify it. The doctrine of selectivity is as old as recorded history. God chose Noah to build the ark and Abraham to be the seed of the chosen people. He named Saul, David, and Solomon kings of Israel. Jesus chose the Twelve to carry the message of the kingdom. Faithful men were Christ's method. Jesus advised we take great care in choosing people to take on ministry responsibility (see Luke 16:10). Paul carried on the tradition by qualifying for Timothy the kind of person who should be trained to pass on the gospel (see 2 Tim. 2:2).

Paul instituted the school of Tyrannus, where at times there were up to twelve men under apprenticeship. Paul gave more detailed information than any other New Testament author concerning qualifications for the careful selection of leaders (see 1 Tim. 3:1–10; Titus 1:5–9).

Selectivity is the process of applying scriptural qualifications to the selection of leaders. Notice the target and purpose: the selection of leaders. The doctrine of selectivity does not apply to the general church populace in the same way that it does toward leaders.

Contrary to some thinking, selectivity does not threaten an atmosphere of acceptance. Selection is made from among the pool of people who have gone through training. It does not threaten the position of the church member who needs support or encouragement or seeks after Christ. In fact, when the qualifications for leadership are taken seriously, the quality of ministry improves; therefore, the church becomes less judgmental and petty. Those who most need acceptance and love are more likely to get it.

Selectivity also means the intentional training and preparation of people to take the leadership role. Not only do existing leaders apply scriptural standards, they provide training and experience that make attainment to those standards possible.

I stated earlier that often selectivity is the disciple-making pastor's toughest battle. From personal experience I know that few if any issues are more hotly contested. During my first week in the pastorate, I attended a nominating committee meeting. The chairman opened in prayer and proceeded to give a gloom-and-doom message concerning the dearth of willing workers available for the thirty-five nominated positions. He then presented a strategy that I will call "twist and lie": Twist arms and lie about the work required. Put pressure on them to serve and emphasize the great ease of the job.

I decided I should contribute the scriptural view. I suggested that we start with a study of scriptural qualifications, then make a list of those who were close. Then I had the gall to suggest that if we couldn't find the people to do the work, we leave vacancies. There was much coughing, some red faces, and the chairman laughed out loud. "If you take that and a dime, you could make a phone call. Obviously, you are new at this!" He was right: A phone call cost a dime, and it was my first week as a pastor. But fifteen years and thousands of experiences later, I am 100 percent sure he was wrong in discounting the importance of qualifications. As a matter of fact, the integrity of the church depends upon our faithful adherence to them.

Why Is It Controversial?

Why do churches object to selectivity? First, it upsets the balance of power, who has it, and how they get it. Churches have operated for years by what is commonly labeled the "good old boy" system. This system esteems length of membership, faithfulness to the organization, willingness to serve, popularity with the church fathers, and a belief that everyone's opinion is of equal value.

Selectivity threatens this system because it shows no partiality. It does not bow to popularity; it discriminates based upon objective standards and measures the performance of elders. It also calls for training and learning. Too often, training and learning ended years ago for the established "good old boys." Since it shakes up the system, it threatens the power base.

It also changes the rules. A common protest is "For years I have been told that being holy is attendance at church services, singing in the choir, giving my tithe, and serving on the Christian education board. But now you tell me I need to be trained; I should be a fruit-bearing disciple; I'm expected to witness, to study Scripture on my own, to think in terms of teaching and training others. I thought I was okay, now I find out I'm not okay. I don't qualify to be an elder or deacon." This is double trouble, because selectivity shakes up the power base and calls into question the established leaders' qualifications. The rules change, and people don't like that.

Churches also resist by charging that selectivity means playing favorites. This is the objection voiced the most. The first two are as real, but pride prohibits most people from admitting what they really feel. Therefore, accusing the pastor of favoritism is a safe ploy.

In their defense, selectivity quite often can appear to be favoritism, mainly because the people chosen for leadership roles have received the training. In order for the training to take place, the trainees have by necessity been in close proximity to the pastor. This commonly results in friendship between the trainer and trainees which gives rise to jealousy and accusations of playing favorites. I'm sure Jesus' calling of certain disciples while ignoring others was considered favoritism. Selecting twelve out of a group of 120 certainly created some consternation. Even the Twelve felt jealousy concerning special seats in the kingdom and who among them was the greatest. Why shouldn't we expect the same misunderstandings in twentieth-century churches?

Selectivity appears unfair because it is different. For years people have labored under some lethal "church theologies." For example, many congregations have the attitude that we all are sinners and no one is really qualified, so why bother? The sad result of such thinking is to reduce qualifications to the lowest common denominator: church attendance. The fruit of such thinking is to compromise the integrity of the leadership, therefore, of ministry to one another and mission to the world.

Lowering standards to a level anyone can meet does not create a system that eliminates the weak, the self-willed, the self-indulgent, and so on, from spiritual leadership. Leadership then becomes a hodgepodge of personal agendas governed by whim, ambition, and favoritism. Yes, favoritism. If you want to see favoritism in a church, drop the qualifications for leaders, don't provide training, and favoritism will rule the church. When qualifications are not taken seriously, playing favorites is all that is left. This is why Paul exhorted Timothy, "I charge you, in the sight of God and Christ Jesus and the elect angels, to keep these instructions without partiality, and to do nothing out of favoritism" (1 Tim. 5:21).

One more objection felt on a broader basis is dealt with elsewhere: the change in the pastor's role. The cardiovascular pastor concentrates as Jesus did on the few carefully selected men, and many object to this new style of elitism. They wrongly feel it will deprive them of the pastor's time and attention. Of course they have no schooling in the belief that in the long run they must sacrifice personal attention for better pastoral care. They will also receive a better quality of ministry all around because the pastor shares the ministry with the equipped laity. The church gives lip service to selectivity, but in practice it is a bloody battlefield.

Churches are like taxpayers. We all want to see the government cut spending, reduce the deficit, but don't cut anything that touches my life. "Oh, yes, we believe in those things, I just don't think they are for our church at this time."

Why Is Selectivity Important?

It protects the product. In a highly democratic culture where all opinions are created equal, discrimination is a hard sell. But discriminate we must if the church plans to produce a quality product called a disciple. Selectivity protects the product. All members are of equal value to God as His creatures. All members are not equal, however, with respect to God's mission to His creatures. Those outside Christ are not candidates to lead the church. Christians who are too busy, too weak, burned out, disobedient, apathetic, or who have any other disqualifying trait, are not candidates to lead the church. The young and inexperienced, novices at doing God's work, are not in line for leadership. Common sense alone eliminates much of the mass of God's creation; Christian and non-Christian alike are not up to leading God's people.

Likewise the opinions of the above groups are not of equal value with those of mature leaders. Experienced, well-trained leaders' opinions and judgments are the basis on which the church acts. If the church has no process by which to select, train, and gradually move people into leadership, the decisions and quality of the church will be reduced to the lowest common denominator.

A large corporation would not give equal weight to the opinions of the inexperienced novice and the seasoned vice-president. When everyone's opinion becomes equal, confusion reigns. The church suffers from a lack of decisiveness; leaders are not allowed to lead, and paralysis debilitates the body.

The church that thinks everyone must agree before they can take action suffers from the convoy mentality: Until all members can agree on a direction and form a convoy, nothing happens.

A great deal of people pleasing goes on as well. "A camel is a horse made by a committee," the old saying goes. By the time everyone's opinion is taken into account and

God's plan gets out of committee, the compromised church product no longer resembles a disciple or disciple maker. The reason is simple: You have unqualified people making policy. No organization can long survive under such dilution of philosophical purity. Selectivity protects the quality of leadership. When the original product design is protected, when quality control exists, the church will continue to be healthy and fulfill its mission.

It produces a good product. Selection of the highest quality people to be trained to lead and then to fill leadership positions will maintain good productivity. The church will grow, and the creativity and integrity crucial to multiplication will be maintained.

It protects the church from trouble. No philosophy or system will keep the church from conflict. In fact, the church is promised that conflict will be a normal part of the Christian experience (see John 16:33). But some practices reduce the possibility for conflict. Attitudes, systems, and organizational forms can insulate the church from unnecessary conflict.

This provides the church with twofold protection. First, by its very nature, selectivity means choosing only the highest quality person to lead. It also means you base the selection upon an objective standard. The happy result is mature, experienced leaders who agree on the direction and methodology of the church. Therefore, it eliminates much of the pettiness that characterizes a hodgepodge board.

Second, selection provides protection by weeding out the unqualified. The self-willed, the rebellious, the unteachable, those who bully others, and those with personal axes to grind are eliminated by the selection process. Working your way through an objective, standardized selection process takes several years. Troublemakers who politicize the selection process don't make it when selectivity rules.

It models the objective. Models, not rhetoric, change people. This is true in parenting, in business innovation, in church planting, and it certainly applies to communication in the body of Christ. The Great Commission qualifies the making of disciples as "teaching them to obey." The most powerful teaching tool is the model: the father and his son, the innovative entrepreneur and the large corporation, the leaders of the church and the church populace. The son can shut out the words, but can't shake the example. The large corporation can be skeptical, but can't deny what works. The church body can be passive, but if the leadership models the product, they must respect its integrity.

The Achilles' heel of the church has been its internal duplicity. The church is more adept at contradicting its message than modeling it. The pulpit declares that Christians are to witness. But if the church leaders do not introduce others to Christ, fold them into the church, then they pass on the real message, "We say that you should witness, but we don't really mean it, because as you can see, we don't witness ourselves." This is teaching people to disobey. Unfortunately this is what some churches do best.

Unless the church's leadership team models their teaching, the church and the vision lack integrity. Selectivity creates standards, training vehicles, and accountability to model the message. The dynamic teaming of effective rhetoric and integrity of life will draw people to discipleship and will bring beauty to the church.

It gives people something to which they can aspire. When a disciple is fully taught, he will be like his teacher (see Luke 6:40). When standards are set and kept, people accept them as the norm. When a quintessential leader is defined in corporate structure, he sets the standard for all to attain.

This gives the young someone to look up to, a model of what it means to be a Christian leader. It gives the general populace confidence in the integrity of their church and the quality of decisions made. It gives the elder statesmen assurance that what they pass on will be left in good hands. Every endeavor, from athletics to law, needs models and mentors. The doctrine of selectivity gives the church both.

Philosophical Purity at the Leadership Level

Few churches run aground theologically; most break apart on the rocks of methodology. Theology can determine methodology if the theology is thought out and applied. Jesus trained the disciples in a small group of twelve. Therefore, a case can be made for the small group being the primary discipling vehicle. The hodgepodge leadership team would disagree concerning the use and priority of small groups. Some might protest they are hard to control and are a seedbed for cults. Another might suggest that they all die natural deaths or that they form social cliques. Some believe that it requires too much training time with too little results.

Unless the leadership team members have a positive common experience with small groups, there will be friction concerning their use. This is one of hundreds of methodological struggles that debilitate and divide churches. The disciple-making pastor avoids many of these problems by teaching and practicing philosophical purity.

Philosophical purity is agreement among leaders concerning the goal or product of the church. In addition, it concerns the priority of certain ministries over others and the methods used to reach the objective. Philosophical purity is what the Bible calls unity. Unity is harmonious agreement. A quartet sings the same song, but different parts. They start at the same time, stop at the same time, even breathe at the same time. They each sing a little differently, but they have an agreed-upon methodology. Their methodology is music; they have chosen a specific piece of music and have agreed to present it in a specific way.

For some odd reason many church people bristle at the very thought of their leaders agreeing so much. They accuse the leaders of being too friendly, being dominated by one person, or accuse the pastor of being surrounded by yes-men. Even odder is the strange belief that a good leadership team is a fighting leadership team. An atmosphere of suspicion is the rule rather than the exception. They have mistaken unity for unanimity. *Unanimity* means "complete agreement on all issues"; *unity* is "coming to agreement based on a common objective."

Philosophical purity is essential for long-term effective ministry. It also is vital to the multiplication of ministry, in particular the planting of good churches. The products of a disciple-making ministry must possess the philosophical gridwork to reproduce disciple making wherever they go.

Please note that this principle applies to the leadership level, not the general populace. Hopefully the congregation moves toward general agreement, but the issue here is the philosophy of the leadership team. Churches are often unwise at this juncture. They ask people to agree to rules and sign documents in order to join the church. While churches that practice official membership must have standards, that should be just the beginning. There should be steps that every member is expected to take toward full Christian potential. This should be taken just as seriously. But the church has put most of its energy into gaining broad agreement among the total membership upon entrance into the church, while asking for no stronger agreement for leadership. The requirements for agreement concerning philosophy and methodology are vital to the church's future.

There are four hallmarks of philosophical purity that every leader needs. I will describe them here and explain how to implement them in a later section.

Has a heart for disciple making. "Having a heart for" is the same as "possessing a conviction concerning"—the potential leader devotes himself to disciple making because he is a product of the discipling process. Convictions are bone-deep beliefs hammered out in life experience. I know it intellectually, I've experienced it practically, therefore, it is a fundamental belief that governs my life.

A heart for disciple making burns with the desire to get into the harvest field and reap the harvest Jesus promised (see Matt. 9:36–38). It means that the number one priority is to make disciples, to find and spend time with eager learners who want to reproduce. He sees disciple making as the fountainhead for effective, reproducing ministry. He believes that disciple making is the key to multiplication, and the Great Commission will not be completed without multiplication.

The question is, how do you get people to this point with this attitude? The general answer is that you need a training program. Trained disciple makers don't just automatically pop up at the church. They must be developed over a period of years. The disciple-making pastor sets the course, then asks all interested members to work their way through the course. The training track should include character building, skill development, philosophical and biblical training. It should be heavily seasoned with a variety of ministry tasks to test spiritual giftedness and to build faithfulness.

It should take people through the six-step teaching method employed by Jesus: "tell them what," "tell them why," "show them how," "do it with them," "let them do it," "deploy them."[1]

Presently, it takes a person a minimum of three to four years to work through this process at our church. Only after the successful completion of such a training track is a person considered for leadership in the church. Time is critical for development: time for maturity, wisdom, expertise, character and skill development; time for the self-willed, the rebellious, the ambitious, the troubled to reveal the contents of their hearts and eliminate themselves. This protects the church and insures philosophical purity.

Is a proven disciple maker. He can name those he has trained who are now discipling others. To name those he has led to Christ is not enough, to identify disciples whom he has established in the Word, prayer, fellowship, and witness is not enough. He must be able to name those he has trained who are disciple makers themselves. This means they establish others in the basics, and those others will reproduce as well.

In addition, he can point to trained disciple makers with the gift of leadership who are leading corporate ministries. One example would be a trained disciple maker who has planted a church. The proven disciple maker can point to reproduction of a leader who creates corporate environments where disciple making and multiplication are honored values.

This means that not only has he reproduced disciple makers without the gift of leadership, but disciple makers with the gift of leadership who have reproduced entire ministries. The local church doesn't need any more armchair theologians, those who talk good ministry but have no product, no proof that they have actually done it.

It is not crucial that leaders maintain a grassroots ministry throughout their lives, but they must earn the right to lead by productive, proven disciple making. Yes, these standards are high, but leaders of a disciple-making ministry must be proven disciple makers. Otherwise credibility is lost, there is no modeling of the desired objective, and once again people are being taught to disobey.

An even more disastrous end is that leaders are not equipped to do their work. If I am to be an elder in a disciple-making church, I must understand how to motivate, teach, delegate, and coach others who report to me. I must teach those under my care the philosophy of ministry that is a top corporate value. I must train them in how to reproduce and multiply throughout their ministry tasks. If I haven't, it is quite unlikely they will do it. If I can't, the entire system breaks down, the work suffers, and the disciple-making philosophy comes under attack.

Never put an unproven disciple maker in a leadership position that requires proven disciple-making experience. This is obvious, but it is done more often than not. Make him earn it, otherwise he won't appreciate it, and the general populace won't respect him.

Has strong biblical knowledge. Earlier I strongly advocated that a disciple-making pastor must have a philosophical framework to guide him. It must be biblically based, well thought out, and possess appropriate vehicles to apply the philosophy. This is equally true of the church leaders if philosophical purity is to be maintained. What does this mean in practical terms?

It means he has a working knowledge of Scripture. He can defend, explain, and teach basic doctrines of the Christian faith. Specifically, if all potential leaders can explain, defend, and articulate the church's doctrinal statement, they would be sufficiently knowledgeable. In addition, they must be able to explain, defend, and teach the scriptural foundations for disciple making.

The means employed to have all potential leaders arrive at the desired destination are as follows. Special seminars are held to teach specific doctrine. Basic doctrine is taught in the two-year discipleship group. This is followed up for those moving into the "Come and be with Me" stage by a workbook self-study covering the doctrine of the church. Special meetings are held as part of the training to learn the specialized doctrines relating to disciple making. The most effective learning tool is to have them teach the content that they need to understand. By teaching what they are learning, they learn it well and own it.

When a trained disciple maker is being considered for a major leadership position, the screening process checks his knowledge. He takes two written exams, the first covering general Christian doctrine and the second testing his philosophical foundations for disciple making. This has proven a good filtering system thus far for straining out those who truly haven't learned. The testing procedure measures where he is in process. It protects the church by identifying those who appear to be ready but are not. It protects the person from being placed into a position in which he will fail. It provides a means of counseling and recommendations for further development. The written exams are followed by an oral examination of his writing. The selecting of leaders for the local church deserves at least the screening that pulpit committees give pastoral candidates. In fact, the screening process for leaders, lay and professional, deserves upgrading.

Often I am asked how I train my elders. My reply surprises many: "When a person becomes an elder, he has already been trained." I don't mean that a trained elder has nothing new to learn, but the character, skills, and giftedness required for the work should already be developed. The qualified church leader learns more in his leading than he did in his formal training. In leading he is learning more about what he already knows. He's learning to do it better, more efficiently, on a broader scale, and he acquires wisdom.

A church that takes these principles seriously will, in time, possess a large pool of qualified leaders. In fact, I promise that you will have more qualified leaders than you will have positions to fill.

Agrees with methods and priorities of the church. You can't be too careful. While anyone being considered for major leadership in a disciple-making church should already agree with methods and priorities, one last checkup saves heartache. In the disciple-making church, methods grow out of philosophical objective. Some of the issues to cover are the use of the small group as a primary disciple-making vehicle, the process of selection of leaders, standards for leaders, and people being required to earn their way to leadership. There must also be agreement in the priority of decentralization of ministry: such as, pastoral care, evangelism, administration, and creative outreach into the community. Other critical areas of agreement are the role of the senior pastor, the professional staff, and the elder board. Do they believe in church planting, in giving at least 10 percent of church income off the top to missions? These and many more quirks that form the local church personality should be covered.

Never deploy workers without philosophical purity. Why not? Because you won't multiply what you want. If you shoot a missile to the moon, it doesn't mean much at the point of origin that you are one degree off course. But by the time the missile nears the moon, that one degree has become thousands of miles. If we desire to reproduce disciples, to create healthy Christians and a healthy church that reproduces and multiplies, the leadership must be philosophically pure.

Accountability

You can't make disciples without accountability. To believe you can is like believing that you can raise children without discipline, run a company without rules, or lead an army without authority. Accountability is to the Great Commission what tracks are to a train. Without rails, a fully powered train will dig itself into the ground. The train's energy will be wasted; it will actually work against the wishes of those driving it. Rails provide a means for the engine's vast power to be properly used.

So much desire and creativity are lost to the cause of Christ because no one harnesses them. Without loving direction along with ground rules, the church is handicapped by every person going his own way, doing his own thing. Laissez-faire seldom works.

Why Is Accountability Necessary?

It is a means for quality control. Accountability provides the individual and the church with the necessary discipline and support to reach godly goals together and the means to channel an individual's desires to reach the goals that God has placed before him. Jesus qualified the command to "make disciples . . . teaching them to obey everything I have commanded you" (Matt. 28:19–20).

Teaching to obey means more than telling people they should obey. It means providing the encouragement, discipline, support, and training that is vital for prolonged spiritual development. Its purpose is to facilitate spiritual growth, to maintain godliness among the body, and to rid the body of people who would pollute, destroy, and bring shame to the name of Christ (see Titus 3:10; 1 Tim. 5:15–19).

Accountability is necessary because Christians are self-willed. "We all, like sheep, have gone astray, each of us has turned to his own way" (Isa. 53:6). Christians will not work together as a loving team without authority. Add to human nature the influence of a rebellious society, and you have two powerful forces militating against authority.

Chuck Swindoll describes modern culture:

> Not even the President of our nation carries the clout he once did. Ours is a talk-back, fight-back, get-even society that is ready to resist-and-sue at the slightest provocation. Instead of the obedient Minute Man representing our national image, a new statue with a curled upper lip, an open mouth screaming obscenities, and both fists in the air could better describe our times. Defiance, resistance, violence, and retaliation are now our "style."[2]

The disciple-making pastor knows he is swimming upstream. He understands that he can't make disciples without accountability. He understands, as well, that he wastes his time unless people learn to obey God. There is no discipling without obedience. There is no real obedience without submission to authority. Submission to authority is a test of submission to God.

A football team whose members won't listen to the coach, learn the plays, and work hard to perfect their game will lose. A church that won't follow leaders, learn the foundational truths of the Christian faith, and practice those principles will fail as well. There must be discipline; people discipline themselves only with the encouragement and inspiration of others. They humble themselves and submit to corporate rules; they submit their personal goals to the larger goals; the result is joyful effectiveness in the body.

The body should work together like a symphony orchestra. The word employed by Paul in his first Corinthian letter is derived from the same root word as our English word *symphony*. "But God has *combined* the members of the body" (1 Cor. 12:24, italics added). Some translations say "composed," but "combined" works as well. In order to produce the desired product, orchestra members must share a corporate desire to reach the larger objective and follow directions with great discipline.

The pastor commits himself to teaching disciples to obey Christ. Accountability is a necessary ingredient to teaching. Humility is necessary for submission (see 1 Peter 5:5–6). If people are not willing to humble themselves before God and before His imperfect appointed leaders in the church, they simply will not be disciples, and the Great Commission is lost.

One of the church's greatest paradoxes has been the neglect of the biblical commands for practicing selectivity and accountability. There are no tougher assignments for the pastor. To convince today's Christians that leadership should be earned and that all members are accountable to local church authority is equal to any task that exists. But the disciple-making pastor devotes himself to teaching these vital truths. They must govern the church, or disciple making is diluted and the quality of the church's product reduced to the lowest common denominator. Accountability insures quality control.

It facilitates leadership. I have heard some great sermons on personal accountability to God. One day I will stand before Christ, and He will evaluate my works. In 1 Corinthians, Paul likens works done for the right motives to gold, silver, and precious stones. The works done for selfish motives he compares to wood, hay, and straw. When God's searching eye penetrates the inward workings of such service, the fire of His judgment will either refine or destroy our life work (see 1 Cor. 3:10–15).

One of the church's most poignant moments is when the preacher has delivered a moving message on making one's life count. He then whispers those words all Christians long to hear, "Well done, my good and faithful servant." The room is filled with amens and other affirmations of this important goal and moment in the Christian's life.

I've always found it interesting how accepting Christians are about one day answering to God. The thought that He will hold us accountable for every word and action doesn't seem to worry most believers. I find it a strange paradox that the same Christians who accept accountability, which has eternal ramifications, fight the hardest against accountability in the church. Why is there resistance?

On its face, the answer would seem obvious: *I will accept accountability from an all-knowing, all-powerful, just God, but I have no intentions of doing what Brother Elder says.* This kind of thinking reveals two flaws. The first is pride, *I will accept God's authority, but not man's.* For the moment, let's forget how inconsistent that is. Let's not mention the police, the IRS, city, state, and federal government, and the line rules at Disneyland. Christians are notorious for giving God lip service, but not real service. As the maxim goes, "People are willing to give God credit, but not cash." As long as accountability is in the future and suspended in space, I will accept it. But if it actually starts interfering with my personal life, forget it.

This returns us to the issue of teaching people to obey. If the church member will accept only futuristic, ultimate, pie-in-the-sky accountability, how can he be taught to keep a commitment to God? How can he learn the importance of making a commitment to a small group? On what basis can a small group leader approach him and encourage him to do the right thing, when he is resisting?

To be frank, there is little hope for a person who will not accept the authority of the local church. There is no basis on which to guide him. He will respond when he wants; he will resist when he wants. He will live a life filled with blind spots that will keep him from God's best. His life will include unnecessary suffering, because he didn't accept the protection of his brothers and sisters in Christ. Some suffering is necessary, but a great deal of it directly results from resistance to the church's authority in his life.

The person who will not accept the authority of the local church has a second flaw. He believes there is a difference between God's authority and the authority in the local church. There *are* some important distinctions between God and His leaders. God's authority is perfect, and God's leaders are imperfect. God doesn't make mistakes, but God's leaders do. God's judgment is perfect; His leaders' judgments are flawed. In spite of the fallibility of the church's leaders, their authority is God's authority. Their authority comes from God, and to disobey, resist, or deny their authority is to rebel against God.

The same principle applies to leaders in the church as does to leaders in other realms:

> Everyone must submit himself to the governing authorities, for there is no authority except that which God has established. The authorities that exist have been established by God. Consequently, he who rebels against the authority is

rebelling against what God has instituted, and those who do so will bring judgment on themselves.

Romans 13:1–2

The well-accepted teaching of the above passage is that in secular society the Christian has the duty to submit to all authority unless that authority directs him to disobey God's law. If the city council tells Christians they cannot pray, then they must disobey the city council. If the IRS tells the church they cannot preach against abortion and keep their tax-exempt status, the church must ignore the IRS and take the consequences.

The other issue in the text is that all authority comes from God. This does not seem to trouble the Christian populace. If secular authorities such as non-Christian police officers, mayors, and meter maids apply to Christians, then does this not apply to the church as well? Of course it does! If church leaders ask Christians to violate God's law, then Christians must reject their leadership. Otherwise, Christians have a special responsibility to follow the leadership of the church.

Local church leadership is not perfect. At times, it's terrible. On occasion their leadership should be rejected. When leaders step outside of clear scriptural directives in the area of morality or doctrine, they should be held accountable. If it is proven they have failed in their leadership task, they should be rebuked, even removed, if necessary (see 1 Tim. 5:17–21).

It takes two thoughts to submit to authority. First, authority is from God. To rebel against it is to rebel against God. Second, God wants me to humble myself. He is opposed to the proud, but gives grace to the humble. Humility makes it possible for me to live under the protection of His authority; it makes me teachable; and it will one day make me a much better leader. With these thoughts as a backdrop, the next step is to look at the clearest command for Christians to obey leaders. It will tell us why leaders need accountability in order to lead: "Obey your leaders and submit to their authority. They keep watch over you as men who must give an account. Obey them so that their work will be a joy, not a burden, for that would be of no advantage to you" (Heb. 13:17).

How the local church leaders became the leaders is not at issue. Perhaps the only germane comment is that since leaders are to be followed, their selection should be carefully made. The church should have objective criteria for measuring suitability. The selection process is critical to the quality of leadership.

Leaders are expected to give direction; others are exhorted to follow their direction. Obedience and submission are different sides of the same coin. As a church member I give obedience and submission to their authority—not to their expertise, their giftedness, their personalities, but their positions. Who the leaders are is not the issue; it is what they represent in my life.

In exchange for their protection, I give my obedience. Obedience is submission with feet on it. I obey specifically because I have decided to submit generally to authority. Obedience implies that sometimes the conflict between my will and the larger corporate will is inevitable. If there were no conflict, obedience would be a moot point. There are benefits for both leaders and followers when accountability works.

It protects the congregation. Leaders are to keep watch over you. Too often people understand this in a negative way. Most people have had a negative experience with corporate accountability. It amounts to the church board coming down on people who have done something wrong. At times church discipline is important. Keeping watch over you in this case, however, is much broader and has a positive tone.

Keeping watch not only means correcting people when they do wrong, but helping them do right. The disciple-making pastor and his leaders are dedicated to helping people by teaching them to live right and to do ministry right. This is why establishing corporate values is so vital to the success of leaders. The leaders are to set the course, to take their delegated authority and lead the church toward agreed-upon values and goals.

Remember, pastoring is helping people do what they don't want to do so they can become what God wants them to be. This means that leaders need the freedom to lead and must have the authority to get people to follow. Otherwise, obedience and submission become nothing more than rhetoric.

What I receive by submitting and obeying is direction in ministry, encouragement, and protection from my own excesses. I also am an important part of a team effort, because the corporate values of teamwork and submission to authority are being practiced.

It makes ministry a joy. Leadership can be and often is miserable. It has destroyed many a person's vision and vitality. As the text indicates, it becomes a burden. The problem of leadership becoming a burden is directed toward the general populace. Leaders and followers equally share the responsibility for leaders' success. Followers tend to throw the entire weight for the organization's corporate success or failure onto the leaders.

If leaders are to be successful, part of the groundwork is the agreement of the followers to submit to and obey their leadership. Accountability is necessary for leadership to work. The most telling statement in Hebrews 13:17 is obey them, because if you don't, "that would be of no advantage to you." Excesses exist in both leaders and followers. But if forced to choose where the excesses exist in the larger degree and create the most grief, the followers win. Most modern-day problems in the local church stem from the general populace's unwillingness to submit and obey their leaders.

Some congregations treat suspicion of their leaders' motives and decisions as a treasured corporate value. To follow their leadership without fighting them is considered irresponsible. Historically these congregations challenge all ideas and programs their leaders suggest. Their church business meetings shame the name of Christ. There are bickering, political power plays, and petitions. *Roberts Rules of Order* have more clout than Scripture.

The root causes are multiple, but at its core such a church would have a lack of trust and confidence in leadership, which occurs because the congregation has not been taught the benefits of following good leadership. Often they don't have good leadership because they don't value leadership. If you don't value it, you won't place a priority on training leaders or maintaining high standards for those becoming leaders. You will not have a good selection process in place. When people understand the importance of leadership and the rigors of training that leaders must undergo, they will be more likely to follow. Standards, trust, training, objective standards for selection: When these are missing, followers will make leaders regret leading.

The writer to the Hebrews says that an atmosphere of suspicion will not be to the advantage of the followers. This means that much of the good God desires to do among such groups will be denied. If the congregation will not follow and submit personal agendas to the larger corporate agenda, they reduce all decisions to the lowest common denominator.

This kind of atmosphere is much like asking a group of children what they would like to do. "Would you like to go to school, take exams, mind your manners, and make something of yourself, or would you rather play all day, eat candy, and do what pleases you?" Which route would the children take? The answer is obvious. Frankly, most congregations are not capable of deciding what is good for their spiritual lives. They are sheep; they need to follow the shepherd.

The sad result is that the church is less than it should be because the followers have compromised what God wants. That is why the writer says resisting leadership is not good for the followers. The principle is clear: Leaders must be given the authority to lead so that the church can become effective. If not, the leaders will be filled with grief, the followers will deny themselves what they need and want. Not to follow your leaders is the worst kind of self-betrayal.

When the writer states that obedient followers make their leaders' work joy, that joy spreads to the congregation. Joy is not happiness. Happiness is derived from happenstance, which is related to circumstance. When circumstances are good, I'm happy; when they are bad, I'm sad. There may be many good circumstances in the well-led, faithfully followed church. This text teaches that there will be better circumstances and less grief if its commands are heeded. But joy is experienced independent of circumstances. Joy is a deep sense of well-being, based on the knowledge that one's life is obedient to God.

Leaders having joy does not mean they have it easy. In fact, leaders can be very unhappy but experience great joy. Jesus experienced joy in going to the cross. Many Christians have joyfully given their lives for Christ while undergoing extreme physical torture. Joy comes from knowing that your life counts, that you are making progress, that you have pleased God with your actions.

The joy comes to leaders when they see their efforts paying off. While it may be difficult and the obstacles are many, if they can lead a congregation that works with them toward a common goal, they will have joy in that leading, and the congregation will have joy in the following. This is the way to build trust: Leaders lead responsibly, followers submit themselves to the larger agenda. This kind of teamwork is effective and builds equity between leaders and followers.

A church must start somewhere. Good leadership and followership develop over a period of years. The starting point is faith. The leaders are selected and given authority to lead. The people follow by faith; in effect they say, *We think you can lead us; it's your authority, respect, and honor to lose, not to win.* In other words, we will give you every chance to succeed; we will allow you to make mistakes, and except for a major doctrinal or moral misdeed, we intend to follow you. That is the necessary foundation on which to build. If someone cannot follow the agreed-upon congregational position on respect and honor of appointed leaders, he should seek another church where he can submit. If he insists on staying within the church and rebelling, he should be disciplined.

It helps people keep their commitments to God. People can't keep commitments to Christ in isolation. Much help is required if a person is to sustain a lifetime of commitment to Christ. Throughout a life cycle, almost every person will need every kind of help. There are various ways to categorize this help, and the one I have chosen is found in Paul's first letter to the church at Thessalonica: "And we urge you, brothers, warn those who are idle, encourage the timid, help the weak, be patient with everyone" (1 Thess. 5:14).

Here is the full-orbed work of accountability. Three major categories: warning, encouraging, and helping—among three distinct need groups—the idle, the timid, the weak.

First of all, this fuller picture of the ministry of accountability dispels the myth that accountability breeds "gulag Christianity," where one loses all privacy, freedom to choose, and right to question, that its purpose is to control people, not help them. This myth has made the work of leaders much more difficult. By considering the details of this verse, I hope we will understand not only the categories of helping but the spirit behind accountability as well.

WARN THE IDLE. This category is legion. Their label is *idle*. The Greek word is a military term meaning "to be out of rank or disorderly." The army is marching in a direction;

those out of rank are going their own way. In this case it applies to those who, by rebellion or neglect, are not fulfilling their duty to Christ or His church.

The leaders are to hold this group accountable by warning them of their condition. The word translated "warn" is *noutheto*; its meaning is "to verbally admonish one who is in error." It is a very directive and strong word. Subsidiary meanings of *noutheto* indicate that the confronter identify the error, then exhort the violator to specific corrective action. *Noutheto* is used by Paul for instruction (see Rom. 15:14), to admonish (see Col. 1:28), and to warn (see Acts 20:31). This action is taken when something has clearly gone wrong. The New International Version translation in this instance is a bit weak because the unruly are anything but idle. The two categories of people who need help are the rebellious and the neglectful.

WARNING THE REBELLIOUS. Warning the rebellious is unpleasant work that most leaders avoid. They consider it a lose-lose proposition, and usually they are right. They lose in congregational perception because the confrontee slanders the leader and plays the martyr. Since the confrontee is rebellious or bitter or revengeful or all three, the confrontee is lost as well. Lose with the congregation, lose with the one confronted, a lose-lose proposition.

The reasons for the lose-lose mentality are three. First, it lives for a lack of positive experience with respect to confrontation. Since honest, straightforward exhortation of the rebellious is rare, few understand its benefits. Most leaders cannot see past the pain, congregational ire, and the potential loss of church families. This is not a book on confrontation or even a major study of it. But the benefits are there if confrontation is practiced properly. The fact that it hasn't been practiced widely or understood well is due to the lack of a foundation upon which its practice can succeed. The next two reasons for the lose-lose mentality tell why.

Second, confrontation is not commonly practiced because of the lack of respect for authority in the local church. This has already been discussed above, but the benefits of confrontation cannot be realized by a church body until they are willing to respect authority (see Heb. 13:17). They must trust their leaders and understand confrontation, warnings, and discipline as helping people keep their commitments to God. Accountability is worthless unless it acts at the point of rebellion. Confrontation restores the repentant rebellious and rids the church of the unrepentant rebellious (see Titus 3:10). For the church, it becomes a win-win proposition.

The third reason confrontation is not widely appreciated is that it has been practiced outside relationships. Too often one well-meaning Christian boldly confronts another, tells him where he has gone wrong and how he can make it right. Even if the confronter is right, if he doesn't have a meaningful relationship established, the confronted will not take the suggestions well.

Paul's exhortations make an assumption that the person confronting and the person being confronted are committed to the body and to each other. If a stranger or even a casual acquaintance confronts me about a weakness in my life, I will bristle. But if I know the person loves me and has my best interests in mind, I will listen. The difference is in attitude and established relationship. I don't mean to indicate that a rebellious or unruly person should be ignored if no one knows him. In most cases, however, leaders can find the right person with some sort of relationship to confront a person.

Paul's exhortation of Timothy was built on a meaningful love relationship (see Phil. 2:19–24). If the general church populace appreciated the benefits of confrontation, much of it could take place on the peer level. Scripture is clear on the benefits of the "buddy" system (see Prov. 27:17; Eccles. 4:9–11; Gal. 6:1; Col. 1:28–29). Confrontation of the rebellious and unruly is tough work. Even those who understand its benefits don't like it. But like surgery, trips to the dentist, and filing income-tax forms, it is necessary to a good church. Now let's move on to the other group that needs confrontation or warning.

WARNING THE NEGLECTFUL. Confronting the rebellious is personal and very threatening for both the confronter and the confrontee. Warning the neglectful is a normal part of church life that is impersonal and nonthreatening. Confrontation is one on one; warning the neglectful is a group experience. Correcting a person is unexpected and intrusive; exhorting the apathetic is expected. Christians have been reared on strong public exhortation. The churchgoer expects to be told in general terms that he is not living up to expectations, that he needs to give more, work harder, and live better. Most people do not take offense, because they are not being singled out.

Do not discount the benefits of confrontational preaching. Many a Christian's life has improved because he responded to a strong exhortation. Paul advocated pressurized preaching, "Preach the Word; be prepared in season and out of season; correct, rebuke and encourage—with great patience and careful instruction" (2 Tim. 4:2). Part of human nature is the need to hear the same thing over and over. The exhortation and the desire to serve will hopefully intersect in the believers' heart. A steady diet of this type of sermon is not advised, but used with caution and calculation, it can yield wonderful results. The disciple-making pastor possesses no better tool in helping people keep their commitments to God.

Helping people walk with God requires strong warnings. The unruly, rebellious, and disobedient must be confronted. If the leaders care, they will confront. The confrontation of the unruly restores the repentant and rids the church of those bent on disobedience.

The idle, the apathetic, and the uninvolved must be continually called to action. This, too, is a sign of love by the leaders when they insist that every member is in ministry. If accountability is to work, it must include the strong warnings advocated by Paul. This is what it means to teach people to obey.

ENCOURAGE THE TIMID. The words employed here specify the action and enrich the understanding. The word translated "encourage," *paramuthia*, means to "cheer up, console, to speak close."[3] The word translated "timid," *oligophuchos*, means "worried, discouraged, fearful."[4]

Accountability has many faces, and this one has been hidden from public perception. Warning the unruly and encouraging the timid are not normally considered under the single rubric of accountability. People stop walking with God for many reasons. Fear, worry, and discouragement are indeed strong culprits. Many more Christians falter here than in "raised fist" rebellion. All people are vulnerable to this triad. In such cases people need the supportive encouragement of other caring Christians.

This provides a balance to leadership's care of the body. Leaders prove their love by confronting the disobedient, calling the uninvolved to action, and supporting those languishing in emotional turmoil. The attraction of such work is that it is almost void of controversy. Congregations agree that supporting the discouraged is vital to a loving, caring church. Another attractive feature is that many more people are qualified and willing to encourage than confront. The disciple-making pastor teaches confrontation and encouragement as different sides of the same coin. Both are part of a necessary package of ministry that teaches people to obey.

HELP THE WEAK. This represents a distinct category. Strong people can be discouraged, fearful, and, at times, worried. But they would not be categorized as weak or unable to help themselves. Once again, the word meaning helps us classify. The word translated "help," *antecho*, means "cling to, help, take an interest in."[5] The word translated "weak," *asthenes*, means "without strength, to be sick."[6]

Another dimension of accountability is taking an interest in those who cannot help themselves. Whether the weakness be emotional or physical, the church is to take a major role in propping up those who cannot stand on their own. This accountability works both ways. The leadership calls the body to be accountable to support its weaker members.

The opposite way it cuts is that by being the person helped, you feel a love and sense of obligation to the body that will spur you on when you become well. Normal human beings cared for in their time of need feel motivated to be part of that ministry. It can be a life-changing event. Being helpless and weak can motivate a person to ministry in ways no sermon or exhortation can. Indeed, God uses sickness and tragedy for His purpose.

I find it interesting that the rebellious or the idle, who would never respond to confrontation or warnings, will change after a crisis. When God's people rally to their aid, they see the hand of God in others; they experience the power of God; and for the first time the church means something.

Yet another benefit is the general feeling of love the body feels when the weaker members are cared for. It breeds a confidence that the leaders care and the people care. Each knows that if it were he, the same loving care would be given. This has a Velcro effect on the body; people stick around.

The three commanded acts of accountability are like a loving parent wrapping his arms around his children. The arms provide strength to warn, to protect, to discipline. They provide the support, the pat on the back, the ability to pick us up when we fall. They give the constant care that is needed to hold us up when we cannot stand for ourselves. The arms hold us, protect us, and direct us. That is accountability, and without it, the church is seriously flawed, and the leaders are without a means to teach people to walk with God.

The Small Group and Disciple Making

Disciple making exists in three primary forms: the large group, the small group, and one on one. The primary tool of the large group is public address. Drama, film, music, and the spoken word are effective vehicles that can communicate powerfully.

The greatest weakness of the large group is that it serves only to tell people what they should believe and why. It lacks the personal touch, the fine-tuning. The large-group communicator fires a shotgun: He sprays out the principles, and they land where they may. This is a first and important step in disciple making, but only a start.

One on one provides a great deal of fine-tuning, but it takes too long and is an insufficient use of a person's time. One on one is important to the discipling process, but becomes a problem when it is considered the primary method. One on one as a primary means for disciple making leads to waste. The disciple maker spends unproductive time with many who are not valid candidates.

Let's say I wanted to find ten people in a group of five hundred to sell my product. I could spend time interviewing all five hundred, and I very well might find the ten, but the time required would be prohibitive. It would be much better if I spoke to the entire group, explaining the requirements, the goals, and objectives for product and salespersons. Then I could ask those interested to meet with me for an interview.

The above scenario would be in order if I were visiting a city or campus for a two- or three-day stint. It would be the best use of my time under the circumstances. But there is a serious missing link without which my selection of the ten best would remain suspect. If I had more time, and the church does, I would put into place the missing link, which would insure that I would get the ten best salespeople. That missing link is the small group, which consists of three to fourteen people.

The small group is the most effective vehicle that exists for full-orbed disciple making.

The Small Group Is Jesus' Example

Jesus demonstrated the superiority of the small group for training. He ministered to the multitudes with much of His teachings. The feeding of the five thousand, the Sermon on the Mount, the parables concerning the kingdom of God, teaching concerning discipleship: All were done before large groups. Jesus also engaged in a great deal of one-on-one work. The Gospel of John alone describes over twenty-five personal interviews. His ministry included both large group and one on one.

At different times and phases of His ministry Jesus' followers were numbered as 500, 120, 70, and the 12. But when it came to training, Jesus chose the small group as His primary vehicle. The fact that He chose the Twelve "to be with Him" is proof.

No one can "be with" thirty, fifty, or even twenty-five; the number must be sufficient to provide enough variety to make it interesting, but small enough so there are no spectators. Jesus chose twelve for functional reasons. He planned to do a quality job of training; twelve was just about right. From the small group as training headquarters, Jesus ministered to the multitudes and did one on one as well. The small group gave Jesus the proper platform to continue ministry to the masses and those who personally approached Him without sacrificing the all-important training of His men.

The Small Group Provides the Proper Ministry Flow

Effective group ministry requires three vehicles. The large group is used for inspiration and motivation as well as interesting people in Christ and the work of Christ. It can tell people what and why, but then its effectiveness comes to a screeching halt. Since true teaching and training of people requires more, employ another vehicle.

The small group takes people to the next logical step. If the large group interests people by telling them what and why, the small group trains them by showing them how and doing it with them. The next link, then, to the discipling process is not the fine-tuning of one on one, but people becoming established in the basics. Jesus waited until the Twelve were well established before He chose them to be with Him, and He spent five months of further training before He commissioned them to ministry.

The small group allows the cream to rise to the top. If people faithfully master the basics, keep their commitments to God and the group, then they should be given more personal attention. Some one on one should be done with every group member. Some for correction, some to deal with weakness or crisis. But taking on someone as a trainee for future ministry responsibility should be carefully done after the person has proven himself in the small group. The flow of people is like pouring the entire group into the top of the funnel. Only a select few make it through the filtering process of the small group. Those who make it through are prime candidates for leadership. Chapter 9 will include the nuts and bolts of such a process.

The Small Group Provides a Controlled Environment

Teaching a person to obey requires some ability on the part of the teacher to control the learning environment. The teacher must be able to measure the student's progress. For disciple making, nothing beats the small group. It possesses all the necessary ingredients to fully teach people to obey, that is, to make disciples. The key areas are skill development, peer relationships, outreach projects, and training disciple makers.

Skill development. Ministry skills teamed with spiritual giftedness make for an effective Christian. Christians need the basic skills of a working knowledge of Scripture, the belief in and understanding of prayer, the benefits of sharing one's life with others, and the ability to communicate the message of Christ. The controlled environment of the small group can teach and measure the development of these skills. The key to the training is the attitude and competence of the group leader. That, of course, depends on the training he has received and his continued development.

Group members are taught basic Bible-study skills, which are reinforced by weekly assignments, followed by group discussion. The final stages of Bible study teach book analysis, inductive study, along with how to research more difficult issues. The goal is twofold: that the members would become self-feeding and that they would understand the major themes of Scripture.

Group members learn to pray, to keep records of how God answers the entire group's prayer requests over a two-year period. This demonstrates the effectiveness of prayer in a special way.

Another important aspect of skill development is learning how to share one's life with others, being open, learning to love others in a concrete fashion, experiencing the benefits of supporting others.

The fourth area of skill development is outreach, learning to tell their own stories, building bridges to non-Christians, and learning how to use basic evangelistic tools. This is the most difficult area for most, but in the long run, the most rewarding. If Christians don't become comfortable with outreach, Bible study is academic, prayer is boring, and fellowship is superficial. Without outreach, the church has failed, and Christians fail.

Peer relationships. We've already considered accountability by leadership. The small group adds another dimension sometimes called peer pressure. Normally this subject conjures up negative images related to teenage rebellion. But properly employed peer pressure can be greatly used of God.

Making disciples requires a training that demands the group members' best effort. It will stretch them, and as a result there will be discomfort, fear, and at times the strong desire to flee the constraints of the group. The leader will do his best, through his influence and authority, to help people keep their commitments. But the leader can't do it alone and needs the help of group members to hold the line and support corporate values. Group members helping and encouraging one another creates the strongest form of accountability.

If the commitment has been fully explained to the group at its inception, if each member has signed a covenant stating he will keep his commitment to God, himself, and other group members, then the group will have agreed-upon corporate values. Therefore, the group possesses built-in peer pressure to help members get over the rough spots.

This is extremely helpful to a person's growth. Most people will take rebuke and correction better from a peer than an authority figure. Such bonding cannot be experienced in a large group or one on one; it is the private property of the small group. This spurs people on to do the Bible study, to spend time in prayer, to do Scripture memory, to invite non-Christians to an outreach, to come to the group when they are tired and want to stay home.

People grow in the mundane, sometimes tough trenches of life. Spiritual growth comes an inch at a time; it consists of little daily battles over Scripture memory, prayer time, Bible reading, faithfulness to attend a group, or to share their faith. Without help, normal people cannot sustain protracted spiritual growth. Therefore, they are left to haphazard, sporadic growth that is generated by crisis or special events.

Outreach projects. Outreach training in the small group consists of attitude adjustment and skill development. The attitude adjustment naturally evolves over a two-year period. The person's mere presence in the controlled atmosphere of the discipleship group changes his outlook. That outlook needs to be changed because Christians are sufficiently affected by culture to have two debilitating attitudes.

The first is that religion is a private matter and it is rude and intrusive to push it on others. The second is that Christians should stay separate from the world and not associate in any meaningful way with the unbeliever. Sadly, this results in no meaningful contact through clubs, social networks, or neighborhoods. The average Christian has no non-Christian friends, therefore, sharing one's faith must be "cold turkey." Most people don't like direct sales; most Christians don't like and fear confrontational evangelism.

Many Christians enter the discipling environment of the small group with the handicaps of not believing they have the right to talk to others, and even if they did, of not having anyone to talk to. The small group's genius is that it provides both the time and training to challenge and then change these attitudes. The means to change are twofold.

First is teaching the Christian's responsibility and authority for proclaiming the message of Christ. This is done through Bible study, discussion, even debate among group members.

The second means to attitudinal adjustment is both a mental adjustment and a skill developed. One reason Christians fear evangelism is a lack of know-how. The small group trains them to think in new ways and gives them new skills. The training starts with simple tasks that focus on others. The first step is small, but significant, for it challenges the insulary selfishness that naturally hinders evangelism. This first step is to encourage another person. Peer pressure comes into play because no group member is allowed to move on to the next project until everyone has completed the first.

Resistance begins almost immediately. The combination of peer pressure, the leader's authority, and the fact they have agreed to do this ahead of time, through a signed document, all work to spur the person to risk. The outreach assignments then move on to writing and memorizing one's personal story. Next, they tell their story to a non-Christian. They progress to learning to use various evangelistic tools, how to begin and direct discussions on spiritual matters, and how to invite a person to an evangelistic event. Other skills taught are how to assimilate people into a church, how to do basic follow-up on a new Christian, and so on. All these skills are basic but revolutionary to most Christians. They equip people to reach out with confidence and effectiveness.

Another added dimension is the group doing outreach together. The power of the group is that they are in this together, a team; they sink or swim as one. Therefore, when they plan to reach out, they define success in several ways.

First, success means doing your best to get a non-Christian to an event. An individual person or couple has succeeded when they have prayed in faith, invited someone in faith, and have done everything possible to get the person there. Even if the invited guest does not come, they have been successful.

Second, there is group success. If 75 percent get non-Christians to attend the event, but everyone has done his best, the group has a 100 percent success rate. Even if I don't get anyone there, I am successful because I am part of the larger group success. At the close of the two-year period, the group is successful in outreach if there has been the attitude adjustment and the skill development. When people graduate from this kind of discipleship group, they are equipped for effective service.

The outreach training must be part of the small group discipleship. Without outreach, the group will die a natural death and produce lopsided Christians. Christians who know the Bible, love to fellowship with other Christians, and pray on a regular basis, but don't do outreach militate against the cause of Christ. They form a wing of Christianity that is selfish and nitpicky. They are much like an untrained army. The only thing they can do is be obsessed with the cleanliness of the barracks, the parade grounds, and the mess hall. They read military history and talk about battle, but when they are called upon for action, they are unarmed and helpless. Like the picture portrayed in the old television series *McHale's Navy*, they make a laughingstock of the real thing.

The small group has it all; it provides the disciple-making pastor with the best means to teach people to obey. By its effective use he can provide proper ministry flow, moving people through the discipling process. He has a controlled environment for training people in ministry skills, relationships, accountability, and outreach skills. There is one more advantage, as well: It is a ready-made training ground for disciple makers.

Training disciple makers. At the close of the two-year small group training cycle, every member is assessed as a means to help him take the next logical step on his spiritual development. Graduation from the training group is not the finish line, but the starting line for fruitful ministry. A few of the group graduates will become leaders. They have the gifts of leadership, teaching, exhortation, administration, and so on. They have the necessary package to become disciple makers. A *disciple maker* is what the words mean, "one who makes disciples." The best training for such a person is to lead a small group himself.

Everything he has learned as a group member takes on new meaning when he teaches it to others. The truths, the environment, the dynamics that facilitated his becoming a disciple, he will now have the privilege of teaching others. After being a member of the discipleship group for two years and then leading for two years, the trained disciple maker has had the time to own the principles, skills, and convictions concerning the disciple-making process.

Hands-on training is the best. Jesus modeled feeding His men back into the ministry as the preferred means of training. This accomplishes two things: It trains them to be disciple makers, and it provides more ministry for those who need it. Jesus modeled a six-step teaching method: "tell them what," "tell them why," "show them how," "do it with them," "let them do it," "deploy them." The two-year discipleship group is steps three and four: "show them how" and "do it with them." A disciple maker in training must experience steps five and six: "let them do it," then "deploy them." Leading a training group is letting them do it, but it is only partial deployment. There is no substitute for hands-on training; the small group provides the best environment for it. The disciple-making pastor considers the small group crucial to obeying Christ's command to train people to reach the world.

Decentralization of Pastoral Care

The disciple-making pastor's belief in and practice of the decentralization of pastoral care grows out of the New Testament's most comprehensive pastoral job description, in Paul's letter to the Ephesian church. The text's main thesis is that leadership has the role of preparing God's people to do ministry. Pastoral care, one part of that ministry, is a work given to the entire body of Christ, not to the clergy alone. Indeed, in most cases, the least prepared by gifts, professional training, and desire are the clergy.

Earlier we made a distinction between the word *pastor* and the office of pastor. The word *pastor* means "to lead, protect, feed, taking the overall responsibility for sheep." *Care* means "to pay close attention to people and their needs." Placing together the word *pastor* with the word *care* has led to some faulty thinking. For example, it concludes the person filling the office of pastor has pastoral gifts: showing mercy, help, encouragement, giving, and so on. The exact opposite is true; most people filling the office of pastor are gifted in leadership, teaching, administration, exhortation, and so on. They are not strong in traditional pastoral care areas. They do it because people expect it. People with gifts of showing mercy, helps, discernment of spirits, giving, and so on are strong and willing to minister. It comes naturally to them.

The traditional definition of pastoral care refers to the clergy's role in counseling, hospital visitation, and crisis intervention. Even the most radical advocates of decentralization of ministry do not suggest the clergy remove themselves entirely from the above list. Decentralization of pastoral care does not mean the person filling the office of pastor no longer does them. It is a question of degree; is it a primary responsibility of pastors, is it the exclusive domain of the clergy? I strongly believe the answer is no.

Does the pastor visit the hospital? At times, yes. Should it be his job to visit every person in the hospital? Certainly not. It is the pastor's role to unleash those gifted by God with pastoral gifts to take on that responsibility. The pastor uses common sense, gauging his personal involvement by the severity of the case. The same principle should apply to counseling, home visits, involvement in times of grief, crisis, and similar situations. The need for the pastor's personal presence should be gauged by severity of situation, the amount of support people already have, and many other factors. But the belief that the pastor's job is to be present at such events, or he doesn't care, is a devilish canard that debilitates churches and pastors and robs gifted Christians of ministry opportunity.

Pastoral Care: A Ministry Given to the Entire Body

Paul teaches that the role of leadership is to prepare God's people for works of service: "some to be pastors and teachers, to prepare God's people for works of service" (Eph. 4:11–12). How many are to be engaged in works of service? "From him the whole body, joined and held together by every supporting ligament, grows and builds itself up in love, as each part does its work" (v. 16).

Every Christian is to be part of the total team effort. The full potential of the body can be realized only when every person exercises his or her gifts. Pastoral care is part of the works of service given to the body. God gave it to the entire body, not just the clergy. To be more precise, it is given more to those gifted for caring than those who are not. The exhortation to preach is directed to those gifted to preach and teach. All Christians have the responsibility to communicate Christ, but some are specially gifted. All Christians are to care for one another and those outside the faith as well, but some are specially gifted.

More often than not, those gifted in caring are not the professional church staff. The staff needs to care, as any Christian is to care. But the expectation that they will be the best at caring is unrealistic and unbiblical. Their job is to train and deploy those who are.

Pastoral care is a corporate responsibility. The entire team combines their gifts and makes it work. The leader hears of a need, the treasurer writes the check, the caring minister delivers the check, another spends time fixing the family's car. The leader, the treasurer, the caring minister, and the mechanic each plays a part; all are caring, but not all have direct contact with the person in need. Pastoral care is given to the entire body, because no one part of the body, including the professional staff, can do it right alone.

Why Is Decentralization of Pastoral Care Important?

Decentralization of the church's caring ministry is God's plan. It means more ministers working; therefore, people are better cared for. What does the church want: good pastoral care or the pastor doing pastoral care? It can't work both ways! Whenever and wherever the professional staff is expected to manage and be present in a wide range of pastoral-care situations, two bad things happen.

First, the staff does it because others expect it, not necessarily because they desire it. This leads to a cloaked disdain for hospital visitation, home visits, and other obligatory duties. The congregation may never realize it, but many pastors strongly feel this manufactured pressure to care. When congregational members hear of someone in need, too often their first act is to call the church office, because "the pastor is supposed to do something about it." The unwritten rule that we have trained people to obey is *The pastor is paid to care about the people*. This is not the congregational member's fault; it is his training. Others have taught him he is not as competent to minister as the clergy.

The congregational membership desperately needs a transformation that helps them immediately meet the need themselves. The call to the church office should be secondary and informational in nature. The staff should be asked to help when all else fails. Under the present system, the church staff is asked to go it alone, taking primary responsibility in an area in which they are generally not gifted or intended to work.

This philosophy also allows many people to fall between the cracks, because the staff cannot know every need. The expectation also keeps the staff from their primary work. Frankly, in 90 percent of America's churches, the staff consists of one person, the pastor. The entire arrangement is a serious flaw in the modern church.

The second bad thing that happens is that many gifted ministers are locked out of the caring workforce. They can never really care well enough to satisfy. Twenty gifted, loving people could visit a hospitalized person, but in the present atmosphere, until the pastor comes, he hasn't been visited. This diminishes the caring of the nonprofessionals. Under the present system they are second-class ministers.

The clergy find themselves in a no-win situation. If they try to change the system, they may be accused of being cold and uncaring. If they continue to perpetuate the system, they contribute to an unbiblical environment that creates weakness and unrealistic expectations. It also keeps the pastor from his most important work.

Decentralization of pastoral care is essential for two reasons.

The proper use of the pastor. The pastor is primarily a trainer of people, not a prophet foretelling the future, or a priest representing people to God, or a counselor leading people on therapeutic journeys through their pasts. His main task is to train people to do ministry.

How the church uses its pastor will determine the quality of that church's ministry. If the church chooses to follow the traditional pastoral model of the generic pastor, ministers will not be trained, and the ministry quality will remain low. If, on the other hand, the church insists that the pastor prepare people for ministry, ministers will be equipped, and the quality of work will be high.

The pastor's work is to declare the what and why of ministry, then to train all willing members to do that work. After that he must manage the ministry. *Declare, train, and manage:* That is the commissioned work of the pastor. Requiring him to focus on doing the work of service himself trivializes his role and hinders the body's function.

Evangelical churches tragically waste pastoral talent. Eager, well-trained young men are being abused by the traditional model. They are required to be jacks-of-all-trades, and they are failing. Their lives become a series of rabbit trails that take them off the main route to pastoral faithfulness. They find themselves officiating at Awana dinners, Sunday school parties, Christian camp fund-raisers, vacation Bible school, and Bible-study breakfasts. Add to that the congregational desire to have the pastor attend every committee meeting, and you have a traditional pastoral lifestyle. The most difficult and debilitating expectation is that the pastor is at the beck and call of every congregational member. If anyone has a need, it is his duty to meet it. If he does not drop everything and posture himself in that person's image, he is considered unloving, uncaring, and in the pastorate for personal gain.

The other debilitating aspect is treating an area of nongiftedness as a spiritual weakness. This takes place because of unrealistic expectations. Not many people champion the belief that the pastor can and should do everything. But if you combine total congregational expectation, you get exactly that. Sadly, for most pastors this results in failure. A pastor fails because he can't live up to congregational expectation; he fails again, because he doesn't live up to scriptural expectations. He fails because he does not please the congregation; he fails because he does not please God. He fails the congregation because he is not superpastor. He fails God because he does not prepare people for works of service. This is tragic by God's standards.

The seminary, denominational leadership, and local churches must rethink pastoral models. There should be genuine effort to help pastors develop a ministry philosophy and style that leads to the equipping of the church. Until the general church populace is inspired, trained, and deployed to ministry, the church will remain weak and self-serving.

The proper use of the body. Equally tragic as the trivialization, abuse, and waste of the pastor is the trivialization, abuse, and waste of the entire body of Christ. It takes two in order to make this waste work: a pastor who will be the generic pastor and a congregation that will accept it. Both perpetuate it. The arrangement can be broken by either party insisting that change must be made.

Pastors can change it by insisting that people be trained for ministry. That means more than "spear-carrying" ministry. "Spear-carrying" ministry is the unskilled work that pastoral superstars need laypeople to do in order to make their performance possible. I am careful not to label some ministry as unimportant and other ministry as vital. But I must say that equipping people to minister means more than stacking chairs, mowing the lawn, and passing out bulletins. These tasks are important, but that is not what is meant by preparing God's people for works of service. Hopefully, the above tasks are testing grounds for a person's faithfulness, not the Everest of ministry.

The abusive character of traditional pastoral models has led to a waste of God's people by treating them as second-class ministers. They can support the religious professional by freeing him to do important things, like preach. While it is important that a pastor has time to write sermons, meaningful ministry is for the benefit of the minister and the needy, not the religious professional.

The goal of the decentralization of ministry is the grand picture of Ephesians 4:16: every member doing his part, pulling together for the purpose of God. The picture also teaches that the people will be fulfilled, productive, and the body will grow and build itself. This is the most loving thing a pastor can do for the church. Why does the pastor as minister and the congregation as spectators grieve God? Because the pastor burns out and the people rust out.

The proper use of the body can be achieved. Remember that the pastor's job is to declare the vision and inspire people to ministry. That is followed by training, and then by management. A training vehicle must exist before people learn how to minister. Otherwise, the pastor is telling people to obey, not teaching them to obey.

For training people in basic ministry skills and the development of new leaders, I have advocated the small group as a primary vehicle. For training in pastoral care, I would suggest a subgroup of the church composed of forty to seventy adults. This subgroup will help people learn to love one another and develop a sense of community.

The name we have chosen for such a group is *mini-congregation*. From day one, we promised our congregation that regardless of the size of the total church, they would always be members of a smaller church. The mini-congregation provides members with a built-in training experience in caring for others. People are encouraged to be creative in meeting needs. Needs are openly discussed so that members become aware of those whom they can help. Some ministries of the mini-congregation include prayer chains, meals for the sick, communion, baptisms, hospital visitation, socials, and support groups for families undergoing abuse from alcohol or violence. Much of the ministry once assigned to the clergy is taken on by the ministers. They baptize, serve communion, visit the hospital, pray for the sick, even dedicate children.

The mini-congregation is special in that it operates with a leadership team. There is a director, a treasurer, a teacher, a hospital visitation director, greeters, social chairman, a small group coordinator, and more. People are asked to join; no one is assigned; people join because they desire it. Training precedes the launch of a group, and it provides an excellent training ground for disciples. The genius of such a system is that regardless of church size, a member will always be part of a group that knows his name and misses him if he is not present. If a need arises, the others will have enough proximity to be aware of it. People are able to engage in community, the kind of real sharing that took place in the early church. Members are no longer like ships passing in the night.

In almost every case, the pastoral care of the church improves. The church gives up a little to get a lot. Members give up their pastor's personal attention for gifted, heartfelt caring of many gifted others. The pastor is not locked out of such situations; he just no longer has primary responsibility. His job is to create environments and provide training to employ gifted ministers where they work best. Once again, the disciple-making pastor declares the vision and inspires people to it. Then he provides the training and finally manages the ministry.

Obeying God's clear directives relieves the pastor of the trivialities that can make his ministry taste like mush. He does what God called him to do: training people to do God's work. He senses that he is making his life count on God's terms. Many pastors who have made the switch from generic to disciple-making pastor experience a deep sense of joy. For the first time, what they read in the Bible, what they were taught in seminary, and what they are experiencing in the church agree. It all makes sense, and it is worth the struggle, the adjustments, and yes, even the disputes with others, to bear such wonderful fruit, much fruit, fruit that remains.

If decentralization of pastoral care is good for the pastor, it is better for the parishioner. It provides people with a means of achieving spiritual self-respect. For too long equipping people to do the work of ministry has meant laymen doing the dirty work. It has meant sermons masquerading as training and pastors/tellers pretending to be pastors/teachers. It meant the layperson as a "spear carrier," as a second-class minister.

When the disciple-making pastor does his work, people are delivered from the yoke of ministerial discrimination and unleashed to do the work God intended. It is a reformation of ministry vitally needed among evangelicals today. Decentralization of pastoral care is nothing more than Ephesians 4 with caring hands. It is multiplication with an emphasis on compassion; it is the principles of the Great Commission practiced with the body of Christ.

The disciple-making pastor commits himself to the decentralization of pastoral care because it is the right thing to do. Under the guidance of Paul's pastoral model, the pastor finds his desired goal, and the corporate body becomes mature and effective. The disciple-making pastor is left with no choice; he must, by his nature, take the church in this fulfilling direction.

I often struggle to describe the disciple-making pastor in an abbreviated form. If forced to, I can give the sum total in three words: *conviction*, *skill*, and *intentional*.

He is passionate concerning disciple making. *Convictions* are the fruit of being properly taught (see Luke 6:40). The disciple-making pastor can inspire because he has convictions. When one feels deeply about an issue, it is natural to move others to action. The disciple-making pastor inspires others out of a strong convictional base.

The second word is *skill*. Motivated from conviction, he seeks to develop the proper ministry skills to accomplish the task. He strongly advocates training and skill development in others. He realizes that skill development comes second only to devotion to Christ. In fact, devotion to Christ and skill development stand shoulder to shoulder in the cause of Christ. The disciple-making pastor possesses the right skills to declare the message, train the people, and manage the results.

The third word is *intentional*. The disciple-making pastor has a target, and he shoots straight. He is *measured*, *calculating*, and *precise* in the best sense of those words. Specific goals forged from Scripture are the driving force. The disciple-making pastor leaves home with a map and knows it when he reaches his destination. Sadly, many a pastor has spent his ministry life driving in circles, his only goals to stay on the track and to keep people happy.

Driven by convictions, armed with ministry skills, and intentional in practice—these characteristics mark the disciple-making pastor. It should be said that many successful people have the same traits.

Further Reflections

The reason that the practices of the disciple-making pastor are controversial is because they require submission. The community of Christ is to be a culture of submission.

A person's character can be measured by his or her willingness to submit. The evidence of being filled with the Spirit is how a person serves and submits to others in the community (see Eph. 5:18–6:3). The community can't function without submission, but many people resist it because they don't understand how it could improve their lives. Submission today implies a group of dim-witted disciples drinking Kool-Aid.[7]

But submission is really about positioning yourself for spiritual growth. Fitting into the community of Christ has power. That is why I like Richard Foster's pithy statement, "The one and only compelling reason for submission is the example of Jesus."[8]

Submission is a word that often raises the hair on the backs of our necks. Submission is what religious extremists demand from their wives and followers. Submission is what the religious and political left deplores and will do anything to stop. It is what millions of people fear will destroy their lives. After all, no one in their right mind would submit to tyrannical governments and amoral corporations. Isn't liberty life's greatest treasure, and haven't many died in the pursuit of it or to protect it? Yes, but the greatest truth about submission is that we submit to what we trust. In the realm of political and religious leadership, integrity and trustworthiness are prerequisites for submission. The good news is that God doesn't require us to submit to governments or churches that violate our consciences. But we must be prepared to pay the consequences when we resist.

Resistance to authority runs much deeper than cultural experiences; it is hardwired into humankind. The most basic human trait is the desire to run our own lives, to maintain control in order to get what we want.

You may have heard the story of a mother trying to control her seven-year-old at a restaurant. Johnny was running from table to table, trying to be cute; this brought great embarrassment to his mom. "Sit down, Johnny," she ordered. Johnny continued his little show, so in desperation his mom grabbed him by the arm and sat him down in the booth, saying, "Now you stay there in your seat." Then Johnny said those words for the ages: "I may be sitting down on the outside, but I'm standing up on the inside." Johnny spoke for all of us who hate being told what to do. And like Johnny, we do comply, but only because we have no other options.

I would like to propose an understanding of submission that would make it our first option. Suppose I told you that submission is the door to liberty and the most empowering act of the human will. What if submission were understood as a love word before it became an authority word?

Submission: Resisting It Will Cost You

Without the practice of submission, the following is true:

1. I won't get my needs met. Therefore, I will live as a needy person trying to fill the holes in my life. All events, good or bad, will be about me and what I need.
2. I will lack humility. Therefore, God cannot bless me.
3. I will shut out others from loving me. Therefore, I will live a life of isolation with an undeveloped character.

These three traits are part of the high cost of non-discipleship.

Jesus' Core Character Trait

The essence is this: One of Jesus' core character traits was submission. If it does not become ours, then how can we believe we are being transformed into His image? Submission was the heart of Jesus' life and mission, and everything else flowed from it. There is no way to read Paul's teaching on this subject and draw any other conclusion.

> Let this mind be in you which was also in Christ Jesus, who, being in the form of God, did not consider it robbery to be equal with God, but made Himself of no reputation, *taking the form of a bondservant*, and coming in the likeness of men. And being found in appearance as a man, He humbled Himself and became obedient to the point of death, even the death of the cross.
>
> Philippians 2:5–8 NKJV, italics added

I am attracted to radical ideas, but this passage is so radical even I don't like it. As a marginal iconoclast, I enjoy breaking more than being broken. Brokenness before God means to relinquish all rights and dreams, to submit them to God's greater good and purpose.

This passage reminds me of Henri Nouwen's words that following Jesus means resisting the temptation to be relevant. He wrote, "I am deeply convinced that the Christian leader of the future is called to be completely irrelevant and to stand in this world with nothing to offer but his or her own vulnerable self."[9] Nouwen could be dismissed as a brilliant nonconformist whose monkish tendencies created such an impractical statement. But it could be that irrelevancy is the road to world impact.

The gurus of the inner life have been preaching to us for hundreds of years to slow down, be quiet, and kill the monster within that insists on being first, being noticed, and being praised. Many have written off those gurus as necessary reminders of an ancient life of contemplation and peace, a life locked away behind the thick walls of retreat centers. The prevailing evangelical mind-set is that we need soldiers charging into the battle, mounted on the engine of technology and armed with strategic plans and procedures. Could it be that we have been terribly wrong?

That we have ignored Jesus as our leader and have chosen lesser gods? It very well could be that we should drop our notebooks and Treos and reconsider. Life experience has documented our ineptness. We are well meaning but ineffective in reaching the world around us. We might be able to dismiss the desert fathers and Benedictines, but we can't dismiss Jesus. He is the one we are to become like, to follow, to learn from, and to imitate in character, methods, and every way we can identify. I want to dig in here and explore what Jesus' example in Philippians 2:5–8 means.

"Let This Mind Be in You"

Many translations say "attitude" (rather than "mind"), from *phronos*, meaning "mind-set" or "frame of mind." This phrase is given to us in the imperative, so it isn't a suggestion. The attitude that Jesus models for us is therefore necessary to any relevancy in mission. Could it be that Jesus has delivered another paradox to our lives? He is viewed as irrelevant only by those who don't have ears to hear. But to those of us who know His voice, His "irrelevancy" becomes the desire of our hearts. So the churchy platitude "we just want to be like Jesus" becomes radical and revolutionary.

What we find at the heart of this mind-set are the words "did not consider equality with God something to be grasped" (Phil. 2:6). What torments most of us is that we are not considered equal to others we work with, to those whose homes are closer to the beach, higher on the hill, or near the seventh green. And how do we feel about those whose cars are shinier, faster, and bigger? Still, being equal isn't enough; down deep we want to be considered superior.

I live six blocks from the beach, and many people walk past my home to get to the beach. Sometimes I feel pleasure knowing they live farther from the water than I do.

When I get upgraded to first class, there is a feeling of pity for those regular minions who must fly coach. Smugness is written on the faces of first-class passengers as others file on after they are already seated and are sipping their drinks.

The radical nature of thinking like Jesus is to not care about what everyone is grasping for. Their hands are extended as they strain to grab hold of the immediate pleasures offered them. But this passage is not speaking only of the material booty. It speaks of the false promise of fame, recognition, and praise from others. Jesus didn't consider those things valuable. He saw them all as a fine meal that satisfies only for a short period.

"Made Himself of No Reputation"

The passage says not "bad reputation" or "notorious reputation" but "no reputation." Now, everyone has a reputation, so this doesn't mean no one had an opinion about Jesus. We know that Jesus was famous in His time; He had thousands of admirers and hundreds of followers. This fact had more to do with His mind-set than with those around Him. He lived based on His own view of who He was and who His Father said He was: "You are My beloved Son, in whom I am well pleased" (Mark 1:11 NKJV). The trust of their relationship overpowered every other opinion and force. It overpowered who the religious establishment said He was, who His disciples said He was, and who the multitudes of people following Him thought He was. They considered Him a healer, a marvelous teacher, a worker of miracles, a maverick, and/or a blasphemer. Jesus saw Himself as a servant:

> You know that the rulers of the Gentiles lord it over them, and those who are great exercise authority over them. Yet it shall not be so among you; but whoever desires to become great among you, let him be your servant. And whoever desires to be first among you, let him be your slave—just

as the Son of Man did not come to be served, but to serve, and to give His life a ransom for many.

Matthew 20:25–28 NKJV

How many of us are driven to serve, to sacrifice our rights and privileges? Jesus was committed to a different kind of greatness, a greatness that slays the power that reputation holds over us.

> The most radical social teaching of Jesus was His total reversal of the contemporary notion of greatness. Leadership is found in becoming the servant of all. Power is discovered in submission. The foremost symbol of this radical servant-hood is the cross. . . . He flatly rejected the cultural givens of position and power when he said, "You are not to be called Rabbi . . . neither called masters." He took women seriously and was willing to meet with children; he took the towel and washed his disciples' feet.[10]

The model and message of Jesus is that submission is the greatest force on the earth. He submitted to His Father, and the world's sins were paid for. We submit to Him, and that same power radiates from us to others. The daily challenge of following Jesus is living in the truth of who He says we are and in the light of His definition of greatness, which is service. In the end the rewards are as He promised: "Whoever loses his life for me will save it" (Luke 9:24).

"Humbled Himself and Became Obedient"

Jesus' humility was based on who His Father said He was, not on what others said He was. When I get angry and upset over not being treated like I think I deserve, I am working from a false and fragile identity that depends on what others around me think of me. This is the way of the proud and high-strung. If Jesus would have followed this method, His mission would have failed. He accepted an appearance that was humble and looked unimportant. We can only imagine the slights of those who needed Him, the cold stares of those for whom He was prepared to die.

It is outside my comprehension to grasp the depth of that kind of love. It is one thing to return good for evil in the mundane of life. But a love that will take the rejection when it doesn't have to, when it has other choices—that requires more than our admiration; it must have our worship.

Jesus was in His very nature a servant. In appearance He looked like a man, but He was much more than a man. When you have the rock-solid identity that you are loved and valued by God, you can take on any role and be satisfied.

The power of humility is seen in service. A humble person does what many won't. He or she desires to give a gift, not take. Submission to our mission in life is the cornerstone of humility, of living in the light of who God says we are. In laying aside our culturally driven dreams and submitting to His plans, we find our feet walking in the good works that He has prepared for us (see Eph. 2:10). Paul's authorial intent in penning his treasures of Christology is for us to find ways of living out the power of humility and submission.

> Therefore, my dear friends, as you have always obeyed—not only in my presence, but now much more in my absence— continue to work out your salvation with fear and trembling, for it is God who works in you to will and to act according to his good purpose.
>
> Philippians 2:12–13

Paul means that Jesus' example is more than beautifully framed words on church walls or in Christian homes. This is really what it means to follow Jesus: to work out what God works in us. God works in us to will, which means He puts His desires in us. How does one distinguish the culturally driven dreams from God's impulses? Paul speaks of a process through which the Holy Spirit conforms us to Christ's image, an image that pleases Him. There is a guide in this passage: That process starts with the frame of mind that was in Jesus, in His values, and in what He considered important. His greatest value was to submit to His Father, because their hearts were connected.

As Jesus did, we need to live in light of who God, rather than the surrounding world, says we are. The culture defines us by look, pedigree, and achievement; God says we are His children, with an eternal inheritance and a specific purpose He has prepared for us.

Those of us in this frame of mind will listen for God's voice; we are humble enough and committed enough to lay aside all other agendas to find God's. We have chosen the life; we are willing to become servants, to take off the limits of sacrifice. In this frame of mind, we recognize the impulses of God, and we begin to act, to obey the desires He plants in us. This is not a static experience but a dynamic and daily one.

Jesus' core character trait was submission, which led to obedience, which led to the cross, which led to our rescue from the death grip of sin. Submission is a love word because it was based on the relationship between Jesus and His Father. Jesus considered His Father trustworthy, and therefore submission was possible. The core character trait of the disciple is also a life of submission and humility based on who God says we are. To choose the life means to choose submission and humility, which are the doorways to power and impact. It means being what Jesus was—mirroring His character—and doing what Jesus did.

Submission and the Community of Christ

A Spirit-filled community is a culture of submission (see Eph. 5:21). There are very few truths in Scripture without dispute. One of them is that Spirit-filled people speak in positive, graceful ways to others. They have deep, abiding joy and hearts of thanksgiving. And they are submissive to one another based on reverence for Christ (see Eph. 5:15–21). The opposite is also true: Critical spirits are without joy and contentment, are resistant to authority in their lives, and are not filled with the Spirit.

Submission is a choice to follow and be like Christ. It is all voluntary "as to the Lord." We submit to the Lord by faith. Faith is the act of obedience to authority, which we submit to because of trust in God's truth. We do so from the heart because we believe in God's love and goodness. Faith is the conviction that the plan He has developed for me is better and more affirming than my own.

The Pastor as Coach

Earlier I presented the thesis that the contemporary analogy of coaching fits the pastoral task better than any other. With respect to principle, the pastoral task is the same as coaching. The pastor tells people what and why, then must assist people to put the teaching into practice. Elton Trueblood wrote, "The glory of the coach is that of being the discoverer, the developer, and the trainer of the powers of other men. But this is exactly what we mean when we use the Biblical terminology about the equipping ministry."[1]

This modern analogy is built on an ancient example: Jesus Christ. The teaching model of Christ gives credence to the modern coaching analogy for the pastor. The pastor/teacher is well advised to imitate Christ as a teacher, rather than his successful colleague over at First Church. Jesus taught the disciples many things. What He taught them is vital; how He taught them is crucial as well. There are several ways to express Jesus' teaching method, and the one I have chosen contains six steps:

"Tell them what."
"Tell them why."
"Show them how."

"Do it with them."

"Let them do it."

"Deploy them."[2]

I will take one element of Christ's teaching and follow it through the six steps. The six steps are true teaching as the Bible describes, as Paul advocated, and as Jesus demonstrated. The chosen element is the methodology of the Great Commission.

Jesus built convictions concerning the dream of the kingdom, and He demonstrated that conviction by commitment to the cross. Sometimes we forget that Jesus was equally committed to the importance of a special methodology. This is precisely where the disciple-making pastor and the generic pastor part company. Let's review how Jesus implanted this methodology in His followers.

"Tell them what." The Great Commission is delivered five times, once in each gospel and then in Acts 1. What is less emphasized is the precross issuing of the commission. During the first four months of ministry training, Jesus exposed His first five disciples to the nature of ministry. The "come and see" phase is recorded in John 1:35–4:46. It is not found in the synoptics.[3]

PRELIMINARY COMMISSIONS. At the close of the four-month introductory period, Jesus first mentioned the task before Him. "Do you not say, 'Four months more and then the harvest'? I tell you, open your eyes and look at the fields! They are ripe for harvest" (John 4:35).

He planted the seed in the good soil of four exciting months of exposure to the supernatural. It is well established that shortly after this the disciples returned to fishing.[4] The seed began to take root, and they began to see the importance of telling others about the Messiah and His kingdom. The fish began to smell, the hours in the boat became tedious, the mending of nets excruciating. This was the beginning of Jesus telling them *what*.

The second precross mention of the task was the inauguration of the second stage of the disciples' training. "As Jesus walked beside the Sea of Galilee, he saw Simon and his brother Andrew casting a net into the lake, for they were fishermen. 'Come, follow me,' Jesus said, 'and I will make you fishers of men'" (Mark 1:16–17).

The seed had time to germinate, take root, and grow. Now they were prepared to enter the next phase of ministry training. They dropped their nets and followed Jesus because He had prepared them to take this important step. During the next ten months, known as "come and follow Me," Jesus delivered on His promise. He made them fishers of men. They had caught the vision for what was truly important. Fishing was a living, fishing for men was a reason to live.

The next recorded declaration of purpose was the second call of the four to fish for men. They had returned to fishing once again. Reasons given for this return range from financial ones to disillusionment. The theories abound, but the fact remains that it did occur, and the restoration of Peter, in particular, is highlighted. Jesus appeared, then instructed the weary fishermen to launch out into the deep once more, after a night of frustration. The result was a record-breaking catch. Peter realized what a fool he had been and flung himself at the feet of Jesus. Jesus responded, "'Don't be afraid; from now on you will catch men.' So they pulled their boats up on shore, left everything and followed him" (Luke 5:10–11).

Each time Jesus confirmed commitment with the disciples, He seasoned it with the vision. Jesus did not let them forget what they were to do; He always made the connection. After all, all work and no vision makes the ministry drudgery.

A fuller and more poignant declaration of the task at hand took place just before the Twelve were commissioned.

"When he saw the crowds, he had compassion on them, because they were harassed and helpless, like sheep without a shepherd. Then he said to his disciples, 'The harvest is plentiful but the workers are few. Ask the Lord of the harvest, therefore, to send out workers into his harvest field'" (Matt. 9:36–38).

Once again the task was placed before the Twelve. There was massive need and not enough workers to meet the need. Immediately following this pronouncement, He sent them out two by two to make the application. Jesus made that important connection between the work that needed to be done and the reasons for the work. While Jesus went far beyond the "tell them what" phase of teaching, He didn't forget to remind them. As one can easily see, Jesus was building in His declarations toward the Great Commission.

He built the disciples' convictions through a healthy portion of life experience. They had a great deal of hands-on ministry in and around the calls to reach out. The Great Commission didn't suddenly plop into the disciples' laps just prior to the ascension. It was a simple culmination of priorities already taught. For thirty-four months Jesus progressively and gradually taught the disciples what they must do.

It's much like training our children to brush their teeth, comb their hair, and clean their ears. We plant the seed, remind them, and fight what seems like a losing battle to establish good grooming habits. Then, one day, when they reach their early teens, they go into the bathroom and never come out. They become so concerned about their looks that we start threatening them for taking so much time on their grooming.

Like handing a person pieces to life's puzzle one at a time, Jesus gradually built the disciples' understanding of what must be done. The continual challenges to fish for men, to work in the harvest, and to preach to all nations laid the foundation for what we now term the Great Commission. Once the disciples witnessed the resurrected Christ, all the puzzle's pieces formed a picture around which the disciples built their lives.

THE GREAT COMMISSION. Following His resurrection, Jesus appeared to His followers several times. Part of those appearances were the commands called the Great Commission:

> John 20:21: "As the Father has sent me, I am sending you."

> Mark 16:15 (NASB): "Go . . . and preach the gospel to all creation."

> Luke 24:47: "Repentance and forgiveness of sins will be preached . . . beginning at Jerusalem."

> Acts 1:8 (NASB): "You will receive power . . . you shall be My witnesses both in Jerusalem, and in all Judea and Samaria, and even to the remotest part of the earth."

A composition of the Great Commission passages would read something like, "Go, preach the gospel to the ends of the earth. Make sure that signs of God's power are present with you. Start at home and work your way toward the remotest parts of the globe."

The four occurrences mentioned above are a beginning, but are incomplete. It would be much like declaring, "Go build houses, make them special, award-winning houses. I will provide the money; build them all over the world and make them nice." This could get the builder moving, but what about a blueprint, what does a nice house look like? There is very little said about methodology.

That is why Matthew's account of the Great Commission is the most often quoted. It provides a specific methodology, it gives a blueprint to follow, a prescribed plan for taking the good news to the ends of the earth: "Therefore go and make disciples of all nations, baptizing them in the name of the Father and of the Son and of the Holy Spirit, and teaching them to obey everything I have commanded you. And surely I am with you always, to the very end of the age" (Matt. 28:19–20).

Going, baptizing, and teaching are considered subservient to the imperative verbal action "make disciples." *Going* indicates establishing a presence for Christ wherever you may be. *Baptizing* new believers means they make a public stand on commitment to Christ. *Teaching* to obey is the core of making disciples. The command is to evangelize the world and make disciples, because disciples will be obedient followers of Jesus Christ.

When we take the Great Commission as a unit, we see that Jesus didn't command simple evangelism. He asked for more. His plan required more than baptized converts. It would call for people who reproduce. The church was commanded to produce a kind of person who would obey Christ, evangelize his world, and set off a chain reaction called multiplication.

Disciple making means developing Christians who have the desire and skill to reproduce themselves. Just as reproducing is a learned skill, so is multiplication. A Christian can introduce another person to Christ, and that means he has reproduced. If the convert is not trained to do the same, then reproduction has taken place, but not multiplication. Christ calls for men and women who not only reproduce, but then teach others how to reproduce. When those converts become practicing disciples, winning and teaching others, then multiplication is set into motion.

The reason the church's evangelistic efforts do not keep pace with the population growth is the absence of multiplication. It is not a priority; it is taught as a result rather than a commissioned methodology. It is considered an esoteric quirk of a few disciple-making ideologies. A commitment to disciple making and multiplication through trained disciple makers is resisted. So while the American church continues to build monuments to itself, 50 percent of the world remains unreached because we have disobeyed the Great Commission.

Much contemporary success proves that if you demand little and put on a good show, you can get a crowd. In the long run, however, large crowds mean nothing. Obedience to the commission is the determined dedication to disciple making. When Jesus told them what, He taught them the importance of multiplication.

"Tell them why." The axiom says, "If a person knows why, he can bear almost any how." Jesus has told them what must be done, but in order to sustain commitment, He must give them a passion for why. Jesus made it easy for us to find out. "For the Son of Man came to seek and to save what was lost" (Luke 19:10). "For even the Son of Man did not come to be served, but to serve, and to give his life as a ransom for many" (Mark 10:45). "For God did not send his Son into the world to condemn the world, but to save the world through him" (John 3:17).

Why disciple making, why dedication to multiplication? Because people need forgiveness, new life, to be rescued from the penalty for sin and eternal separation from their Creator. Jesus came to save His own and to populate heaven with His children. Disciple making for disciple making's sake is heresy. Disciple making and multiplication are a means to an end; they must never take on a life of their own.

The Word must be proclaimed to all nations. People must go out if the Word is to get out. It will require personnel, disciples committed to reproduction and multiplication. Obedient disciples are the only ones with the commitment and stamina to fulfill the task. Without multiplication in place, there will be a shortage of trained personnel, and the status quo will reign.

Tell them *what*: the multiplication of disciples for world evangelization. Tell them *why*: salvation of mankind and the establishment of Christ's kingdom.

The pastor/teller stops here. He tells people what and why, and that's it. There is too much emphasis on sermons, Sunday school lessons, and academic Bible-study programs. The evangelical church is Word oriented. Learning, to the middle-class white church, is sermons and Bible study.

If a pastor primarily focuses on preaching, without vehicles to apply the preaching, he does two things wrong: He does not teach, because he does not teach them to obey. He tells them to obey, but does not provide the means for true learning, which takes place apart from mere communication of content. Second, he creates an environment for guilt and failure. This takes place when people are continually told what they should do, yet there is no means to get them there. This is the prostitution of the pastorate and the exploitation of God's people.

Telling them what and why is the foundation on which the pastor builds. He should be dedicated and committed to teaching the Word. He should spend long hours preparing the very best sermons possible. But he had better provide a means for application, or he isn't doing his job. He must constantly think through how he wants his teaching applied. Jesus is our model for such an approach.

Coaches spend a great deal of time talking to their teams, telling them what and why things must be done. They review films, study play books, prepare game plans, then they go to the practice area and begin to apply the *what* and *why*. The coach goes to the practice field with the players. The public generally sees coaches on the sidelines, dressed in street clothes. But the players remember their coaches more in athletic attire, with whistles around their necks. Ninety percent of coaching is the nitty-gritty of the gym or the practice field. Pastors preach thirty to forty minutes, once a week. The question is, apart from fifteen hours preparing that sermon, how are they spending their time? A smart and responsible pastor also spends time making sure his teaching is applied, training people, and providing vehicles for both training and ministry expression.

"Show them how" and "do it with them." The disciple-making pastor as coach now steps out from behind the pulpit and shows people how to apply this teaching. How did Jesus model His own commitment to multiplication? The very fact that He chose them and they were together demonstrated His interest in training them. The "come and see" phase was both introductory and brief. "Come and follow Me" lasted longer, ten months, and Jesus took the responsibility, "I will make you fishers of men." In the third call, "Come and be with Me," He separated out the Twelve and gave them special responsibility and authority. When Jesus commissioned the Twelve and sent them out, they knew it was for keeps. He planned on passing on the work to them.

As the time for Christ's departure drew near, He increased the personal time with the Twelve. His first priority was the cross; His second was the training of the Twelve. As with children, where investment of time and effort communicates love and importance, so the same dynamic was at work with Jesus and his men. Jesus spent His time demonstrating, explaining, experimenting, and clarifying over and over.

If a pastor teaches that evangelism is important, he must lead the charge. Start a class, teach the principles, then take people out to practice them. After sufficient demonstration, the students should do it. Show them how it's done, then do it with them. They might start by giving testimonies, then build toward a full gospel presentation. The pastor demonstrates his commitment to multiplication by teaching others how to witness. Then his students teach others. This is obvious, but it is as rare as it is obvious. The cause of Christ is debilitated because we neglect the basics.

The most effective teaching tool is a model. Whether it be athletics, art, sales, or driving a car, modeling must be done. Gradually the student is allowed to try out what has been shown to him. Jesus demonstrated, by His practice, that men were His method. He was dedicated to building men who could multiply. His commitment was demonstrated by His willingness to give His ministry away to trained men.

They knew how to teach, because they saw Him teach. They knew how to cast out demons, pray for the sick, care for the weak, because He modeled it. They understood the importance of working through others, because He demonstrated it through them. Because it had been done to them, they could do it to others. The disciple's golden rule is "you will do unto others as it has been done unto you."

DECENTRALIZATION OF MINISTRY. Earlier I spoke of the decentralization of pastoral care. The only reason the disciple-making pastor believes in and practices such a thing is because Jesus was committed to the decentralization of all ministry. The six-step teaching method modeled by Jesus is a testament to the decentralization of ministry. What other reason would Jesus have for such a frustrating experience as trying to work through the Twelve? They were self-serving, fearful, ego driven, competitive, forgetful, jealous of one another, slow to learn, even slower to unlearn. Working through this ragtag bunch must have been like Michael Jordan trying to play basketball in Woody Allen's body. They slowed Jesus down; they tempted Him to disobey His Father; they were more trouble than most people thought they were worth. Everyone except Jesus, that is.

Jesus could see the world through others. In fact, the Great Commission requires that the disciple-making pastor sees the world through others as the core of his work. How the disciple-making pastor is doing is how the people of the church are doing.

Jesus' method of teaching is just as controversial today as ever. Most evangelical churches will not allow their pastor to teach like Jesus. They will resist the disciple-making pastor. If he desires to concentrate on a few, select out some for training so he can multiply his work, he will be opposed. When the disciple-making pastor starts talking about selecting the best, training standards, and insisting that board members be trained disciple makers, he will find himself in a battle.

If the church is to take the example of Jesus seriously by teaching the way He did, and to take the Great Commission just as seriously by demonstrating a commitment to multiplication through disciple making, it will require some tenacious disciple makers who can endure the bumps and bruises of ecclesiastical battle until the fruit begins bearing. Given enough time, the decentralization of ministry proves itself far superior. It gets more done, and the work is done better. It gives more people fulfillment and a life of purpose. It gives the church leadership a new sense of accomplishment, which is very satisfying, and makes all the struggles of leadership worthwhile.

THE BEST TRAINING VEHICLE. By selecting the Twelve, Jesus identified the best training vehicle. The Twelve were a small group—enough to give variety, but not so many that anyone could spectate. It provided a launching pad for either the multitude ministry or one-on-one fine-tuning. They could experience most things together, then discuss, argue, respond, and dialogue with Jesus.

The disciple-making pastor considers the small group the most valuable tool in his ministry. Most of the principles and skills that need to be taught can be done in the small group context. If it's prayer, Bible study skills, giving a testimony, learning evangelistic skills, how to do evangelistic entertaining, and so on, the small group fits the bill. If the people of the church need to get acquainted with one another, require support during crisis, or work on a ministry project, again the small group is the best vehicle.

If I were starting a ministry from scratch, I would begin by inviting all who like to "come and see" to a small group Bible study. Then, in that context, I would allow the cream to rise to the top and elect those who respond to the "come and follow Me" call into another small group for training.

From those who finished that basic training, I would select a few more to "come and be with Me." These I would train to replace me, and I would work through them. Therefore, I get multiplication; I get decentralization; and more gets done by a wider group and in a more effective fashion.

Showing them how and doing it with them are crucial steps that are the bridge to both multiplication and decentralization of ministry. If we were to relate the six-step teaching method of Jesus to the three-phased training plan built around Christ's calls to the disciples, it would look like the following.

> *"Come and see"* = 1. "Tell them what." 2. "Tell them why."
>
> *"Come and follow Me"* = 3. "Show them how." 4. "Do it with them."
>
> *"Come and be with Me"* = 5. "Let them do it." 6. "Deploy them."

"Show them how" and "do it with them" compose the bridge that makes the trip from knowing what and why to doing it and getting it done through others. It is equally apparent, when the training is not provided, why multiplication will not take place. Jesus showed them how for ten months during "Come and follow Me" and for twenty months during "Come and be with Me." Gradually, throughout, He turned more and more responsibility over to them. This is the model for the disciple-making pastor. Just as the coach tells what and why, then follows it with demonstrations and critiques, so will the pastor committed to the Great Commission.

"Let them do it." Too often multiplication falls apart here, because people are given too much too soon. There must be final testing, fine-tuning, and solid instructions to insure the integrity of what is multiplied. Great care is required. Jesus showed us how.

"He called his twelve disciples to him and gave them authority to drive out evil spirits and to heal every disease and sickness" (Matt. 10:1). This is the first mission of the Twelve without Jesus. They were on their own; Jesus wasn't looking over their shoulders. Now their judgment, their words, their courage, their ability had to bring God's power to bear on human need. Before a ministry is handed over to another, letting him go it alone is vital. The terms on which he goes it alone, however, are crucial.

The disciples went out to work under specific instructions that detailed everything from the message preached to the amount of luggage. Jesus didn't ask them to go beyond their training. Second, they would return to Jesus for debriefing, evaluation, and affirmation.

The Twelve were not totally unleashed. They remained tied to Jesus, but they were on a long leash. This phase of training provides the "fine-tuning" necessary to a successful deployment. During this phase the disciples become disciple makers. They prove that they can do more than evangelize; they can build people to maturity who, in turn, reproduce themselves as well. There is no substitute in the disciple's heart for the personal knowledge that he can get the job done. The only way to find that out is to go out and try. Jesus sent them out in this case; later He allowed them to lead the seventy in a special mission (Luke 10).

The notable difference between a disciple and a disciple maker is the ministry of multiplication. The disciple maker not only reproduces, he leads those who are disciple makers themselves, people who make disciples two and three generations away from where they started. The people Jesus called to ministry leadership could not only make disciples one on one, but in a corporate structure as well. The step of letting them do it is crucial to protecting the integrity of what you reproduce. How the product is protected is the next issue.

"Deploy them." The disciple-making pastor as coach makes sure that those chosen for deployment have mastered the necessary skills. This select group composes about 10 percent of the congregation. The first reason such a small percentage reaches this level is that 50 percent of the church never leaves the comfort zone called "come and see." They attend worship, church dinners, and possibly special events. Ninety percent of the remaining 50 percent move into the "come and follow Me" phase. They join a group that teaches ministry skills; they do some form of ministry with the church. They are disciples; they reproduce; they have a wonderful ministry in reaching others as well. The difference between these faithful disciples and the remaining 10 percent is leadership ability and spiritual giftedness.

Those chosen for multiplied leadership responsibility must have the proper gifts and must possess leadership ability. What sets this group apart is not spirituality as much as suitability. One can only guess why Jesus chose the twelve He did. The disciple-making pastor better have some criteria for selecting those entrusted with ministry leadership.

In our selection process, those who have successfully completed the "come and follow Me" phase are then assessed and directed to areas of ministry. Those selected to "come and be with Me" have the gifts and skills to lead and create environments where disciple making and multiplication are effectively developed. Let's take a look at some objective criteria for measuring suitability for leadership.

The Foundation for Ministry Skills

Character. Part of the training is that over a period of two or three years a person reveals the content of his heart. The person is evaluated, based on the character issues recorded in 1 Timothy 3 and Titus 1. Progress, not perfection, is the issue. Those charged with the selection process must be sure there are no major character flaws, no skeletons in the closet. If a person doesn't measure up at this point, there is no reason to continue preparation for leadership.

Faithfulness. Passages such as 1 Corinthians 4:2; Luke 16:10; and 2 Timothy 2:2 teach faithfulness as a nonnegotiable prerequisite for leadership. The inherent suggestion from Luke 16:10 (NASB) provides a formula for establishing faithfulness: "He who is faithful in a very little thing is faithful also in much; and he who is unrighteous in a very little thing is unrighteous also in much."

The disciple-making pastor gives assignments to disciples who, over a period of years, establish a track record either of faithfulness or dishonesty. Faithfulness is on equal footing with character as a necessity for leadership. Again, the distinctive of the disciple-making pastor is that he monitors progress and intentionally moves people through the process. He knows who is on first and second and third; he sees people through his philosophical grid.

Spiritual Gifts/Suitability. The proper gifts for corporate spiritual leadership are teaching, leadership, administration, exhortation, and other similar gift clusters. Most people are not cut out for leadership. It makes perfect sense that only 10 percent of the congregation would be candidates for leadership. Only 10 percent of a group needs to be leaders; a church filled with chiefs and no Indians would make for anarchy.

Those who excel during the "come and follow Me" phase are the pool in which the disciple-making pastor fishes for leaders. The two teaching steps that correspond to "come and follow Me" are "show them how" and "do it with them." He looks for those who have proven they can lead, who influence others positively, and who have made it through the process to that date.

Character, *faithfulness*, and *suitability* are the foundations on which a disciple-making pastor can build. Taking people with these basic qualities, he can fine-tune them just as Jesus did for major leadership. This is so vital, it determines if there will be significant multiplication. When this fifth teaching step is neglected, the Great Commission begins to unravel.

The next issue, then, is what are the skills required for a person to become an effective disciple maker? Keep in mind we are speaking of a leader who can create corporate environments for disciple making and multiplication.

The Ministry Skills

The key to developing strong ministry skills is letting potential leaders practice the skills. It takes more than a pilot in a simulator; it requires live action with real people with real needs. The disciple-making pastor must trust his trainees with valuable treasure. This is the only way they will really learn. That is what Jesus did; it is what the pastor must do.

The most effective means of training we have found is to feed those chosen for leadership back into our system. This gives them the hands-on experience they need. Because academic models dominate our training thinking, we experience the temptation to give increased classroom experience, but we must resist this. While more content is required to develop their philosophical grid, the more important need is to make what they already know work.

Can effectively communicate Scripture. Without communication there will be no multiplication. The disciple maker must be able to teach others. By *teach* I mean the ability to transfer knowledge, convictions, and passion concerning values; to be able to transfer these values sufficiently that they can be passed on without a decline in quality (see 2 Tim. 2:2). Teaching means to take people through the six-step method.

The effective communicator need not be a gifted speaker. Too often we associate the gift of teaching with highly polished public speaking. Effective public address is helpful, but not required. What is necessary is the skill to get others to understand the content and reasons behind what must be passed on. The indispensable quality is conviction. If a person has passionate conviction, he will be able to infect others. Therefore, if the foundation of character is laid and the convictions are developed by the six-step teaching method, the disciple will become a disciple maker because he passes it on. The forum for such teaching includes public address, group discussion, reading, self-study, and informal association.

"Everything we do teaches," "Values are caught more than taught," the axioms go. The best teaching combines all the above forms. Character and convictions, however, must head the list of qualities that make communication most powerful. The testing and training ground is to turn the potential disciple maker loose on people. If he can transfer values, convictions, and skills to people assigned to his care, he is on his way to a lifetime of disciple making. The pastor as coach provides vehicles of opportunity for those selected to "come and be with Me."

The ability to manage. Managers are not pencil pushers or people who shuffle papers well. In this context, *manage* means "the ability to get work done through others." The main thrust is human relations, how to work effectively with others, how to bring the best out of others for the cause of Christ. Tom Peters claims that the toughest issue in leadership today is delegation. It is hard to assign someone a task, make sure he understands it, and make sure he can do it and do it well. I agree with Peters that the toughest issue among Christian leaders is creating an atmosphere for multiplication. Whether we call it shared ministry, unleashing the laity, multiplication, or discipleship, it means bringing full and meaningful ministry to the body of Christ.

The first step in training managers is to develop convictions concerning the decentralization of ministry. The second aspect is to help them understand the steps in delegation. The third phase is to monitor their attempts to work through others in their ministry assignment. Multiplication on this level requires more than basic ministry skills such as sharing the faith or how to follow up with a new believer. The goal is to multiply disciple makers, leaders, those who lead ministries. That is the reason for such emphasis on the ability to get work done through others. It means the ability to influence groups of people, not just the individual.

The ability to motivate and inspire. The disciple maker effectively communicates; he gets work done through others; and he must motivate others. Leaders always fight inertia among followers. Apathy is to be expected among the general populace. Experienced leaders don't waste time lamenting its existence; they channel energy toward a solution. The prescription for apathy is inspiration. To be inspired is primarily an emotional game. God uses emotions, and we may validly frame important issues to speak to them. While useful, inspiration is also short-lived. Emotion's partner is motivation. Motivation is distinct from inspiration because a motivated person has reasons.

The experienced disciple maker should seek to inspire, but it is more vital to motivate. The ability to motivate combines the first two ministry skills: communication and management. The Christian is taught why serving Christ is important, then receives tasks to complete under the supervision of the disciple maker. The disciple maker adds these motivational factors: continual reminders of why it is important, affirming his present performance, pushing him to do better and achieve more, the promise of greater responsibility, storytelling concerning successes in the area of training, and honest evaluation of his work. If the disciple maker feels excited about and derives pleasure from others' success, he will be a great motivator; he will inspire others to serve Christ.

We might call this the lubricant that makes management meaningful. Motivation and inspiration are the oil that takes away the irritating grinding of ministry wheels.

Can counsel others. "I myself am convinced, my brothers, that you yourselves are full of goodness, complete in knowledge and competent to *instruct* one another" (Rom. 15:14, italics added). "We proclaim him, *admonishing* and teaching everyone with all wisdom, so that we may present everyone perfect in Christ" (Col. 1:28, italics added).

The words *instruct* and *admonishing* come from the same Greek word. *Nouthea*, used thirteen times in the New Testament, means "to verbally correct someone." There is some justification for translating it as "counsel." The issue before us is that leaders do have a responsibility to counsel those under their care.

At this level of development, leaders must be able to help people with the basic conflicts of life. The people selected for disciple-maker training inhabit the pool in which we fish for missionaries, elders, pastors, church planters, and other crucial leadership roles. Part of their training then is to take classroom instruction on basic counseling techniques. Depression, anxiety, marital conflict, communication problems, and conflict management in the church are a few of the subjects covered. Once again we have found that small group leadership provided the trainee with opportunity to practice his skills.

Can correct others. "Don't have anything to do with foolish and stupid arguments, because you know they produce quarrels. And the Lord's servant must not quarrel; instead, he must be kind to everyone, able to teach, not resentful.

Those who oppose him he must gently instruct, in the hope that God will grant them repentance leading them to a knowledge of the truth, and that they will come to their senses and escape from the trap of the devil, who has taken them captive to do his will" (2 Tim. 2:23–26).

This is one of several passages that calls upon leaders to correct those who have fallen prey to false teachings or practices. Many disciple makers resist this part of their skill development. It is human nature for most to avoid confrontation. The first hurdle is to convince the trainee that confrontation and correcting others is an act of love. It is part of helping others keep their commitments to God. The faithful leader who cares enough to confront in the context of relationship will save those under his care much sorrow and himself even greater pain. In fact, unless the leader engages in such activity, he is unfaithful, and he will limit his work. When sin lives unattended in the body of Christ, it has the same deleterious effect as untreated disease has on the human body.

The main training vehicle for the development of the five ministry skills is the small group. It requires a potential disciple maker to employ all five skills. An example is the fifth skill of correcting others. The group agrees to allow the leader to help them keep their commitment to God. Whenever a group member fails to keep the commitment, the leader approaches them with the attitude, "What can I do to help you?" The person is either unwilling or unable to keep the commitment. If they are unwilling, it is a spiritual problem; if unable, it is a management problem. Learning to address issues head on and early saves both group members and leader much heartache.

Correcting others is part of the discipling process that is neglected. Too often someone claims to practice accountability, but in reality practices selective accountability. He submits to authority and changes when he wants, but ignores authority when he doesn't want it. In those cases, accountability is a farce, it means nothing. People cannot develop into what God desires until they submit to God's authority through leaders when they don't want to. Until they have to swallow their egos and submit in a moment of crisis, their independence will retard their development. Those selected for "come and be with Me," step five, "let them do it" must demonstrate that they are willing to be corrected and able to correct others.

Deployment. Don't dare deploy without philosophical purity. When you enter a McDonald's restaurant in Pittsburgh, it serves the same menu as one in San Diego. The coffee is good, the ice cream tastes the same, and you can always count on the hamburgers to be consistent. The reason for high quality throughout the country is the emphasis on quality control.

McDonald's has standards for selecting franchisees. Rules and agreements must be maintained in order for the franchise buyers to keep a store. When they sell a product, it looks and tastes the same worldwide. They know what they want to multiply and how to maintain the integrity of their product. The same is true of the church. When a disciple maker is deployed, it is vital that he possess the same philosophy and skills, in order to reproduce the desired product.

As deployment came near, Jesus called the disciples to the upper room for final instructions. He taught them new material; in particular, He introduced the Twelve to the ministry of the Holy Spirit. He explained the change in their relationship. He would be with them, but not in the same way. They would be expected to do more and have greater responsibility. Jesus emphasized that it was necessary for Him to go away. One of the reasons it was necessary was for the disciples' development. They could only go so far with Jesus around. If we combine the upper-room discourse with the postresurrection appearances, we find principles for deployment.

REVIEW THE BASICS. The upper room teaches us that Jesus reviewed some basic factors about love, fruit bearing, maintaining a relationship with the Father and one another. The postresurrection appearances teach us the importance of leaving disciples with the promise of continued support but also with a clear command to dedicate oneself to the task.

For us, the application has been to review the basics through a series of tests. Tests cover doctrine, philosophy of ministry, work-style preference, and an oral exam. The oral exam is a freewheeling discussion in which the person has opportunity to demonstrate his ability to articulate his knowledge and commitment to the philosophy. This gives both leaders and the ready-to-be-deployed disciple maker confidence that he is ready.

The most obvious way in which Jesus carried through the Great Commission to the sixth step, "deploy them," were His last words. The five occurrences of the Great Commission are the last and most important words to His men. His very last words make the point: "But you will receive power when the Holy Spirit comes on you; and you will be my witnesses in Jerusalem, and in all Judea and Samaria, and to the ends of the earth" (Acts 1:8).

He started by telling them the fields were white for harvest. He finished by saying they would be a powerful witness to the entire world. During the interval He trained them; He showed them how, did it with them, then let them do it, and finally He deployed them. Today He continues to enable His disciples to do the same. Because of His excellent teaching, when He said "make disciples," they knew what He meant and how to get it done. Can we say the same about our people?

ESTABLISH A NEW RELATIONSHIP. Jesus told the disciples that their relationship would change. When a trained disciple maker is ready for deployment, the same is true. Jesus told the disciples that they would not be orphans; He would maintain contact through the Holy Spirit. They would have greater responsibility with the same amount of power. The only thing lacking would be the physical presence of Jesus.

When the trained disciple maker is deployed, he will have more responsibility, more freedom, but will maintain the relationship to his mentor as well. The difference might be that the trained disciple maker makes contact with his mentor once a month. They will spend an entire day together twice a year. This is generally the case when the person is deployed to a geographically distant ministry assignment.

In a more common scenario, the trained disciple maker stays in the same church. He is given a major responsibility, a challenge to create and develop a ministry from scratch. While he may have contact with the church leadership team, the trained disciple maker pretty much goes it alone. He is to do so because he can, because by doing so he will recruit and train others. He should not depend on the church leadership for daily help.

The important thing is for the church to produce many trained disciple makers. Some will go to seminary, to the mission field, to church planting, to other forms of professional Christian work, but the majority will remain at home in the workforce. Highly trained people must resist the temptation to "kick back" after such training. The challenge for the disciple-making pastor is to coach people into challenging and fulfilling ministry, help people take the next step, and allow the creativity of the Holy Spirit to provide the ideas for ministry.

We encourage trained disciple makers within the church to lead labor teams, small groups of dedicated Christians who target a segment of society and attempt to help it and reach it for Christ. The homeless, AIDS patients, abused children, or social groups such as parents of soccer players or members of recreational leagues—all are viable groups to penetrate for Christ. To succeed, these ministries must be led by those who have the training and skill to get it done, namely, trained disciple makers.

By training people and allowing them to go as far as possible, there will be much more leadership and more effective ministry. Some will not get past "tell them what and why." The majority will find their place in "show them how and do it with them." That means they will not be leaders, but they are disciples; they reproduce, but they will always need others to lead. Then about 10 percent will become trained disciple makers. You let them do it and then deploy them. They are the cream of the crop; they will multiply their efforts through others. The more of these you can produce, the better.

Further Reflections

Recently I learned that my high school basketball coach, Gene Ring, had died four years earlier. I was disappointed that I was not able to attend his funeral to pay tribute to his impact on my life.

The first time I laid eyes on Gene Ring was at a meeting in the Broad Ripple High School gym. Thirty to forty boys sat on the bleachers, eager to hear from this Indiana legend. Coach Ring spoke with passion as he paced back and forth: "We're going to play fast-break basketball; we're going to work harder, run faster, and jump higher than our opponents." Then we got our first taste of one of his trademark idiosyncrasies: "We're going to get up in there, get up in there. We're going to play hard, defend hard, get up in there, get up in there." The more excited he became, the more he would repeat himself. He had a look in his eye that at the same time excited us and made us want to wet our pants.

At that time, I was fourteen years old and a lowly freshman, so Coach Ring didn't pay much attention to me. The next year I was 6'3", but I was still a freshman and academically ineligible. He pulled me aside to say, "You could be a good player, boy, but you are screwing up. Go to class, study, do your homework. Come on, boy, get up in there."

I wanted his approval. I sensed that he believed in me, and not many did. I was a classic underachiever; on the basketball court I was confident, but in the classroom I was lost. I missed school too much and even got suspended for leaving the school grounds. I chose to change. I started to get passing grades, continued growing in stature, and became much more focused.

Fast forward to my senior year. By then I was 6'6", and a lot was expected from my teammates and me. Coach Ring called me, whom he had nicknamed "Hoss," into his office for a preseason pep talk. (This was 1964, and *Bonanza* was the number one program on television.) He started his now-familiar pacing in front of me. "Hoss, this is going to be a big year, a big year for you, for the team, for our school. We are going to win a lot of games, and you are going to make that happen. And Hoss, whenever we lose a game, if ever we lose a game, it's your fault, it's your fault." Once again those conflicting feelings of excitement and fear were mixing inside me.

A few weeks later we were playing one of our fiercest rivals. My legs were cramping, and they reeked of liniment, the only known treatment for cramps in those days of canvas Converse sneakers and short basketball trunks. At halftime I had four points. Ring was fuming, and I heard him rumbling down the hallway to the locker room. He burst into the room, took one look at me, and lunged for me. I think I did wet my pants then. In the second half of the game, I scored twenty-five points.

Now that's coaching; that's discipleship. Coach Ring knew how to get the best out of me.

I had a great year. We lost more games than we had planned, but we were playing very well going into Indiana's state tournament. Ring had a special speech he would give at tournament time: "Listen up, boys, it's tournament time, it's tournament time." *We know that, Coach*, we would think to ourselves. "I want your complete focus. First, throw those books out the window; I don't want you distracted by books.

Second, no skirts. I don't want you thinking about skirts or talking to them, and if I see you walking down the hall holding hands with one of them, it's Katie barred the door, boys, Katie barred the door." We never knew what "Katie barred the door" meant, but we didn't want to find out.

Our first game in the state tournament was against the other best team in the sectional. The other team ran up a big lead on us, but in the middle of the second half, we pulled even and then went slightly ahead. Ring was going crazy. "Don't let this be your last game, Hoss! Do you want this to be your last game?" I think that was a rhetorical question. The game came down to the wire. A couple of controversial calls went against us, and we lost.

Later I sat in front of my locker in tears. We lost with our last chance, and it was my fault. Ring came into the locker room and sat down beside me, saying, "Hoss, you played great tonight; that loss wasn't your fault." It was amazing how affirmed I felt at that moment. He had used the pressure to get the best out of me, and when the pressure no longer was needed, he let me off the hook.

Gene Ring loved me and I loved him. I still love him. Jesus said, "Every one when he is fully taught will be like his teacher" (Luke 6:40 RSV). I did become somewhat like him—focused, passionate, an overachiever. He taught me that determination and discipline pay off. As a leader, pastor, and writer, I have benefited from his influence.

I don't advocate that you be as wild and wooly as Gene Ring. But I do recommend that you be as passionate and caring. Remember, what you do with others makes a difference for a lifetime. Coach Ring rescued me from a life of disappointment and helped me live a life of joy and achievement. Thousands of people have heard about Gene Ring and know what an impact he had on me. His impact has been multiplied and used for the advancement of the kingdom. I don't know if he was a man of faith, but I do know he had faith in me, and for that I am thankful.

Making It Work in the Local Church

This is the part of the book I normally don't read. It's where the author explains the details of what has worked for him. I avoid nuts-and-bolts sections because usually they aren't transferable. Principles are, programs are not, and applications tend to be programmatic. Before you follow suit and close the book, however, give me a chance to demonstrate that I am still dealing with principles.

This section applies the principles espoused throughout the book. My method will be to summarize each of the four phases of Jesus' training methodology. I will follow with concrete vehicles that put the principles to work. Generally I will describe what each vehicle does and why it is employed. I hope this will put handles on the principles, giving you useful ideas for making disciples in your ministry. But first, some important reminders.

Reminder 1: Make Sure You Have a Plan

A church-centered disciple-making plan is the work plan needed to place disciple making at the heart of the church.

The plan represents how the principles are applied. Don't start implementing disciple making until you know where you are going and how you plan to get there.

Reminder 2: Explain Your Plan

Declare the priorities. The pastor declares the biblical priorities from the pulpit. He expounds the passages, extracts the principles, and illustrates their usage. He clearly points the church in a specific direction.

Publish it in church literature. Bulletins, newsletters, annual reports, yearbooks, brochures all should reflect the declared priorities. The writings should be annually updated and improved; there should be standards for measuring corporate achievement written into the constitution, as well.

Model it at the leadership level. This is a most crucial step, second only to the senior pastor's philosophy. The qualities and priorities of disciple making should be reflected in the life and work of the church leaders. When this is missing, the church populace is taught to disobey declared priorities. Why should they believe that disciple making is top priority, when the leaders do not practice such a lifestyle? These three prerequisites lay the groundwork for installing disciple making at the heart of the church.

Reminder 3: Present a Model of How You Plan to Work

Present your work plan to the leadership of the church. If you have thought out what you want to do and have written it down, you can sell it to others. You will need to persuade others that this is the way to go. Just as important is your strategy to implement the plan. When you explain the concrete vehicles for implementation, the common man can identify and be motivated. This can be as simple as, "I will start a small group to teach anyone who will 'come and see' what it means to be a disciple."

Three reminders: develop a plan, explain your plan, sell your plan. People respond to a leader who knows where he is going. When you present a workable plan with the right goals, people will follow. The suggested model below can put disciple making at the heart of the church; it is presented as a way of implementing principles vital to the development of healthy Christians, the production of disciple makers and multipliers who make the fulfillment of the Great Commission possible.

A Model

In my book *Jesus Christ, Disciplemaker*, I presented the seeds of the model I propose. The model is built around the three training phases of Christ in relation to His disciples. They are common observations; many have noticed and written about them before. A. B. Bruce, in his classic *The Training of the Twelve*, speaks of the three calls of Christ.[1] The calls of Christ were "Come and see," recorded only in the Gospel of John 1:39; "Come and follow Me," found in Mark 1:16–20; and "Come and be with Me," in Mark 3:13–14. I have added a fourth phase that is shorter and less vital, but still important, "You will remain in Me" (John 15:7–8). Chart 1 shows each training phase. At the top of the chart you will notice the six-step teaching method of Christ and how it fits the four training phases.

> *"Come and see"* 1. Tell them what. 2. Tell them why.
> *"Come and follow Me"* 3. Show them how. 4. Do it with them.
> *"Come and be with Me"* 5. Let them do it.
> *"You will remain in Me"* 6. Deploy them.

If we follow the body analogy, the four training phases and six teaching steps are the cardiovascular system. When employed, these principles produce the product called a disciple. The vehicles or methods found under each category make up the body's skeleton. The skeleton gives the body structure. The health of the body, however, is most dependent on the heart, arteries, vessels, and lungs. People don't die for lack of strength; they die when their hearts quit. The body cannot function without a good cardiovascular system. When it works, the rest of the body works.

The four training phases focus on two essentials: time and level of commitment. The six-step teaching method incorporated in these phases focuses on content of training and level of responsibility. The four training phases provide an overall look at the church's disciple-making training, while the six-step training method helps the trainers track the training content throughout the entire process.

Phase 1: "Come and See" (John 1:39–4:46)

Jesus did not demand to be followed; He simply extended invitations. At each stage of development and deepening of commitment, He called people to follow to the next level, and some did. The calls describe the training and relational phases Jesus employed to prepare His followers for multiplication.

"Come and see" was a four-month introduction to Jesus and His work. Five disciples followed Him, learned from Him, and then returned home to consider if they wanted to go further. Jesus exposed curious converts to the nature of ministry. They witnessed water changed into wine, the clearing of the temple, the interviews with Nicodemus and the woman at the well. They were challenged to consider laboring in the harvest field. They left Jesus with the knowledge that reaching others with the gospel of the kingdom was paramount and that they could be part of it.

"Come and see" is characterized by the words *gather, consider, expose, interest,* and *inspire*. These words emphasize introduction to Christ and His work. This is the first

Chart 1
A Church-Centered Disciple-Making Structure

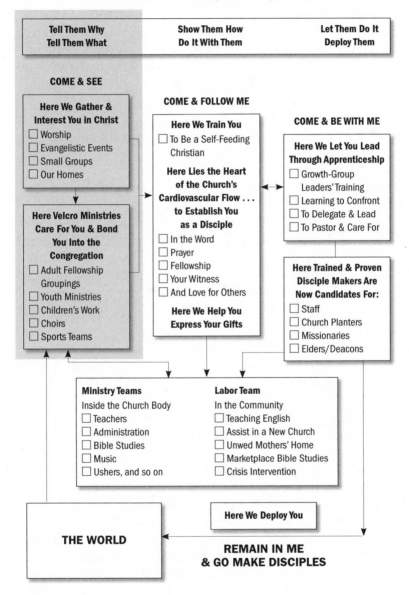

| Tell Them Why
Tell Them What | Show Them How
Do It With Them | Let Them Do It
Deploy Them |

COME & SEE

**Here We Gather &
Interest You in Christ**
☐ Worship
☐ Evangelistic Events
☐ Small Groups
☐ Our Homes

COME & FOLLOW ME

Here We Train You
☐ To Be a Self-Feeding
Christian

**Here Lies the Heart
of the Church's
Cardiovascular Flow . . .
to Establish You
as a Disciple**
☐ In the Word
☐ Prayer
☐ Fellowship
☐ Your Witness
☐ And Love for Others

**Here We Help You
Express Your Gifts**

COME & BE WITH ME

**Here We Let You Lead
Through Apprenticeship**
☐ Growth-Group
Leaders' Training
☐ Learning to Confront
☐ To Delegate & Lead
☐ To Pastor & Care For

**Here Velcro Ministries
Care For You & Bond
You Into the
Congregation**
☐ Adult Fellowship
Groupings
☐ Youth Ministries
☐ Children's Work
☐ Choirs
☐ Sports Teams

**Here Trained & Proven
Disciple Makers Are
Now Candidates For:**
☐ Staff
☐ Church Planters
☐ Missionaries
☐ Elders/Deacons

Ministry Teams
Inside the Church Body
☐ Teachers
☐ Administration
☐ Bible Studies
☐ Music
☐ Ushers, and so on

Labor Team
In the Community
☐ Teaching English
☐ Assist in a New Church
☐ Unwed Mothers' Home
☐ Marketplace Bible Studies
☐ Crisis Intervention

THE WORLD

Here We Deploy You

**REMAIN IN ME
& GO MAKE DISCIPLES**

phase of any spiritual work, and the church has various vehicles to make it work.

Sunday morning church meeting. The most ready-made gathering tool of the church remains the Sunday morning meeting. Our culture is built around it, and there is no better time to reach the majority of people than Sunday morning. When the average person thinks *God*, he still thinks *church*. When he thinks *church*, he thinks *Sunday morning worship attendance*. Therefore, don't fight it; utilize it as a gathering instrument.

FOR THE CHRISTIAN OR THE UNCHURCHED? The Sunday morning meeting, whether it be called celebration, worship service, or teaching hour, should be intentionally designed. Will it be for the Christian or for the non-Christian and the unchurched? Will it be expository preaching with a heavy learning focus or more topical, lighter fare, tailored to the unchurched? Will the music be contemporary or traditional, hymnals or song sheets, hands raised or subdued and quiet?

Some churches, which could be called "come and see" churches, focus on reaching the unchurched. They do a great job of gathering people with dynamic music, drama, and speaking. They have chosen to use other meetings for teaching and training. These churches have made their choice; it is not a wrong choice, but it is a different one. The important issue is that somewhere in their church, teaching and training takes place.

One commonly overlooked aspect to churches that gather large numbers through innovative methods is the entrepreneurship of their leader. Dynamic leaders are required to make such models work. When such a leader is available, this model is an option. I do, however, have some reservations in considering this a common option for the majority of churches. Ninety-five percent of America's churches have a Sunday morning attendance of two hundred or less. The reality is that the great majority of churches do not have a pastor talented in this way, the money, or the innovative skills to benefit from the entrepreneurial models.

The entrepreneurial models intimidate more than they help. Some valuable principles and ideas can prove helpful to the average church, but generally they set a standard that most cannot reach. The cultural tendency to point to these successful churches as models to follow only makes the problem worse. For 95 percent of pastors, the dynamic entrepreneurial pastor and church is a guilt-producing scourge. This is not the entrepreneurial pastor's problem or fault. The posture I recommend is simply to thank God for these talented few, take from them what we can apply, and leave it at that.

We need a model any person can employ with his talent and resources. The issue is not how many you have but what you do with what you have. If you do well with what you have, God will give you more, but not as many as some others. The question remains: As a disciple-making pastor, what are you trying to accomplish with the Sunday morning service?

INTEREST, INSPIRE, AND GATHER. We chose to address the Sunday morning service to the Christian. The primary reason to gather is for encouragement, instruction, consolation, and motivation (see 1 Cor. 14:3; Heb. 10:24–25). Scripture does not command or expect non-Christians to attend church. The Christian, however, is commanded to be there on a regular basis (see Heb. 10:24–25).

Another reason we focus on the Christian is that Christians are to gather for edification and scatter for evangelism. The test of a church's effectiveness is the penetration of its members into society. The commanded focus is not to bring non-Christians to church, but for equipped Christians to take Christ to the world. There is an expectation that new converts will be assimilated into the church environment, but as a by-product of the members' witness.

The Sunday morning service, then, provides an atmosphere in which a group of Christians can praise God, learn more about the Bible, and be moved toward ministry. Sunday morning is where we intend to interest Christians in ministry. Through the use of the pulpit the pastor instructs, inspires, but most important, interests Christians in the work of God. He calls them out of the stands and onto the field for action.

This provides the disciple-making pastor with his greatest opportunity. He declares the priorities and calls people to participate. This is akin to Jesus' multitude ministry. The pastor tells people what is important and why it is important. He tells them who they are and what they are to do. He gives the reasons why it would be in their best interest to be a part of God's work. The pastor uses the pulpit to build church environment. The music, the prayers, the ritual, and the teaching work together to motivate people to action. But the bottom line of the Sunday morning meeting is to interest people in living for God and working for God: becoming disciples.

The mini-congregation. The Sunday morning service is where we interest you. The mini-congregation is where we care for you. The "come and see" phase of ministry must possess both dimensions. People must be interested, and they must be cared for. Very often, unless people feel loved, they will not allow God's Word into their lives.

The mini-congregation provides the church with congregational life. Congregational life means development and maintenance of relationships. We have promised each member of the congregation that regardless of the size of the total church, he would always be a member of a smaller congregation, where he would be known and loved. If he is not present, he is missed; if he is in the hospital, he is visited; if he is sick, someone delivers meals to his door.

The groups are much more dynamic than a normal Sunday school class. They meet on Sunday morning in our church, but they can work at other times as well. They play the important role of better caring for people by decentralization of ministry. Communion, baptism, and child dedications are handled through the mini-congregations. This is consistent with the "every member is a minister" theology.

They provide greater ministry opportunities. Recently our mini-congregations have collected and taken clothes to prisons. They have provided clothes, toys, food, and money for minority groups. They have helped some of our ethnic church planters with various needs. When people start experiencing the vitality of ministry, they sell it to others, and a dynamic atmosphere results. Recently, one of the mini-congregations brainstormed how to pay a member's medical bills. Talk of forming a lawn-care business to put street kids to work followed. They are ministers; they create the ministry, facilitate the ministry; they don't need to have everything screened by the church board.

The mini-congregation is led by a well-trained leadership team. They are almost always lay led. A team consists of a leader, a teacher, social director, small group directors, benevolence coordinator, and so on. People learn to love one another in the congregation. Various small support groups can grow from them as well. When people get to know each other, needs are identified and then met. It is vital to good care of people that the church provides such a vehicle.

This is what I mean by decentralization of ministry, including pastoral care. People start to believe in themselves; they gain self-respect; they understand that they are not dependent on the clergy for ministry ideas or implementation. It breaks the chains of professionally ruled ministry.

The "come and see" phase is designed to interest and care for the general Christian population. The main tools most Christians will come to are Sunday morning worship and a Sunday morning meeting that is different from worship, but dynamic in its approach. The reality of this phase is that 50 percent of Christians never leave it. If the Sunday morning worship celebration involves 100 percent of the congregation, then about 45 percent of the adult population will join a mini-congregation. "Come and see" represents that pool of humanity in which the disciple-making pastor fishes for those who want to go on. About 50 percent of the congregation will move on to the "come and follow Me" phase.

With such realities in mind, it should be stated that the church has a responsibility to the 50 percent who never go further than "come and see." They may not be as productive as those who do, but they are God's children, and the church is responsible for them.

Velcro ministries. Most Americans have seen Velcro. It is that stick-to-itself strip that replaces zippers on wallets and purses and the laces on children's shoes. Velcro ministries help people stick with the church. The Sunday morning worship and mini-congregation have considerable "stick" to them. Other vehicles that fit "come and see" hold people in the church as well: choirs, sports teams, men's clubs, retreats, children's activities, social-action committees, small informal Bible studies, and so on. Such groups aim to keep people together. Velcro ministries play an important role because they hold people in the church until they respond to move on to greater ministry. A person may be "on hold" for years in one or more of the Velcro arenas, then one day say yes to "follow me and I will make you fishers of men." Not only does the Velcro ministry do much good; it holds a person until he is ready to move on.

The disciple-making pastor works hard at "come and see." He makes sure that come-and-see vehicles are high quality. He puts interesting ads in the paper and utilizes many means of getting people to visit the church. Once he has them in a pew, he's got them right where he wants them. Through the major come-and-see vehicles, he attempts to interest them in service and commitment to Christ. At the same time he employs all vehicles available to hold people in the church environment until they are ready to move on.

Like the hurdler, the pastor keeps one eye on the process and the other on the finish line. The process is to take people through the training phases. The objective is to make every willing person a healthy, reproducing believer. The come-and-see phase is telling people what and why they should move forward on their spiritual pilgrimages. It involves framing the issues, describing the goal, pointing the way. Anything that will hold people in the environment where they are consistently exposed to the message is important to the disciple-making ministry.

Phase 2: "Come and Follow Me" (Matthew 4:18–22; Mark 1:16–20)

We tell our congregation that in "come and see" we interest you and care for you. During "come and follow Me" we train you, establish you as a mature disciple. Steps three and four of Christ's six-step teaching method were primary to the "come and follow Me" phase. Jesus showed the disciples how and did it with them. He established them in the Christian's life-support system during this ten-month training phase. "Come and follow Me" provides a prolonged exposure to the foundations of ministry. Jesus established that four essentials were needed to sustain a lifetime of commitment to Himself and the mission: to be rightly related to the Word of God, prayer, relationships or a shared life, and witness or mission. Jesus' training showed them how to do this. There was limited participation; Jesus did a great deal of modeling. His objective was to teach them what was important and then work it into their lives.

Making the transition. Every Christian needs time to get his feet firmly planted on a solid foundation. "Come and follow Me" was such a time for the disciples. The disciple-making pastor faces the challenge of moving people from "come and see" to "come and follow Me."

While 50 percent of the congregation never leaves the come and see phase, the happy focus is that the other half will. The psychopathology of not moving from "come and see" I will leave to the analytical. I think the disciples responded to the invitation "come and follow Me, and I will make you fishers of men" for three reasons.

THEY HAD ALREADY BEEN WITH HIM. The four-month "come and see" phase served as necessary introduction to both Christ and the nature of ministry. The seeds were planted; Christ exposed them to the supernatural and then challenged them to the task. They had two months to think it over, to make a solid choice concerning their future. They knew Jesus would come and challenge them; when He did, they were ready.

The disciple-making pastor knows the importance of "come and see." Without it, people are challenged to too much too soon. They get in over their heads. They make commitments they don't understand and therefore cannot keep. The transition from "off the street" to the world of Christian commitment is buffered by the "come and see" experience. When the believer hears the same priorities over and over in a loving and caring environment, the chances are good that he will desire more. People move from "come and see" to "come and follow Me" because their hearts are prepared. They know what they should do and why. They take a loving step of obedience, becoming mature disciples.

HE EXTENDED AN INVITATION, NOT A RESPONSIBILITY. People hesitate risking something when you leave the how-to and the know-how to them. The attractiveness of Christ's invitation is that He shouldered the responsibility. "I will make you" says it all. *I know where you want to go; I know how to get you there; trust Me, follow Me.* Jesus proceeded to show them what He meant by demonstrating the priorities of the Word, prayer, fellowship, and witness.

Chart 2
A Church-Centered Disciple-Making Structure

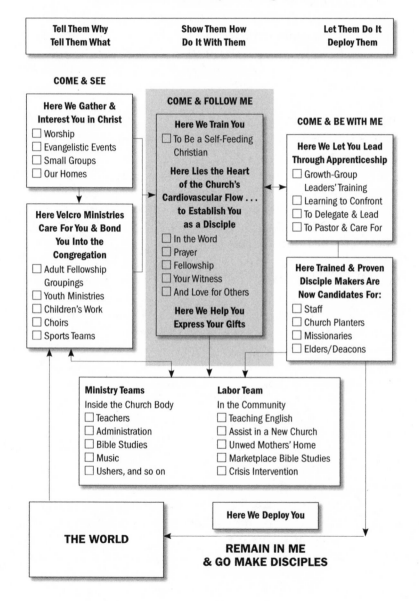

| Tell Them Why | Show Them How | Let Them Do It |
| Tell Them What | Do It With Them | Deploy Them |

COME & SEE

Here We Gather & Interest You in Christ
- ☐ Worship
- ☐ Evangelistic Events
- ☐ Small Groups
- ☐ Our Homes

COME & FOLLOW ME

Here We Train You
- ☐ To Be a Self-Feeding Christian

Here Lies the Heart of the Church's Cardiovascular Flow . . . to Establish You as a Disciple
- ☐ In the Word
- ☐ Prayer
- ☐ Fellowship
- ☐ Your Witness
- ☐ And Love for Others

Here We Help You Express Your Gifts

COME & BE WITH ME

Here We Let You Lead Through Apprenticeship
- ☐ Growth-Group Leaders' Training
- ☐ Learning to Confront
- ☐ To Delegate & Lead
- ☐ To Pastor & Care For

Here Velcro Ministries Care For You & Bond You Into the Congregation
- ☐ Adult Fellowship Groupings
- ☐ Youth Ministries
- ☐ Children's Work
- ☐ Choirs
- ☐ Sports Teams

Here Trained & Proven Disciple Makers Are Now Candidates For:
- ☐ Staff
- ☐ Church Planters
- ☐ Missionaries
- ☐ Elders/Deacons

Ministry Teams
Inside the Church Body
- ☐ Teachers
- ☐ Administration
- ☐ Bible Studies
- ☐ Music
- ☐ Ushers, and so on

Labor Team
In the Community
- ☐ Teaching English
- ☐ Assist in a New Church
- ☐ Unwed Mothers' Home
- ☐ Marketplace Bible Studies
- ☐ Crisis Intervention

THE WORLD

Here We Deploy You

REMAIN IN ME & GO MAKE DISCIPLES

The key to getting people to make the transition is to provide a vehicle which is consistent with the objective. If the objective is to be a mature disciple, then the vehicle should build those characteristics that form the disciple's profile. It begins simply with inviting the willing ones to an orientation meeting, where they can make a decision concerning such a vehicle. Various ways of accomplishing the task will serve, but a smart church focuses on one to begin with and only a few in a mature form. Doing a few things well is more important than having every option known to man.

The transition is marked by the person clearly understanding what and why he should push on spiritually. An invitation that provides a means to get where he is convinced he should go follows. He must also believe that the leader can get him there.

HE CALLED THEM TO A VISION, NOT A JOB. Jesus also promised that if they would follow Him, the disciples would become fishers of men. The driving force behind commitment is vision: vision of what I can become and what I can do as a result of the training. In "come and follow Me" people establish the basic characteristics and skills that classify them as disciples who, in turn, glorify God.

To do that, people need vehicles. The two training steps vital to "come and follow Me" are "show them how" and "do it with them." This requires a controlled environment. Jesus required His men to travel with Him, and they lived together twenty-four hours a day. The traveling band was a controlled environment. Their ten months of intensive living together equals several years of today's forms of togetherness. Therefore, today, any training experience that attempts to model itself after Jesus requires longer than ten months. Working with people with families, jobs, and various competing choices requires a reachable opportunity.

We have chosen the time frame of two years. Since we believe that every Christian is to be a reproducing disciple, we must create vehicles that make their participation pos-sible. Too often Christians see discipleship as something only possible for full-time Christian workers who, like Jesus and the Twelve, give all their time to service. This belief is both untrue and harmful. It tends to make the average working person think that important dedication to Christ and ministry is out of reach. The church leadership must find a way to make it happen for the layman.

The discipleship group. The small group provides the best environment for disciple making. The group is designed to provide a means for the average person to become an es-tablished disciple and is built around several principles:

ONLY PEOPLE WHO MAKE THE COMMITMENT ARE APPROVED. Those who have said yes to Christ's invitation, "Come and follow Me, and I will make you fishers of men," attend an orientation meeting. The commitment is explained in detail. They agree to attend the meetings, to participate in the training, and to be held accountable. The growth group covenant is shown below. People have one week after the orientation meeting to make their decision.

Commitment is essential for progress. "Teaching them to obey" (Matt. 28:20) is not possible without the signed agreement. This makes it possible for the leader to refer to the covenant when group members waver. "What did we agree to do?" is a starting point for discussing the is-sues. The group covenant is the glue that holds the group together. It is their common ground; the "we are in this together" feeling makes the group dynamic.

THE GROUP MUST BE SMALL ENOUGH TO AVOID SPECTATORS BUT LARGE ENOUGH TO PROVIDE VARIETY. The group works best when varieties of gifts and life experience exist within it. The leader does not possess the multiplicity of giftedness or experience to sufficiently disciple group members. Interplay between group members is a vital part of the training.

Growth Group Covenant

Commitment to Grow in Christ

Introduction: The following covenant sheet is to identify clearly the description of what is involved by joining a Growth Group. After attending our orientation meeting and prayerfully considering the challenge, opportunity, and commitment, you need to sign this sheet and hand it in to our church office.

What is involved in a Growth Group?

- A desire to become a self-feeding Christian in prayer, accountable fellowship, the Word, and your witness.
- A willingness to come regularly to the meetings of the Growth Group and to always phone your Growth Group Leader of potential absence.
- A commitment to be on time.
- A goal orientation to prepare all lessons in advance as part of your weekly devotional time with Christ.
- A willingness to place yourself under the leadership and direction of your Growth Group Leader's spiritual guidance.
- A determination to:

    1. Memorize 30 verses of Scripture in two years.
    2. Complete five Design for Discipleship study books, one book analysis within the New Testament, and spiritual gifts assessment for ministry.
    3. Write out and share your personal testimony.
    4. Aggressively cultivate friendships with the un-churched.
    5. Participate in all outreach events of your group and the church.
    6. Make prayer a regular part of your devotional life.

Covenant

After reading these expectations I/we feel unworthy yet challenged to attempt what you have asked. I/we have prayed about this commitment and feel God is leading us to become Growth Group members. I/we desire to grow in pursuit of faith in Christ, love for others, and the expansion of Christ's kingdom. Therefore, I/we agree to channel our efforts to comply with these expectations for the next two years as God leads me/us. We give you permission to confront us whenever we fall short of this covenant as a friend and loving guide for our spiritual well-being.

Names _____, _____, _____

Date _____

The group should be no larger than fourteen. Too many members make it difficult for everyone to talk, to share their learning, their needs, within the time allotted for the evening. If a person doesn't have the repeated opportunity to participate, his learning will be slowed, and dropping out becomes a greater possibility.

THE GROUP MUST MEET OFTEN ENOUGH AND LONG ENOUGH FOR THE TRAINING PROCESS TO WORK. By meeting once a week for two hours, the group provides the consistent exposure needed for learning. Training requires weekly reinforcement of Scripture memory, Bible study, outreach projects, and so on. Another vital part of the training is the expected attitudinal transformation. The Bible study helps transform the mind; the outreach projects put the finishing touches on the transformation. The one aspect to training that cannot be rushed is time. In our two-year time frame attitudes gradually change because of repeated experience. It is very much like learning a foreign language. A seven-week "cram course" may get you by, but is inferior to learning the same material over a one-year span. If the student can practice the language and allow time for assimilation, the learning is more exciting, and he will retain the lessons much longer. The learning process naturally ebbs and flows; the two years provides a cushion for members to work out problems.

THE GROUP MUST TEACH BASIC SKILLS THAT ACT AS TOOLS TO REACH THE OBJECTIVE. Four areas compose the disciple's life-support system and must be established: a working knowledge of the Scriptures; an effective prayer life; meaningful relationships, including an appreciation for accountability; and a positive attitude toward evangelism and the ministry skills to do evangelism.

Bible study. Group members need to have sufficient knowledge of the Bible's contents to possess a working knowledge of scriptural principles. Material should simultaneously increase in difficulty and cover major biblical themes. The degree of difficulty should include transition from filling out blanks to inductive book analysis. At the close of the two years, members would know how to feed themselves from the Word of God.

Prayer. Many Christians do not know how to pray. They pray in general terms, they don't ask for specifics, they are unacquainted with intercession. The members are taught to pray specifically, to be bold in their requests, to pray conversationally, and to keep prayer lists to remember the good God has done. Another dimension is the half days in prayer in which the group engages. Many members feel threatened by the prospect of spending a protracted time in prayer. They are taught how to develop intimacy with God, how to spend three hours praying, meditating, praising, and reflecting; that is, spending quality time with God.

Being rightly related to God in both the Word and prayer form the foundation for the effective Christian life. But without the remaining two dimensions, Bible study will become academic and prayer boring. In fact, most Bible studies that simply meet for study and prayer die a natural death. The group needs more if it is to be dynamic; it needs the strength of relationships and outreach.

Relationships. The discipleship group relationships are much more dynamic than those of the generic small groups. The difference is accountability, both in life and in task. Many small groups have accountability in lifestyle, where people encourage one another to live godly lives, to do the right thing ethically. I would not discount this feature at all; in fact, I would place it at the top of a priority list. But like many other important issues, if it is done in isolation, it loses its punch.

The discipleship group also holds people accountable for elements of the task: the challenge of evangelism, Scripture memory, reaching out to others, doing your Bible study lesson, or coming to group regularly and on time. The group's peer pressure is built in and is the most powerful form of accountability. The expectations of others in the group test the relationships. Positively we could say, "Accountability helps us keep our commitments to God." This goes back to the covenant group members sign and the determination of the group leader and members to keep the covenant. This sets the group apart, because when people are challenged, confronted, encouraged, and corrected, the façade comes down, people get authentic, it creates cathartic crisis.

The group will go through a series of cathartic crises, and there will be casualties. This is necessary to the growing process, and by maintaining the covenant, the integrity of the group and the members' spiritual self-respect remain intact. The key to creating this kind of environment is simple. First, set forth the expectations. Second, allow in the group only people who agree to meet the expectations and are willing to sign on the dotted line, that is, the covenant. Third, be determined to keep the covenant, correct and encourage those who waver, restore those who are open, dismiss those who are not. This will create a dynamic environment of crisis, conflict, healing, and growth. This is the way to make disciples. If people practice selective accountability and they are allowed to get away with it and be considered disciples, we have failed.

Outreach training. Group members are given projects to complete. The theory behind projects is the same as homework. If a student is given an assignment related to what he studies, his learning accelerates. The outreach objectives are twofold: to create in members a positive attitude and conviction concerning the importance of outreach, and to develop a series of evangelistic skills to make outreach possible.

The very first group meeting includes an outreach assignment. Each member is asked to encourage someone. This starts the wheels turning, it gets them thinking of others; now they must take off the blinders. When all group members have completed the first project, the group moves to the second. This creates the peer pressure and built-in accountability that is so vital to success. Over the two-year period the objective is that group members will develop the attitude that they can effectively reach others.

The skill-development objective is that group members will become able to reproduce themselves. The specific skills are: knows how to engage others in spiritual conversations, knows how to invite others to evangelistic events, knows how to tell his personal story and transition into asking clear questions that facilitate movement toward the sharing of the gospel. The group members are trained in how to verbalize their faith, how to follow up a new convert, how to assimilate new believers into the church. The group's main objective is not conversions, but helping members become competent in reproduction. This is essential, since Jesus said a proven disciple reproduces (see John 15:8).

In two years the group has many opportunities to practice skills and to become effective. Repetition is integral to the learning process. When shortcuts are taken through crash-course disciple making, the sad result is that it doesn't take and one must start again.

It is worthwhile to start slowly, not to take shortcuts, and to make sure a solid foundation is laid. If the heart of the cardiovascular system is properly maintained, it will insure the future health of the body. The two-year discipleship group is the very heart of the church body's cardiovascular system.

GROUPS MUST LAST LONG ENOUGH AND BE DEMANDING ENOUGH TO SURFACE NEW LEADERS. Vital to perpetuating the future of groups and leadership development is the identification of new leaders from the group process. Leadership development begins when a group member exhibits qualities in attitude, aptitude, and skill. Several months into a group, the "chargers" become apparent. Some will aspire to teach, to lead, to influence. The group leader then starts running potential leaders through a series of integrity checks. The potential leaders are asked to carry out some simple functions. These might include tasks outside the group, ushering, for example. There is nothing like a task a person doesn't relish revealing the content of his heart. By giving small tasks, some they like, some they don't, we learn if they are teachable, if they are servant leaders, or simply want power.

Other means of pushing attitudes to the surface are teaching a lesson, followed by critique and further learning through books and tapes. If a person is teachable, has the spiritual giftedness and desire to lead, then the group leader will begin to groom that person for leadership. If multiplication is to be a reality in the church, the group leaders must always develop new leaders who have the potential to be multipliers.

Our group leaders look for potential leaders who have the gift cluster to be pastors, elders, church planters, missionaries—those who create environments and can lead movements. They move on to the "come and be with Me" phase of training. There is another form of evaluation going on, as well. It is just as important as identification of future disciple makers, and it includes much larger groups of people.

Group assessment. In the last three months of the two-year cycle, every group member is assessed. You will notice on the chart that the majority of group members are not candidates for "come and be with Me." Let me say it again: About 50 percent of those in "come and see" will move to "come and follow Me." About 10 percent of the 50 percent in "come and follow Me" will be selected to "come and be with Me." Note the difference: Every believer is called to be a mature, reproducing disciple, but a select few are meant to enter the "come and be with Me" training for disciple makers. Therefore, there remains the 90 percent of the 50 percent in "come and follow Me" to deal with. These people comprise the vast majority of the church's core and are equally important to the effectiveness of the mission. The difference between those selected for leadership and those not has little to do with spirituality. In fact, many who are not selected for leadership are more faithful and godly than those who are. It's an issue of suitability, not spirituality.

The assessment is the means to launch group members into their future ministries. Too often, members consider the completion of the two-year discipleship group a graduation. They have finished their course of study; now they can float out of the controlled environment into whatever work the Lord leads them to do. I wish this were true, but experience teaches that people need more guidance than a pat on the back.

We treat the graduation from a two-year group as the starting line, not the finish line. Therefore, the assessment asks "Who are you; what are your gifts, interests; what would you be good at?" We use various tests to measure work-style preference; the group also studies spiritual gifts and determines into which gift cluster they fit.

The group leader then counsels with each member or couple and asks them to consider what area of ministry they should enter next. The church provides a list of opportunities and needs. The members are asked to be creative, to think of a new means of reaching others for Christ. As the chart reflects, many enter the ministry teams of the church. With new vigor and confidence, they take on such areas as teaching, administration, leading special-need Bible studies, or many other options. Even if a person's gifts do not call him to be more than a behind-the-scenes support person, now he is a reproducing disciple, carrying out that function with new meaning.

It is my firm conviction that every believer is called to be a reproducing disciple. This conviction grows out of the Great Commission itself (see Matt. 28:19). Therefore, a means of moving people out of the gathering, motivating, caring, come-and-see stage to the training phase of "come and follow Me" is required. Over a ten-year period, I have the goal of getting at least 50 percent of the congregation to the "come and follow Me" phase. Then I will feed them back into the congregational workforce to give new life and vitality to the body of Christ. This is why the two-year small group is the heart of the cardiovascular system. It provides the church with a continual flow of healthy, reproducing disciples who can minister.

Life is not lived on a chart. The chart is only an imperfect model and teaching tool designed to help communicate the process of spiritual development that must take place in a healthy church. It is a means of applying the teaching of our Lord to the local church. Please do not make the model more than it is; try to glean what you can and leave it at that. To make more of it than that could lead to great danger.

In the quest to make disciples, the chart shows that in the first two phases the people have been told what and why. That was followed by showing them how and doing it with them via the two-year small group. The question remains, however, "Don't the vast majority not selected for the come-and-be-with-Me phase benefit from the let-them-do-it and unleash-them training principles?" Yes they do! The difference is that we "let them do it" in the area they have chosen. We "let them do it" with mini-congregations, special Bible studies for groups such as single parents or parents with teens, working with antiabortion counseling, and many other options. The future development of this group is doing the task and in the process reproducing themselves.

The people not selected to "come and be with Me" really are the most powerful feature of the church. When unleashed, they exhibit greater creativity and ability to reach their friends and associates than do those marked for leadership. The main body of reproducing disciples is the center of ministry action. They have most of the fun; they are on the front lines; they have hands-on ministry; they are the trench troops. They are the key to the disciple-making church's real success. Their role is to reach people for Christ. As I often say, pointing to the congregation, "You are our outreach program." The most effective outreach program unleashes the trained disciples of the church. But if you don't train them, you won't have them. If you don't have them, either you will have to prop up evangelism with expensive programs and outreach events, or you won't do it at all. If you have the money, you will, if not, you won't. It's your choice!

Isn't this too narrow? Common questions about the model are "Isn't this a bit narrow? Is the two-year group the only way?" There are many ways to train people to be reproducing disciples. I have presented what I consider the best way for a church to do it, and I have no reservations about claiming the small group as the superior vehicle for such work. The important issue is that the principles presented in this section are maintained. We also employ other means: intensive weekends, summer courses, breakfast meetings, and Bible studies.

Existing ministries in the church can be used to teach the same thing. For example, a person leading a mini-congregation or teaching high-school students the Bible or how to witness can suffice. The nature of this book is such that I will not advocate too many methods peculiar to my church or personality. As I say again and again, "If you have the right convictions, you will figure out how to get the job done."

A word about "one on one." Some consider one-on-one discipleship as the best methodology. While one on one can be important to the process, it cannot be primary to disciple making in the church. The natural discipleship flow was modeled for us by Jesus. First there is the come-and-see phase demonstrated by the multitude ministry. By teaching the Word to a large group and then calling those willing spirits to "come and follow Me," the disciple maker saves himself both wasted time and needless hurt. If I wanted to reproduce myself and I had a hundred people to choose from, I would not personally interview and try to develop them one by one. I would tell them what and why, then call them to the training phase, "come and follow Me." Then, through the small group, I would further identify those who should be the future leaders. Finally I would work one on one with the select few. One on one works best in concert with the large group exhortation and small group training.

The next training phase, "come and be with Me," churches have largely left to the seminaries, Bible schools, and mission agencies. The sad result is that many professional Christians are well trained, but gifted leaders from the laity world are not.

Chart 3
One-on-One Relationship

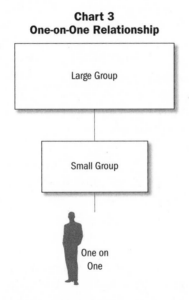

Phase 3: Come and Be with Me (Mark 3:13–14; Luke 6:13)

This phase is for a few. Not many are interested, not many are qualified. It is done quietly, out of the sight of most of the congregation. But like much behind-the-scenes work, it is vital to the survival of the organization. All churches engage in the come-and-see activities of gathering, inspiring, and interesting people in Christ. Approximately 50 percent of churches would provide some training as demonstrated in the come-and-follow-Me phase. Very few churches, less than 10 percent, venture into the third phase of Jesus' modeled training of "come and be with Me." It makes sense that the same percentage of individual involvement in each training phase reflects the percentage of corporate church participation. As the difficulty increases, the participation decreases.

Even the better disciple-making churches quit too early. They treat the completion of the come-and-follow-Me discipleship training as the finish line. The people graduate, then they are on their own. They are assigned various duties within the church and are not challenged to greater ministry. Too often the very principles and skills learned in the discipleship groups have nothing to do with what the church asks of them next. Therefore, in large measure, the training goes to waste and the people go to seed on "church work." In the come-and-follow-Me section, I described the assessment process and how we attempt to intentionally launch graduates into ministry matched to their temperament and skills.

The come-and-be-with-Me phase is for the select few who have the suitable gifts, character, and skills to be trained to be disciple makers. This trained disciple maker with leadership gifts is the key to multiplication. The neglected part of even the better disciple-making churches is their failure to intentionally address the careful selection and training of the few who can lead ministries. These future elders in the church and leaders in the outreaches into the community are the pool from which the church gets church-planting pastors, missionaries, and dynamic disciple-making leaders for the Great Commission.

Too often those leaders who emerge from the local church do so by divine accident. That is, they have some basic training, but only the hungry, the self-starters, the highly motivated climb to the top. Many others who have equal ability, but not the same drive, are left behind. The come-and-be-with-Me training makes it possible for more potential candidates to be exposed to the information and experience needed to be leaders.

Jesus went out to pray concerning the next phase of His ministry. He was faced with the challenge of vast unmet need and not enough workers to meet the need. He also needed to prepare others to carry on the work after His departure. The next morning He chose twelve disciples to be with Him.

He prayed all night, called the Twelve, and delivered the Sermon on the Mount. They immediately left on a short tour, which ended with a retreat for review and critique. From the time Jesus appointed the Twelve, in Mark 3:13–14, until He commissioned them to go out two by two, in Matthew 10:1–42, was five months.

The Twelve knew that they would be given a special position and authority; still, Jesus didn't let them try it alone for five months. He gave them some assimilation time, a short time of review for them to lock in on a few basics before they were deployed. "Watch Me closely, because soon it will be your turn," Jesus very well might have said. If someone is demonstrating how to paint a house, you watch much more closely if you know he will shortly pass the brush to you. The disciples paid much closer attention to Jesus' actions, knowing they would soon be on their own.

In the remaining months of training, Jesus sent the disciples out to practice and learn. The process of practicing ministry, followed by a critique, was a repeated method employed by Christ during this phase. He later gave them additional responsibility by having the Twelve lead the seventy (see Luke 10). A fuller biblical description of "come and be with Me" can be found in this work's progenitor, *Jesus Christ, Disciplemaker.*

The greatest challenge of the come-and-be-with-Me stage is making the necessary transition from doing the ministry with them to letting them do the ministry. This is moving from step four to five in the six-step teaching method mod-

Chart 4
A Church-Centered Disciple-Making Structure

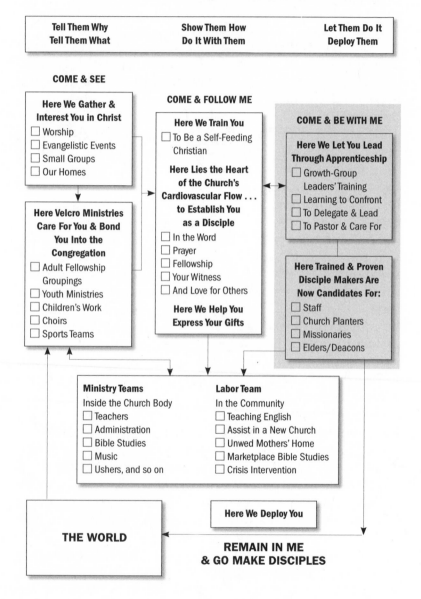

Tell Them Why Tell Them What	Show Them How Do It With Them	Let Them Do It Deploy Them

COME & SEE

Here We Gather & Interest You in Christ
- ☐ Worship
- ☐ Evangelistic Events
- ☐ Small Groups
- ☐ Our Homes

COME & FOLLOW ME

Here We Train You
- ☐ To Be a Self-Feeding Christian

Here Lies the Heart of the Church's Cardiovascular Flow . . . to Establish You as a Disciple
- ☐ In the Word
- ☐ Prayer
- ☐ Fellowship
- ☐ Your Witness
- ☐ And Love for Others

Here We Help You Express Your Gifts

COME & BE WITH ME

Here We Let You Lead Through Apprenticeship
- ☐ Growth-Group Leaders' Training
- ☐ Learning to Confront
- ☐ To Delegate & Lead
- ☐ To Pastor & Care For

Here Velcro Ministries Care For You & Bond You Into the Congregation
- ☐ Adult Fellowship Groupings
- ☐ Youth Ministries
- ☐ Children's Work
- ☐ Choirs
- ☐ Sports Teams

Here Trained & Proven Disciple Makers Are Now Candidates For:
- ☐ Staff
- ☐ Church Planters
- ☐ Missionaries
- ☐ Elders/Deacons

Ministry Teams
Inside the Church Body
- ☐ Teachers
- ☐ Administration
- ☐ Bible Studies
- ☐ Music
- ☐ Ushers, and so on

Labor Team
In the Community
- ☐ Teaching English
- ☐ Assist in a New Church
- ☐ Unwed Mothers' Home
- ☐ Marketplace Bible Studies
- ☐ Crisis Intervention

THE WORLD

Here We Deploy You

REMAIN IN ME & GO MAKE DISCIPLES

eled by Christ. Making this transition is absolutely crucial to creating multiplication.

Jesus helped the Twelve make the transition by twenty months of gradual increase of responsibility. The church, then, is called to do the same and to provide a means for this critical process. The remainder of this section's material will be the practical "nuts and bolts" of how to make that transition.

Who gets selected? The uniqueness of "come and be with Me" is that potential disciple makers are chosen. They choose only after being chosen. As Jesus told the eleven, "You did not choose me, but I chose you . . . to go and bear fruit—fruit that will last" (John 15:16).

SUITABILITY, NOT JUST SPIRITUALITY. In the first two phases of "come and see" and "come and follow Me," the lone criteria was that the individual responds to the invitation to commit to Christ and to be a disciple of Christ. In this phase, many can aspire, but few are chosen. It would be a terrible mistake to allow anyone who desired to enter the disciple-maker training. Even if he qualifies on many issues and in many cases is as spiritual—or more so—than another who is selected, he may not be right for this level. The issue is suitability, not just spirituality. Many godly people have no business leading God's work. This is a distinction that many have not made, and it has spelled disaster for both the misplaced person and the misguided ministry. By choosing the Twelve, Jesus did not choose hundreds who followed Him. The unique aspect to this model is the careful selection of a few qualified persons to prepare for the ministry of leadership and multiplication. We use three primary criteria to make our selections.

Character, faithfulness, and gifts. Observation of the members of the discipleship groups over a two-year period provides ample information to evaluate character. The scriptural criteria of 1 Timothy 3 and Titus 1 are used as guides. We do not expect perfection; we are looking for progress with respect to the character issues.

The general knowledge acquired by the group leader and members gives clear indicators. The condition of a man's family, business, and social interaction are known by the end of the two years. The group leader has spent personal time in the ministry of fine-tuning, which delves into personal matters that do not surface in the group. This is the value of a system that does not make exceptions and requires the motivated growers of the church to share the same training experience. A system where no person is selected for "come and be with Me" until he has been tested for two years closes many loopholes and eliminates much guesswork in the selection process. You don't need to fish for future leaders outside the pool of discipleship-group members.

The second important dimension is the prospective leader's faithfulness. Faithfulness means he follows through on his commitments. This is absolutely required for anyone to be considered. Paul told Timothy and us as well to pass on the responsibility of leadership to only the faithful. Jesus taught that only if a person would be faithful in the small things could he be trusted with big things. Only if he knew how to handle the world's riches could he be trusted with "true riches," the spiritual responsibility for others. Early in the two-year group, those with leadership potential are identified and assigned simple tasks. This is the intentional and careful testing of their faithfulness. If they demonstrate a faithfulness in the small things, then they will be candidates for larger responsibility. If not, they will not be candidates.

A third issue is spiritual gifts. At the close of the two-year discipleship group, each member studies and is led to discern his gifts and abilities. The personal bias of our church is to limit those selected for "come and be with Me" to those with leadership gifts. Leadership gifts are that cluster of gifts such as teaching, preaching, leadership, administration, exhortation, and the like. We want those who can lead others. Since the issue is multiplication, putting the ministry into the hands of those who can multiply, who are trained disciple makers, requires leadership. Yes, leaders can be made, but only if the raw material is present. We use a series of tests and simple observation of their assigned work to determine if they can lead.

Completed the two-year discipleship group. Simple graduation from the discipleship group is not enough. Those selected for "come and be with Me" are magna cum laude. This caliber of person finishes hard, strong, and with flying colors. He has excelled in every area of the group. He has been strong in Bible study and prayer, has developed good relationships, and has assisted the leader in helping others be accountable by his words and actions. In addition, he has been outstanding in both attitude and behavior in evangelism.

Once again, those who cannot finish the boot-camp experience are not candidates for greater training and responsibility. This weeds out the malcontents, the troublemakers, the self-willed, and the proud. It not only makes disciples of the members; it tells you which ones are your future leaders and which ones are not.

Desire. Those who can go on must desire to go on. "Here is a trustworthy saying: If anyone *sets his heart* on being an overseer, he *desires* a noble task" (1 Tim. 3:1, italics added). To "set your heart" means you stretch yourself; the word *desire* serves to confirm the same willingness to go for it. The candidate must be willing to stretch himself to the limit in order to prepare for the work. Paul describes the object of affection as a "noble task." Other translations say "fine work." It is the work of ministry to others that a person stretches for, not the position.

The process could be likened to a soldier first excelling in boot camp. Subsequently, he could go to Officer Candidate School (OCS). To be successful in OCS a candidate must be filled with desire for the goal. He must be willing to pay a big price, to push himself to the limit, to stretch himself toward the goal. The goal is to be equipped to do the work. The person selected for this kind of spiritual training must possess the same desire and willingness to sacrifice and to work. If he is to multiply disciple makers, he must have the ability, which comes from training. His heart must be set on the work of ministry to others and getting ministry done through others. If he has not reached this point, he has no business in the come-and-be-with-Me training.

Who gets selected? Those who have the proper character, faithfulness, and gifts. Those who have completed the two-year discipleship group with flying colors. And those who have a burning desire for the work of a multiplying disciple maker.

What does the trained disciple maker look like? This description can be framed in various ways. I have divided the description into two categories: character and ministry skills—what a person is and what a person does.

CHARACTER. What the person is governs his activity. Character is the foundation. It is impossible, however, to separate a man's character from his actions. A person must have a spiritual depth equal to the task at hand. A spiritual leader is required to engage in a level of spiritual warfare unknown to most Christians. The judgment and staying power required for effective ministry is a nonnegotiable and is described in the previous section.

MINISTRY SKILLS. *Can effectively communicate the Scriptures.* The emphasis here is not classic preaching and teaching. If the person is gifted there, consider it a bonus. If he wishes to move into pastoral ministry, then some professional training would be in order. Primarily this requires the skill of passing on the gospel and the truths of Scripture to others in a small group setting. This calls for the ability to lead a guided discussion, to ask good questions and guide people to the biblical text and help them apply it.

Effective communication of Scripture means that the trained disciple maker knows systematic theology. By *systematic theology* I mean he has a framework into which he can put additional information and has a gridwork to defend against false teaching.

The trained disciple maker must be a solid student of Scripture and possess a working knowledge of its contents. Biblical and systematic theology along with a sound hermeneutical grid are essential for the communicator of Scripture. This is the description; the process of their training will be covered in the next section.

Can effectively articulate the philosophy of disciple making. From the foundation of a strong biblical knowledge, the trained disciple maker builds his philosophy of disciple making. He is driven by convictions firmly rooted in Scripture. This means he can effectively defend and explain the reasons for the priority of disciple making. This ability is acquired by a very simple process. First, you are exposed to the teaching. Second, you try to apply it through your teaching and practice. Third, you are challenged, and you attempt to defend your thinking. Fourth, you go back and study harder and go back to your challengers to clarify points. This repeated process will make it possible for a trained disciple maker to become a convincing advocate of the disciple-making philosophy.

Unless and until a disciple maker can articulate and defend, he won't multiply in a significant way. With passion, he must be able to persuade others to adopt his plan. That is how you find and develop others to multiply the work.

Can manage or coach others. As you can see, the disciple maker's skills focus on multiplication, getting things done through others: communicate the Scriptures, articulate and defend a philosophy, and now management of others. This skill is the toughest for most of our people. It involves shaping a vision, organizing the work, and choosing the right people to do the work. Properly assigning the work, along with appropriate guidelines and accountability comes next, followed by the ability to teach others to teach others. Therefore, delegation and working through others are still the number-one challenges in management today.

If you recall, this skill is much like coaching. Tell people what and why, show them how, do it with them, then let them do it, and finally deploy them. If multiplication is going to take place and more people are going to get involved in ministry, leaders will need to work effectively through others.

Can motivate others. No long-term motivation exists without conviction. Jesus developed convictions in His disciples through the six-step teaching method. When you believe something to be true and follow it with a related experience that confirms the belief, you are on the road to a conviction.

Passion normally follows convictions. A person with passionate convictions will be able to motivate. The most normal thing for him to do is persuade others that his way is right. The techniques of motivation have much less importance than the reasons behind it.

The discipleship-group leaders who experience the greatest problems have lacked the convictions to move group members to positive action. They defend a practice with difficulty because they don't have positive personal experience in that area. Therefore, they have no real passion as a tool for persuasion. The ability to motivate others is necessary to disciple making. People will pay no price, attend no meeting, do no work, until a passionate leader shows them the way and inspires them.

Can correct others. An earlier section covers this subject in detail. The "teaching them to obey everything I have commanded you" part of disciple making requires correcting people. The trained disciple maker has demonstrated his willingness and ability to help people keep their commitments to God. The disciple maker is trained to find out if the person who needs the correction is unwilling or unable to do right. The same question applies to a person who does the correcting. Many leaders will not correct others. That is much more difficult than working with the person who is unable to correct others, but who is willing to learn. The trained disciple maker who leads is both willing and able to correct those who are in error. It is the loving and necessary thing to do, if disciples are to be made.

Is comfortable with and effective in personal evangelism. The trained disciple maker leads people to Christ and is successful in training others to lead others to Christ. Too often church leaders have not been trained in evangelism; they have never reproduced and fear evangelism. This leads to a number of leadership pathologies: a focus on maintenance of local church machinery, whereby the mechanics of ministry become the ministry; a nonreproducing leadership team will create a sterile church populace, then the leadership core will go to almost any lengths to protect themselves from risky behavior and accountability in this area.

The trained disciple maker successfully gets evangelism done through others, because he has convictions. He is passionate because he has experienced the joy of reproduction. He can speak with a clarity of conviction; what he says rings true; he can back up his teachings with storytelling. His convictions and passion can overcome people's fears and objections by motivating them to risk in this area.

We have, thus far, answered two questions: *Who gets selected? What does a trained disciple maker look like?* Now how can a magna cum laude discipleship group graduate into trained disciple makers?

How do you train them? Once again, I have chosen to divide the training methods into two departments: the classroom or cognitive element and on-the-job training.

Several general foundational beliefs govern our training:

1. The best training is the six-step method modeled by Christ.
2. Our best training tool is putting people to work applying the principles we have taught.
3. We have no better method than putting them back into our present system for their training.
4. If you want them to reproduce your philosophy, they must experience all levels of the system. This is the advantage of the person who comes into the church as a new believer and grows through the system. He is a product of the system, is grounded in the principles, and his training capstone is teaching the principles that have created them to others within the system. The products of the principles are the most compelling reason they believe in the principles.

THE CLASSROOM. No person will be selected for training unless we have a place for him to practice what he learns. The classroom is vital, but it produces academic Christians if on-the-job training does not bring it life.

The classroom training is built around the training objective, the six ministry skills described above. Therefore, the training consists of working systematically through each skill. Those selected meet once a week for two hours. The meeting is broken down into two sections. In the first thirty minutes we evaluate their ministry assignments. We go over the areas that are difficult; we share ways in which a problem can be solved or a technique improved. Reports are read, questions are asked, there is a philosophy of sharing ideas and skills that will improve the work.

The second part, lasting ninety minutes, we devote to the information they need for their personal development. Each member has evaluated himself in each of the six skills. Everyone participates equally in all six areas of learning, but the leader also helps in fine-tuning through one-on-one time outside the meeting. The training goes something like this:

Skill 1: Effectively communicate the Scripture. The training includes the study of doctrine. Each week the members do a self-study of a certain doctrine. During the next meeting they discuss the material. This continues until all the major doctrinal areas are covered. An exam covering their knowledge of the doctrine follows the study.

They are taught how to lead a small group discussion and all the germane dynamics of the small group. Almost all members lead a two-year discipleship group; therefore, most of them put this into practice every week. The leader also occasionally attends their groups and observes them teaching.

The remainder of training dealing with special subjects and preaching/teaching instructions is part of the fine-tuning. They are also instructed in hermeneutical principles.

Skill 2: Can effectively articulate the philosophy of disciple making. The same method used above is employed. They are taught the material, followed by an exam that measures their ability to write about the philosophy. Once again, on-the-job training confirms their ability to persuade others to adopt the same thinking.

Skill 3: Can manage or coach others. The students are taught principles of management. They study how Christ got work done through others. The issues previously mentioned, such as identification of the task, organization of the task, selecting personnel, delegation, and follow-through are all taught as information.

The real test is how effectively the leader works through others in his discipleship group or ministry assignment. On-the-job training is most important with this skill. The information becomes important only in bits and pieces as he needs it to refine his thinking and skill.

Skill 4: Can motivate. Motivational skills are considered, but the real issue is the leader's convictions and whether he can passionately communicate them. His ability to move his group members to action in areas people normally fear gauges his motivational ability. This is worked on case by case.

Skill 5: Can correct others. This is the most difficult area for most people. No one really likes to confront. We coach each person through each case and teach the basic skills of confrontation: how to say things and what not to say. This area reveals the people's courage level. A person's willingness to endure pain in order to help another is a vital part of building character. When a leader understands the crucial nature of correcting others, he will do it and do it well.

Skill 6: Is effective in evangelism and in training others to do evangelism. By the time he gets to this point, the prospective leader knows the basics of how to share his faith. In fact, one of the requirements of "come and be with Me" is that he share his faith once a week with an unbeliever. First, he models what he teaches, and second, he motivates others to do evangelism. Is he a multiplier? He has practiced this in the two-year discipleship group. Now he requires fine-tuning in this area: how to handle objections, rejection, difficult scriptural or philosophical questions. This can be handled on the classroom level.

ON THE JOB. If you refer to chart 5, you can see that most "come and be with Me" people lead discipleship groups. They have built in accountability on the group level and on the group leader's level. Their average week includes their discipleship group meeting, their two-hour training meeting with me, and their preparation time for both. In addition, they have retreats, seminars, and other intensive training periods throughout the year. We also expect them to build relationships with their group members outside the group context.

Other on-the-job training includes leading mini-congregations or a labor team that is attempting to reach a segment of society for Christ. The one rule is this: All ministry assignments must put into practice the principles of disciple making. The on-the-job work must add to the classroom training. It must provide the opportunity for the trainee to prove himself, to be productive, and to demonstrate disciple making and leadership technique.

The two-year training called "come and be with Me" should result in a trained disciple maker who is a leader. These two years, as well as the previous two years in "come and follow Me," allow enough time for all the other pieces of the puzzle to fall into place. Character, relationships with others, peccadilloes, and positives have been brought into the light of biblical scrutiny for refining and training. Most wonderful, this person has borne fruit that will last. After completing training, he is ready for step six of Christ's teaching methods.

Phase 4: Remain in Me

Deployment is the exporting of your product. It gives the process of disciple making its real meaning. Here the trained disciple makers of ministry enter into a new relationship with that ministry. Jesus defined this new relationship as "remain in Me." He was leaving them in the good hands of the Holy Spirit. Clearly they faced a major change in relationship. That change in relationship is present in both forms of deployment. It is more noticed in the first, however, than in the second.

Professional deployment. The chart shows that trained disciple makers with the gift of leadership are the resource pool for pastors, church planters, and missionaries, that is, those going into professional ministry. A disciple-making ministry will deploy many who fall into this category. When these people are deployed, they physically leave the church and remain with you in a distant way. The church should encourage this kind of deployment, and these people should be given a grand send-off. It should be a time of celebration of the work of the church, when it can deploy such a well-trained dedicated product of that ministry.

Local lay deployment. First, I want to apologize for the use of the term *lay* or *laymen*. I use it only for communication purposes. These products of the ministry who stay in the church are more difficult to deal with than the professionals. Professionals leave, and that brings a bit of finality to the process. The layman is ready to be deployed locally; this calls for more work and much creativity.

By the time laymen have reached this level they have established themselves as effective and proven leaders in the church. Of course they are the candidates for eldership. These are the ones to whom you entrust the decision making of the church. But eldership is not enough. You have trained them too well for that to satisfy. Remember, you have taught them to love the ministry: leading people to Christ, teaching others how to do the same, making a difference.

Labor teams. The end product of a disciple-making ministry is trained members who will go into the community and lead others to Christ. Then they will bring the new converts into the church environment and get them started on the discipleship road. Trained lay disciple makers are the key figures who dream big dreams and then go out and make the dreams a reality. They should be encouraged to do different and special things that will influence people for Christ.

Target an unreached group, develop a plan, recruit personnel, and go for it. That is their training and hopefully their spirit. The genius of disciple making is that you will produce this kind of people. Too many churches never get to this point because they do not intentionally produce such a product. Whether it is teaching English to refugees, helping the poor or homeless, or sharing Christ with each member of the country club, a well-trained, highly motivated, deployed laity can do it. This provides the discipleship flow. In a church where the system feeds itself, it's a self-perpetuating, growing organism that Paul described: "From him the whole body, joined and held together by every supporting ligament, *grows and builds itself up in love, as each part does its work*" (Eph. 4:16, italics added).

I am convinced that if a church employs the model presented in this chapter, it will serve them well. I have given only one suggested way of putting the principles of Christ to work. However a church handles it, the most crucial issue is that every church do something intentional to make disciples. It must have a means to move people from considering Christ to full commitment to His commanded work to reach the world. The church must lead people to maturity. Their people will honor God, reproduce, multiply, and train disciple-making leaders. They will deploy disciples into the harvest field. Then the church will be healthy, and the good news of Christ will reach every person in the world.

Further Reflections

Making Things Work

I am an idealist. That's why I insist that the best way to lead is from principle. A principle is a fundamental truth, a rule of conduct, and an essential element. Hypothetically, a person working from a set of four principles succinct enough to be written on a piece of paper can be a powerful force. He or she could apply those principles in any culture at any time. That is why this section is based on four principles. They provide a pathway for leading people through their lives and are based on simple observations of how Jesus managed His men. All principles, when applied, become a model. (By *model* I mean "program" or

Chart 5
A Church-Centered Disciple-Making Structure

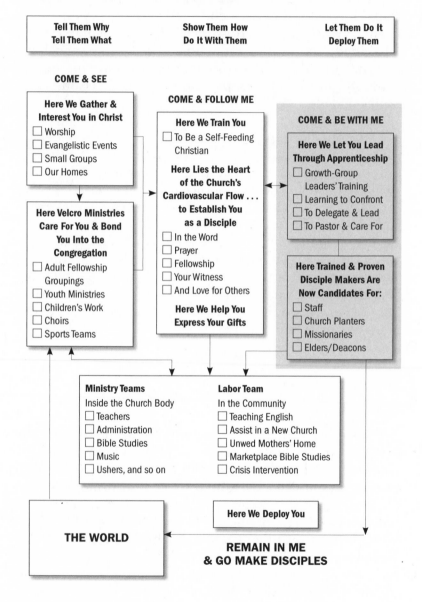

| Tell Them Why
Tell Them What | Show Them How
Do It With Them | Let Them Do It
Deploy Them |

COME & SEE

**Here We Gather &
Interest You in Christ**
- ☐ Worship
- ☐ Evangelistic Events
- ☐ Small Groups
- ☐ Our Homes

COME & FOLLOW ME

Here We Train You
- ☐ To Be a Self-Feeding Christian

**Here Lies the Heart
of the Church's
Cardiovascular Flow . . .
to Establish You
as a Disciple**
- ☐ In the Word
- ☐ Prayer
- ☐ Fellowship
- ☐ Your Witness
- ☐ And Love for Others

**Here We Help You
Express Your Gifts**

COME & BE WITH ME

**Here We Let You Lead
Through Apprenticeship**
- ☐ Growth-Group Leaders' Training
- ☐ Learning to Confront
- ☐ To Delegate & Lead
- ☐ To Pastor & Care For

**Here Trained & Proven
Disciple Makers Are
Now Candidates For:**
- ☐ Staff
- ☐ Church Planters
- ☐ Missionaries
- ☐ Elders/Deacons

**Here Velcro Ministries
Care For You & Bond
You Into the
Congregation**
- ☐ Adult Fellowship Groupings
- ☐ Youth Ministries
- ☐ Children's Work
- ☐ Choirs
- ☐ Sports Teams

Ministry Teams
Inside the Church Body
- ☐ Teachers
- ☐ Administration
- ☐ Bible Studies
- ☐ Music
- ☐ Ushers, and so on

Labor Team
In the Community
- ☐ Teaching English
- ☐ Assist in a New Church
- ☐ Unwed Mothers' Home
- ☐ Marketplace Bible Studies
- ☐ Crisis Intervention

THE WORLD

Here We Deploy You

**REMAIN IN ME
& GO MAKE DISCIPLES**

"curriculum.") Every ministry leader needs a way to sort out who people are and where they belong. Anything less would be pastoral neglect.

This chapter looks refreshingly relevant even though it is based on what my staff team practiced twenty years ago. It seems that regardless of how "hip" we want to be, the "work of ministry" (Eph. 4:12 NKJV) comes back to these basics of helping people through the journey. Learning experts say that around 5 percent of all people are creative and 15 percent are adaptive.[2] That means 20 percent of all people can identify principles and live by them. The other 80 percent need a model, some way to have the principles explained with materials and pathways.

If you as a leader are willing to make a model your own, to apply it with wisdom and care, you can't go wrong. The nice thing about a principled model is that you can take almost any material or idea from others and fit it into your plan. For those of you who need examples or illustrations to grasp the principle, in time they will emerge for you.

"What Do You Mean by 'Work'?"

How do you know when your plan is working? Immediately my mind goes to numbers. Luke's recording of the early church's growth included numbers (see Acts 2:41, 47; 5:14; 6:7; 11:26). It seems like numbers are something we either nearly worship or banish to the fleshpots of culture. We love them, we hate them, we want them, and we rebuke their power over our lives. When they are good, they make our hearts sing; when they are bad, they are sawdust in our mouths. Having more people in our meetings feels good—a packed room raises the energy level, the music is better, the preaching is dynamic, and people sense God's presence. The bigger the crowd, the bigger the buzz. That feeling then creates excitement in the attendees, who tell others, and attendance grows.

It is obvious that people pay attention to what grows fast and big, whether it is a tumor or a church. Numbers do matter; very often they are a good indicator that you are getting through to people. The question is, are they penetrating their worlds with the love of Christ? When the lights in the church are out, the doors are locked, and the parking lot is empty, what are Christians like in their day-to-day lives?

Allow me to be more concrete. You can design application vehicles for the phases of "come and see," "come and follow Me," "come and be with Me," and "remain in Me." This book gives you some ideas. Your plan is working when all willing members are making progress through the phases. Don't concern yourself with the unwilling people. If you spend too much time with them, they will ruin your life.

There is a limit to measuring the changes in the members since so much change takes place in their everyday lives. But let me point out that I believe there is no distinction between the everyday life and the spiritual life. We all have just one life; everything in it is interwoven, and God works in all of it. The physical is just as real as the spiritual and is an integral part of our spirituality. The incarnation of Christ is enough evidence to confirm the unity of the spiritual and the physical. How does one measure joy or acts of kindness? To put forth much effort to detect and measure the fruit of the Spirit can make life a bit too clinical. I would instead depend on two things that are related: First, are people positing themselves in the groups and opportunities you provide? Second, do they testify to the changes in their lives? In the end, these are the most reliable indicators.

Three years after making your plan, there should be a steady new crop of leaders ready to serve. The genius of Jesus' approach is that people are trained on the job, and that training brings to light the motivated—those whose desire is to serve Christ with all their hearts. Another plus is that those people have similar values and can pass them on to others. There are always easier ways to measure change, such as by the number of new groups, the number of the new people in groups, and the ways in which the groups and people become effective and innovative in reaching others.

However, the most potent character traits in making your plan work are the combination of principle, commitment, passion, and patience. The forces of the enemy will collapse in the path of such a tour de force. The longer you work on your plan, the better it will work. When I get discouraged, I take shelter in the symmetry of the apostle Paul's words that God works to will and to work for His good pleasure (see Phil. 2:13). He works His plan in us and then works it out through our spirit and body into life. I cannot escape what He has willed in me. When I obey, I feel His pleasure. Therefore, He keeps working it out. When you think you are going to lose sight of your plan, go to Him and allow Him to impress His will on you once again.

Notes

2007 Introduction

1. George MacDonald, quoted in Ruben Job and Norman Shawchuck, *A Guide for Ministers and Other Servants* (Nashville: Upper Room, 1983), 60.

2. Thomas Friedman, "The Age of Interruption," *New York Times*, July 5, 2006.

Chapter 1: The Need

1. Elton Trueblood, *The Best of Elton Trueblood: An Anthology* (Nashville: Impact Books, 1979), 34.

2. Gallup poll.

3. Elton Trueblood, "A Time for Holy Dissatisfaction," *Leadership Journal* (Winter 1983): 19.

4. Ibid.

5. George Barna, *Vital Signs: Emerging Social Trends and the Future of American Christianity* (Westchester, IL: Crossway Books, 1984), italics added.

6. Os Guinness, *Gravediggers File* (Downers Grove, IL: InterVarsity Press, 1983), 233.

7. Francis Schaeffer, *The Great Evangelical Disaster* (Westchester, IL: Crossway Books, 1983).

8. Dr. Kenneth Kantzer, *Christianity Today* (November 1983).

9. Eugene Peterson, "Doing the Right Thing in the Wrong Way," Spiritual Formation Forum Conference, May 2004, personal notes.

10. Fact sheet in *Christianity Today*.

11. Trueblood, *The Best of Elton Trueblood*, 34.

12. George Barna, *Growing True Disciples* (Colorado Springs: WaterBrook Press, 2001), 54, italics added.

13. Tom Fillinger, newsletter, "Under the Elm Tree."

Chapter 2: The Conflict

1. Lyle Schaller, *It's a Different World* (Nashville: Abingdon Press, 1987), 60.
2. Richard Neuhaus, speech at Congress on the Bible, Washington, D.C., September 1987.
3. Tony Walters, *Need the New Religion* (Downers Grove, IL: InterVarsity Press, 1985), 142.
4. D. Elton Trueblood, in private interview with Jon Johnston, *Will Evangelicalism Survive Its Own Popularity?* (Grand Rapids: Zondervan, 1980), 38.
5. Eugene Peterson, "Doing the Right Thing in the Wrong Way."
6. Eugene Peterson, "Spirituality for All the Wrong Reasons," *Christianity Today*, March 4, 2005, http://www.ctlibrary.com/ct/2005/march/26.42.html.

Chapter 3: The Product

1. Gerhard Kittel, ed., *Theological Dictionary of the New Testament*, vol. 4 (Grand Rapids: Eerdmans, 1967), 441.
2. Ibid., 457.
3. *Webster's New World Dictionary*, second edition, s.v. "Business."

Chapter 4: The Role of a Disciple-Making Pastor

1. R. Laird Harris, Gleeson Archer, and Bruce Waltke, *Theological Wordbook of the Old Testament* (Chicago: Moody Press, 1980), 852.
2. F. Wilbur Gingrich, *Shorter Lexicon of the Greek New Testament* (Chicago: University of Chicago Press, 1957), 176.
3. See Robert Saucy's excellent treatment, *The Church in God's Program* (Chicago: Moody Press, 1972), 140–52.
4. Bruce Shelley, *Church History in Plain Language* (Waco, TX: Word Books, 1982), 85.
5. Paul Brand and Phillip Yancey, *Fearfully and Wonderfully Made* (Grand Rapids: Zondervan, 1980), 24.
6. T. S. Eliot, quoted in N. T. Wright, *Simply Christian* (San Francisco: Harper & Row, 2006), 3.

Chapter 6: The Commitment of a Disciple-Making Pastor

1. See Bill Hull, *Jesus Christ, Disciplemaker* (Grand Rapids: Baker, 2004).
2. Gingrich, *Shorter Lexicon*, 78–79.
3. Online Etymological Dictionary, 2001, www.etymonline.com.
4. See Bill Hull, *Choose the Life: Exploring a Faith That Embraces Discipleship* (Grand Rapids: Baker Books, 2004).

Chapter 7: The Practices of a Disciple-Making Pastor

1. Howard Hendricks, speech at "Disciple Making in the Eighties" conference, October 1983.
2. Charles Swindoll, *Strengthening Your Grip* (Waco, TX: Word Books, 1982), 238.
3. Gingrich, *Shorter Lexicon*, 162.

4. Fritz Rogers Rienecker, *Linguistic Key to the Greek New Testament* (Grand Rapids: Zondervan, 1976), 602.

5. Gingrich, *Shorter Lexicon*, 18.

6. Ibid., 30.

7. "Drinking Kool-Aid" refers to people who unthinkingly believe a line of thought, even if it is untested. The phrase usually refers to a religious or political philosophy and originated with the tragic Jonestown mass suicide. In 1978 Jim Jones, a charismatic personality, led his more than nine hundred followers to drink a deadly Kool-Aid that killed them all.

8. Richard Foster, *Celebration of Discipline* (San Francisco: Harper & Row, 1978), 102.

9. Henri Nouwen, *In the Name of Jesus* (New York: Crossroads, 1996), 17.

10. Foster, *Celebration of Discipline*, 101.

Chapter 8: The Pastor as Coach

1. Trueblood, *The Best of Elton Trueblood*, 140.

2. Howard Hendricks, speech at "Disciple Making in the Eighties" conference, October 1983.

3. A full treatment of this phase is found in Bill Hull, *Jesus Christ, Disciplemaker* (Grand Rapids: Baker, 2004), 29–75. A. B. Bruce, *The Training of the Twelve* (New Canaan, CT: Keats Publishing, 1979), 11–12, also acknowledges a threefold division of training that forms the foundation for the calls or invitations given by Christ.

4. Hull, *Jesus Christ, Disciplemaker*, 79–80.

Chapter 9: Making It Work in the Local Church

1. Bruce, *Training of the Twelve*, 11–18, 39.

2. Bill Hull, *7 Steps to Transform Your Church* (Grand Rapids: Revell, 1993), 39.

Bill Hull's efforts as a pastor and writer have been focused on being a disciple (a follower of Jesus) and making other disciples. He has written several groundbreaking books for leaders and churches and can be heard speaking at www.bible.org. He has also developed curricula that can be reviewed and purchased at www.bible.org.

Bill and his wife, Jane, have been married since 1969 and are the parents of two grown sons. Bill can be contacted at bill@billhull.com.

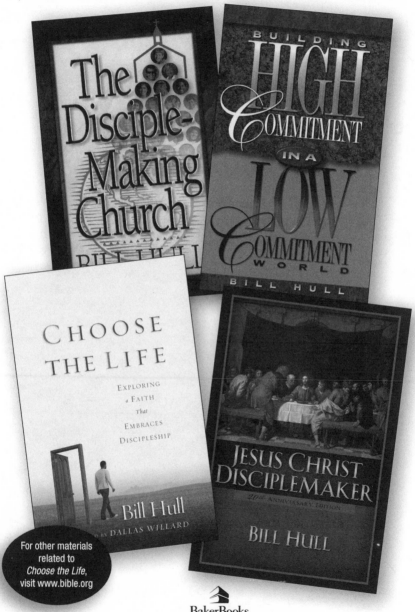